Building with Our

Building with Our Hands

New Directions in Chicana Studies

EDITED BY

ADELA DE LA TORRE

BEATRÍZ M. PESQUERA

UNIVERSITY OF CALIFORNIA PRESS

Berkeley Los Angeles London

University of California Press
Berkeley and Los Angeles, California
University of California Press, Ltd.
London, England

Library of Congress Cataloging-in-Publication Data
Torre, Adela de la.
Building with our hands : new directions in Chicana studies / Adela de la Torre, Beatríz M. Pesquera.
p. cm.
Includes bibliographical references and index.
ISBN 0-520-07089-5 (cloth : alk. paper).—ISBN 0-520-07090-9 (paper : alk. paper)
1. Mexican American women. I. Pesquera, Beatríz M. II. Title.
E184.M5T67 1993
305.48'86872073—dc20 91-39227
CIP

Printed in the United States of America
9 8 7 6 5 4 3 2
The paper used in this publication meets the minimum requirements of American National Standard for Information Sciences—Permanence of Paper for Printed Library Materials, ANSI Z39.48-1984. ♾

This anthology is dedicated to "Las Compañeras" de MALCS.

CONTENTS

ACKNOWLEDGMENTS

This anthology represents a collective enterprise of Chicanas who struggled in their respective disciplines to give "voice" to their issues and research. Mujeres Activas en Letras y Cambio Social (MALCS) provided a forum for many of us to share and develop our research and has given us the intellectual and emotional support we needed to complete this project. We are truly grateful.

We also thank Inéz Hernandez for suggesting the title of the book from a verse in a poem by Lorna Dee Cervantes, "Beneath the Shadow of the Freeway."

Norma Alarcón, editor of Third Woman Press, and Patricia Zavella of the University of California, Santa Cruz, provided valuable assistance in editing the manuscript.

Financial support was pieced together through various programs and fellowships that were made available to us both. We therefore gratefully acknowledge the President's Fellowship Office, University of California, Berkeley; the Faculty Senate Research Grant, University of California, Davis; the Pew Health Policy Postdoctoral Fellowship, University of California, San Francisco; and the Scholarly and Creative Activities Committee, California State University, Long Beach.

Finally, we thank Naomi Schneider of the University of California Press, who valued and supported this intellectual enterprise.

CONTRIBUTORS

Antonia I. Castañeda is Assistant Professor of Chicano Studies and Women's Studies at the University of California, Santa Barbara. El ensayo se dedica a nuestras antepasadas mestizas, indias, mulatas, y negras—cuyas voces, fuerza, inteligencia, y pasión retumbran en nuestras obras.

Adela de la Torre is chair of Chicano/Latino Studies and Associate Professor of Health Care Administration at California State University, Long Beach, and a scholar at the Tomás Rivera Center at Claremont. As a health economist specializing in Latino health issues, she has published several articles in the area of Chicana/Latina health, health-care financing, and rural health-care access.

María de los Angeles Crummett is Assistant Professor of Economics and Women's Studies at Barnard College, Columbia University. She has published numerous articles on Mexican agrarian structure, rural women, and migration. She has been a consultant for the United Nations Development Fund for Women (UNIFEM), the International Labor Organization, and the Food and Agriculture Organization.

Angie Chabram Dernersesian is Associate Professor in the Chicana/Chicano Studies Program at the University of California, Davis. She has published essays on Chicano literary criticism, feminism, ethnography and theory, and Chicano culture. With Rosa Linda Fregoso, she coedited a volume of *Cultural Studies* entitled "Chicano/a Cultural Representation: Reframing Alternative Cultural Discourses" (Oct. 1990). Her primary work, "Conversations with Chicano Critics: Portrait of a Counter Discourse," is forthcoming.

Elisa Facio is Assistant Professor of Sociology at the University of Colorado, Boulder. She has published articles on Chicana aging. Under the auspices of a postdoctoral fellowship from the National Institute of Aging at the University of California, San Francisco, she is completing a book on the social construction of older Chicana lives.

Rosa Linda Fregoso is Assistant Professor in the Chicana/Chicano Studies and Women's Studies Programs at the University of California, Davis. She has published essays on Chicano cinema and cultural studies, and with Angie Chabram Dernersesian coedited a volume on Chicano/a cultural representation for *Cultural Studies* (Oct. 1990). She is currently working on a manuscript on Chicano cinema and cultural identity.

DEENA J. GONZÁLEZ is Associate Professor of History and Chicano Studies at Pomona College, Claremont. She has published an article on widowhood that has been reprinted in *Unequal Sisters,* ed. Ellen Carol DuBois and Vicki L. Ruiz. She is completing a book on Spanish-Mexican women of Santa Fe.

EMMA PÉREZ, a *tejana,* is Assistant Professor of History at the University of Texas at El Paso. She has taught Chicano/a history at the University of Minnesota at Minneapolis; the University of California, Davis; and Pomona College. An award from the Ford Foundation Postdoctoral Fellowship for Minorities in 1989–90 permitted her to continue research on the social history of Mexican American women in Texas.

BEATRÍZ M. PESQUERA is Associate Professor and Director of the Chicana/Chicano Studies Program at the University of California, Davis. She has published articles on Chicanas' employment and familial experiences and on Chicana feminism. She is currently completing a book on the intersection of work and family among Chicana workers and, with a coauthor, is preparing a manuscript on Chicana feminism. During 1990–91, she was a Rockefeller Humanist-in-Residence at the Southwest Institute for Research on Women at the University of Arizona, Tucson.

VICKI L. RUIZ is the author of *Cannery Women, Cannery Lives,* and coeditor of *Unequal Sisters, Women on the United States–Mexico Border,* and *Western Women: Their Land, Their Lives.* She is currently writing a monograph on the history of Mexican women in the Southwest from 1848 to the present.

DENISE A. SEGURA is Assistant Professor in the Department of Sociology at the University of California, Santa Barbara. She has received numerous awards, most recently a 1991–92 Ford Foundation Postdoctoral Fellowship. She has published articles on Chicanas and Mexican immigrant women in the labor market, Chicano education, and Chicana feminism. Currently she is writing a coauthored book on the contemporary and historical dimensions of Chicana feminism.

ANGELINA F. VEYNA is presently a doctoral student in the Department of History at the University of California, Los Angeles. From 1988 to 1990, she served as coordinator of the Chicana/Latina Studies Office at the UCLA Chicano Studies Research Center. Her primary research interest is in the history of Chicana/Latina women.

A NOTE ON ETHNIC LABELS

Among the numerous ethnic labels used to describe persons of Mexican origin in the United States, none is unanimously regarded—by scholars or by the population at large—as the "most appropriate" or the "most correct" one. In the social science literature, *Chicana* and *Chicano* typically refer, respectively, to women and men of Mexican descent residing in the United States. *Chicano* is also a broad term that includes both males and females who claim Mexican heritage (e.g., the Chicano community). These labels offer an alternative to the more common ethnic identifiers *Mexican* and *Mexican American.* The term *Mexican* may also be used to refer specifically to immigrants from Mexico. *Mexicana* and *Mexicano* typically refer to immigrant women and men. Regional and historical differences also affect the use of ethnic labels. For example, *Hispana* and *Hispano* are terms used by the Mexican-origin population of New Mexico.

The term *Chicano* was popularized in the late 1960s during the Chicano movement to affix a political orientation that affirmed the need to struggle against the historical oppression of people of Mexican descent in the United States. *La Raza* was also popularized during the same period and underscores a shared cultural experience and a sense of unity among peoples of Mexican, Central American, and South American heritage. *Latino,* commonly associated with peoples of Latin American origin, has a similar use. *Hispanic* is a term coined by the U.S. Census to identify all Spanish-speaking and/or Spanish-origin populations in the United States. While it is commonly used in data sets, it is considered an imposed identifier.

For further clarification, see J. A. Garcia, " 'Yo Soy Mexicano . . .': Self-Identity and Socio-Demographic Correlates," *Social Science Quarterly* 62 (March 1981): 88–98; A. Hurtado and C. H. Arce, "Mexicans, Chicanos, Mexican

Americans, or Pochos . . . Que Somos?: The Impact of Language and Nativity on Ethnic Labeling," *Aztlan: A Journal of Chicano Studies* 17 (1987): 103–130; M. Tienda, "The Mexican American Population," in *Non-metropolitan America in Transition,* ed. A. H. Hawley and S. M. Mazie (Chapel Hill: University of North Carolina Press, 1981), pp. 502–548; F. Penalosa, "Toward an Operational Definition of the Mexican American," *Aztlan* 1 (Spring 1970): 1–12.

ONE

Introduction

Beatríz M. Pesquera
Adela de la Torre

Building with Our Hands depicts diverse aspects of the Chicana/Mexicana experience.[1] The essays reveal the collective importance of our work as women of color in the United States and express our shared experience in a society that has attempted to render us invisible. Historically, Chicana voices have not been chronicled, yet Chicanas have spoken out—around kitchen tables, in community and political organizations, at union meetings. Our voices have gone largely unnoticed and undocumented; in spite of the academic claims of value-free inquiry, they have not been deemed worthy of study. When they have been studied, stereotypes and distortions have prevailed.

This anthology evolved from our need to document and analyze the Chicana/Mexicana experience. Our scholarship reflects the intricate tapestry of our lives. To contextualize this tapestry, we have included in this introduction, and in our final chapter, interviews with contributors to the anthology and other key Chicana scholars.[2] We hope that our collective voices will make known the impulses that inspire Chicana scholars, as well as the power relationships—in both the academy and our communities at large—that influence our scholarly production. By providing such a forum, we offer our audience a glimpse into our milieu and our analysis of the Chicana experience. We believe this approach challenges and corrects the Eurocentric male bias of "detached," "value-free" inquiry, an underlying premise of traditional disciplines.

Rooted in the political climate of the late 1960s and early 1970s, our scholarship, like other currents of dissent, is a Chicana critique of cultural, political, and economic conditions in the United States. It is influenced by the tradition of advocacy scholarship, which challenges the claims of objectivity and links research to community concerns and social change. It is driven by a passion to place the Chicana, as speaking subject, at the center of intellectual discourse.

Although we were all trained in traditional disciplines, our intellectual enterprise compels us to stretch our disciplinary boundaries, discover new methodologies, and formulate new directions in theory building, in order to comprehend our complex position in a society stratified along lines of class, race/ethnicity, gender, and sexuality. Chicana academics work "many sides of the street," a situation imposed by the need to maintain our presence in our own disciplines, our historical roots in Chicano studies, our political interest in women's studies and feminist theory, and our own "protected" space.

CHICANA SCHOLARSHIP: HISTORICAL AND INTELLECTUAL ROOTS

The Chicano movement and the "second wave" of the women's movement, which emerged during the 1960s, called into question social and ideological patterns that justified systems of racial and gender inequality. Both movements used political action and ideological critiques as weapons in the struggle against oppression. These movements gave birth to Chicano studies and women's studies programs, which developed new conceptual frameworks to analyze Chicanos and women. In theory, the particular circumstances of Chicanas should have found expression in Chicano and feminist discourses, but they did not. The Chicano movement and Chicano studies paradigms have typically analyzed race/ethnic and class domination, neglecting a gender critique. Women's studies and feminist theory have challenged the system of male domination and female subordination, ignoring race/ethnic and class contradictions. Chicana activism and discourse of the late 1960s and early 1970s characteristically reverberate with frustration at the politics and theoretical formulations of these movements, because they denied, subsumed, or neglected the "triple-oppression" status of Chicanas. Although Chicanas sought numerous ways to express their concerns, their discourse was confined primarily to alternative publications within the Chicano movement.[3] When asked to discuss their perceptions of the relationship of Chicana scholarship to Chicano studies and women's studies, our contributors gave voice to the tensions and contradictions characteristic of earlier Chicana positions.

Angie Chabram Dernersesian: Mainstream feminists, many of whom do not know this newly formulated Chicana who has yet to make her way into mainline academia, are now being obliged to think about their own privilege in terms of access to cultural production. Mainstream feminists are being invited by Chicana scholars to reflect on their own convergence with male hegemonic practices that omit minority scholars (in this case women of color) or silence them as speaking subjects in theoretical discourses of race, class, and gender oppression. In their critiques of Chicano scholarship, Chicana scholars have successfully deconstructed Chicano movement discourses that privilege the Chicano male subject and draw on male cultural symbols (Ché, Pancho Villa, brave Aztec figures on sexy calendars) as illustrations of group resistance to domination. By pointing out that Chicano cultural production is replete with male figures—El Pachuco, El

Vato Loco, the political Chicano, the existential Chicano, the indigenous Chicano, the metaphysical Chicano, and their authoritarian fathers, all of whom constitute the essence of Chicanismo for their producers—Chicanas have also brought to light the uncomfortable convergence between alternative nationalist and mainstream hegemonic discourses of culture, which foreground patriarchy. Ultimately, the contribution of Chicana scholarship is that it has begun to populate Chicana/o cultural production with positive, viable images of Chicanas. Chicanas are not only questioning and restructuring feminist and nationalist discourses but also infusing largely unexplored class themes with new forms of identity that have until now been absent from Chicano/a cultural production.

Antonia Castañeda: It's a question of who has power in the society and then how that power is used. At this point, Anglo women and Chicano men out of Chicano studies have more power than Chicanas do, and that's why I keep coming back to political issues. That's what it boils down to: Where does the power lie? Who has it? How is it being used? I don't have in my experience much of a basis for trusting the institutions of society and the people who run those institutions. At this point in women's studies, it's Anglo women; and in Chicano studies, it's Chicano men. I'm not sure that they have the best interest of Chicanas in mind, because I don't think that they have thought about it; or if they have, their attitude has been unfortunately more "How do we control and direct?" than "How do we empower?" It's not that I'm expecting Anglo women or Chicano men to empower me. I'm just expecting them not to be obstacles, and unfortunately I have found that in many respects they either are obstacles or I'm in the position of having to teach them, and that can be very problematic.

Vicki Ruiz: In Chicano scholarship, Chicanas are invisible; and in women's studies, Chicanas are exotic—the "other" of the "other." Chafing against the matrices of invisibility and mystery, Chicana scholars have created their own terrain, both personally and professionally. I believe that Chicana academics share a deeply embedded commitment to their communities, to the women whose voices take center stage in our research. They are our friends, not our informants. We feel a sense of responsibility that exceeds the ethical standards of our disciplines; we care for those who entrust us with their secrets. Whether we meet someone in person or through scraps of physical evidence—for example, diary or testament—we feel that bond of trust.

Norma Alarcón: I think that in the 1980s there have been signs that women's studies programs want to incorporate the literature of women of color; they even want to hire women of color, although they continually run into problems, because sometimes they may find that the work of women of color is too combative, in which case they may say that they are looking for someone more collegial. Thus, the plan to hire women of color is fraught with problems, many of them regarding the politics of feminism itself. Such politics often pivot on theoretical questions and problems. Women's studies programs have been producing successive theories of "correct" women's studies since the 1970s, and as they successively theorize themselves, they do not want to have that construction displaced by the positions of women of color. Ultimately, it is not going to be a curricular problem, because most women's studies programs have demonstrated, especially in the late 1980s, that they are willing to include your article, your book, your novel, your poem, whatever, in their syllabus. What they do not want disrupted are the theoretical underpinnings of that syllabus. So they appropriate the work without retheorizing the syllabus, and I think that is going to be the major battle. You can see that there are parallels here with the Chicano studies project, whereby the theory underpinning the syllabus elaborated by male scholars around male topics is going to be displaced. Basically, we are speaking about an epistemological overhaul. As long as neither group is willing to rethink all of this, we are in a position where we have to keep on doing what we are doing; and, like the women of color at the National Women's Studies Association, we may have to opt for our own organizations.[4]

CONTEMPORARY DIMENSIONS: THE EMERGENCE OF CHICANA STUDIES

Marginalized within traditional disciplines, Chicano studies, and women's studies, Chicana scholars, like other women of color, created alternative avenues, "safe spaces" to develop intellectually and continue the trajectory of political dissent. The creation of such spaces was forged by institutional constraints and fueled by the emergence of a small but critical mass of Chicanas within the academy who persisted in posing "Chicana" questions.

Because of their historic "home" in Chicano studies, Chicana academics have tended to focus political energy within Chicano studies programs and the National Association for Chicano Studies (NACS). At the University of California, Berkeley, for example, several women graduate students and one assistant professor from Chicano studies organized Mujeres en Marcha in opposition to male domination within Chicano studies and NACS. At the NACS conference in Tempe, Arizona, in 1982, they presented a panel on sexual politics.[5] The following year, at the NACS conference in Ypsilanti, Michigan, about a dozen women met and formed the Chicana Caucus, demanding that the next conference focus on gender and proposing "Voces de la Mujer" as the conference theme.[6] In this way, discussion of gender politics was institutionalized at NACS through the Chicana Caucus and the yearly plenary.

The decade of the 1980s demarcates the emergence of Chicana studies. At the organizational level, a separate "safe space" was institutionalized through Mujeres Activas en Letras y Cambio Social (MALCS) in 1983. In 1985, MALCS initiated its annual Chicana/Latina Summer Research Institutes. The Chicana faculty and graduate students who founded MALCS as a support and advocacy group and a forum for sharing research interests declared: "We are the daughters of Chicano working-class families involved in higher education. . . . We are particularly concerned with the conditions women face at work, in and out of the home. We continue our mothers' struggle for social and economic justice."[7] Drawing from a tradition of political struggle, MALCS is dedicated to the documentation, analysis, and interpretation of the Chicana/Latina experience in the United States.

Although a critical mass of Chicana scholars were engaged in gender analysis in the 1980s, it is premature to attempt to categorize their scholarly production. We propose that the vitality in Chicana scholarship springs from its insistence on developing new categories of analysis that reshape and expand established intellectual boundaries. For the first time in the short history of Chicano/a scholarship (about two decades), a visible, viable group of Chicana academics confront the complex intersection of class, race/ethnicity, and gender/sexuality in their scholarship.

In the following paragraphs, Chicana scholars discuss the significant contributions of Chicana studies over the past ten years.

Elisa Facio: I think that Chicana scholarship, its development and establishment, is a struggle for representation and voice in the realm of knowledge. So obviously I would want to see this knowledge contribute to change, not only in communities but in the larger society. But, like most scholarship, ours is not developed in a vacuum. Its most important contribution has been the integration of a gender analysis of the Chicana experience. The methods of investigation of Chicana lives, both past and present, are being seriously questioned, challenged, and tested. And they continue to be part of a larger academic process in building theory and seeking new methodological approaches. Chicana scholarship has not only contributed to the building of knowledge about the Chicana experience but has also helped Chicanas develop as scholars.

Deena González: I think Chicana studies is expanding the categories that it uses, that it relies on. I don't feel any longer that I'm "just" a historian. I'm not so locked into the methodologies and the ways of history. I've found, for example, that literary criticism has helped my work enormously, that it has made me think in different ways. I think Chicana studies is moving to develop its own practices, pedagogies, methods, and treatments in a more public way. I wouldn't divide Chicana scholarship into disciplines, because I don't think we have an equal distribution across disciplines. But I certainly think we have carved out a subfield within major fields, whether those are Chicano studies, history, or literature. We have a presence, a beginning interest and visibility, and that's different. The final thing that I think is important in all this, probably the most important, is our focus on and continuing interest in sexual politics. Many of us never let that die out. In my own work, I never let go of the fact that on some primary level, sex and sexuality, sexual politics, are dimensions that are missing in past analyses of women's lives. I'd say that in the last ten years these are some of the key things that Chicana studies has contributed.

Emma Pérez: As a historian, I'm really seduced by theory, and I know that theories follow practice—what people do in their daily lives. Chicana women are exposing the lack of harmony in gender relationships by focusing on conflict in the family and in women's political and economic positions.

Rosa Linda Fregoso: Chicana scholars are applying available theories to new objects of study; the consequences include revision and modification of previous theoretical frameworks. Chicana scholars insist on the centrality of theorizing about all forms of domination. This is one of the ways that previous theoretical assumptions of many of these academic disciplines are undergoing transformation.

Denise Segura: I think that Chicana scholarship offers critical perspectives on the way society is structured hierarchically. Chicana scholarship confronts a myriad of critical issues: poverty, education, employment, institutional racism, sexism, and classism. I'd say there are several types of Chicana scholarship. One type tries to connect research on Chicanas to mainstream frameworks in the respective fields; another type tries to develop an understanding of the status and oppression of Chicanas, using feminist frameworks as points of departure; another type, connected to postmodernist frameworks, tries to get away from all mainstream thought. It begins with Chicanas as a point of departure and builds from there an understanding of their uniqueness as well as their commonalities with other oppressed peoples in this society.

In sum, Chicana scholarship challenges analytical frameworks that dichotomize the multiple sources of Chicana oppression; at the same time, it posits alternative frameworks grounded in the Chicana experience. Although the field does not yet offer fully developed, coherent new frameworks, it is beginning to reconstruct the often fragmented or incomplete analysis in traditional disciplines, Chicano studies, and feminist theory. Chicana studies places at center the Chicana subject. Thus, its analytical underpinnings are grounded in the multiple sources of Chicana subjectivity. As the contributors to this anthology illustrate, Chicana scholarship draws from diverse theoretical traditions and methodological interventions, at the same time forging into new intellectual terrains.

The contributions to this anthology span several decades and stretch the analytical frameworks usually employed by mainstream scholars. For example, analysis of colonialism (both Spanish and Anglo conquest of what is commonly referred to as the Southwest) has been dominated by economic and racial/ethnic frameworks. Chicana scholars expand our intellectual horizons by incorporating sex/gender domination and resistance within a colonial dialectic. Similarly, immigration—generally viewed through male immigrant lenses—takes on new contours when analyzed through Chicana feminist frameworks. Analyses of cultural practices and cultural reproduction are contested and reshaped when Chicana experiences—the forces that Chicanas contend with in their daily lives—are made a part of these analyses.

ORGANIZATION OF THE BOOK

I. Acts of Domination / Acts of Resistance

Themes of political subordination, sexual exploitation, and ideological domination in sex/gender politics provide the conceptual framework in Part One of this book. Against this backdrop, the contributions in this section analyze diverse manifestations of power relations and opposition to domination.

The first essay, Antonia Castañeda's "Sexual Violence in the Politics and Policies of Conquest: Amerindian Women and the Spanish Conquest of Alta California," focuses on the manner in which sex/gender informed the politics and policies shaped by social relations of domination/subordination during the eighteenth century. Highlighting the sexual assault on Amerindian women, Castañeda points out that the brutality they experienced was not unique to the Spanish Conquest; indeed, sexual violence is generally considered legitimate in the context of war and conquest. Although the political and religious authorities recognized that assaults on Amerindian women severely obstructed the Spanish crown's objective of missionization, they were unsuccessful in curtailing such attacks. By linking domination based on race with domination based on sex/gender, Castañeda illuminates the relationship between sexual violence, racial ideology, and conquest.

Angie Chabram Dernersesian's "And, Yes . . . The Earth Did Part: On the Splitting of Chicana/o Subjectivity" explores the development of Chicana subjectivity through an analysis of cultural production. Moving away from a subjectivity grounded in the Chicano movement's nationalist discourse, Chicanas' cultural production deconstructs the hegemonic singular Chicano (male), challenging his claim to privilege and power. Furthermore, Chicanas contest the Chicano movement's limited codification of the female subject within the confines of "La Familia." Through various cultural media, they offer instead Chicana representations engaged in a struggle against class, race/ethnicity, and gender/sexuality oppression.

Emma Pérez's essay, "Speaking from the Margin: Uninvited Discourse on Sexuality and Power," analyzes Octavio Paz's use of the discourse of the Oedipal-conquest triangle to decode social-sexual-racial hierarchies and Chicana oppression within a historical context. Using Luis Valdez's rendition of the Delgadina *corrido,* Pérez also illuminates the cycle of destructive dependence through an investigation of the Electra complex. Female subordination can be combated, Pérez concludes, through a dialectical process that challenges oppressive social constructs of race/ethnicity and gender/sexuality.

II. Cultural Representations / Cultural Presentations

Fragmented cultural representations of Mexican-origin women are challenged on the basis of the realities of their daily lives. The four chapters in this section document issues of accommodation and rebellion within different historical periods and suggest alternative interpretations of these women's behavior.

In "La Tules of Image and Reality: Euro-American Attitudes and Legend Formation on a Spanish-Mexican Frontier," Deena González discusses doña Gertrudis Barceló, an ingenious New Mexican businesswoman who profitably adapted to Euro-American colonizers. Chafing against prescribed Euro-American views of "proper" female roles, La Tules established a niche in a transitional society. Rather than merely describing a legendary figure, González sets Barceló within the larger framework of colonization and adaptation of New Mexicans. To Euro-American colonizers, La Tules embodied prevailing stereotypes of Mexicans as smoking, gambling, and dancing degenerates. To the people of Santa Fé, she represented a woman who successfully accommodated to colonization, but on her terms.

Angelina Veyna discusses the lives of ordinary women of Spanish-Mexican origin during the colonial period. In her article, "It Is My Last Wish That . . .": A Look at Colonial Nueva Mexicanas through Their Testaments," using primary sources from the Spanish Archives of New Mexico, Veyna focuses on the wills and estate documents of twelve women from northern New Mexico. By reviewing the material goods that women owned and the way they distributed their possessions, she interprets their daily activities and interests and provides a glimpse into family interactions. These documents also allow her an initial interpretation of the dynamic role women played within New Mexican society during this period.

In " 'Star Struck': Acculturation, Adolescence, and the Mexican American Woman, 1920–1950," Vicki Ruiz discusses agents of acculturation that influenced Mexican American women's coming of age in this generation. Focusing on such issues as education, intergenerational conflict, the lure of Hollywood stardom, advertising, and consumerism, Ruiz illuminates conflicting currents in the acculturation of Chicanas in California. On the one hand, Hollywood films, consumerism championed through advertising, and acculturation promoted by the educational system framed illusions of conformity to the American dream. Yet the daily reality of racial prejudice, restricted employment, and parental control thwarted upward mobility. Faced with these contradictions, young Mexican American women navigated a precarious path between acculturation and cultural retention.

In "The Mother Motif in *La Bamba* and *Boulevard Nights,*" Rosa Linda Fregoso deconstructs male cultural narratives by analyzing Hollywood representations of "La Madre" (mother). Both films, one directed and produced by a Chicano, the other by a non-Chicano, center on the mother motif vis-à-vis the "good" son and the "bad" son. Thus, the mother is not a subject but an embodiment of dominant cultural patterns that at the same time idealize and condemn mothers. Fregoso analyzes Oedipal themes of seduction and retribution central to both films. Using feminist lenses, she reveals the patriarchal text embedded in the cultural imaging of Chicanas through both films.

III. Contested Domains: Economy and Family

In this section, women's paid and unpaid labor is examined through a consideration of gender strategies in migration, health practices, and the division of household labor. By juxtaposing the costs and benefits incurred by the participation of Mexicanas and Chicanas in the labor force, the authors critically assess the effects of that participation.

In "Gender, Class, and Households: Migration Patterns in Aguascalientes, Mexico," María de los Angeles Crummett shows that only in the context of a class analysis does the household become a useful tool in examining the uneven impact of migration on gender. Using a case study of migrants from Aguascalientes, Mexico, she forcefully argues that differing patterns of migration by class and gender are critically linked to the household's economic standing in the agrarian structure and to internal demographic features. Among commercial, subsistence, and landless households, the bulk of the migrants are located in the subsistence class. Additionally, women from this class have higher migration rates, greater involvement in household agricultural tasks traditionally assumed by men, and greater unpaid labor in the home. Thus, Crummett elucidates how class status affects migration and women's involvement in wage labor, agricultural production, and social reproduction of household members.

In "Hard Choices and Changing Roles among Mexican Migrant *Campesinas,*" Adela de la Torre examines maternal behavioral changes in infant-feeding practices, migration, and rural employment in California, together with changes in the household division of labor of these migrants. Her essay suggests that the consequences to Mexican women of migration to the California fields may not be completely positive. From her survey of agricultural migrant workers in selected California labor camps and rural clinics, she concludes that traditional infant-feeding practices, such as breast feeding, are limited by these women's seasonal employment. In addition, the increased paid employment in agriculture is not offset by greater male participation in the division of household chores.

Beatríz M. Pesquera assesses the complex dynamics in the division of household labor by focusing on the relationship between Chicana workers' ideological position, gender strategies, and the division of household labor. " 'In the Beginning He Wouldn't Even Lift a Spoon': The Division of Household Labor" delineates differences across occupational categories. Pesquera's data suggest that income differentials among couples and women's employment demands shed light on ideological and behavioral differences among the informants in her sample. Furthermore, she elucidates the manner in which the division of household labor by gender is altered or reproduced.

IV. Social Reproduction: Institutional and "Uninstitutional" Lives

Employing a case study analysis, the last two essays illustrate the tension between formal and informal institutions and social reproduction. These essays are framed within a social reproduction conceptual model. This model analyzes the process whereby institutional practices reinforce existing structures of inequality inherent in the capitalist system. For example, the educational system—through curriculum, tracking of students, and allocation of resources—codifies existing class and race/ethnic relations.

Denise Segura's "Slipping through the Cracks: Dilemmas in Chicana Education" describes the educational experiences of a select sample of Chicana women. She concludes that Chicanas often are unsuccessful in the educational system because of insensitivity, indifferent instruction, and the lack of strong support in the schools. Her findings refute beliefs that Mexican-origin families are not motivated to pursue educational opportunities. Segura emphasizes that Chicanas "slip through the cracks" primarily because of forces in the educational institution rather than as a result of parental educational neglect.

This section fittingly concludes with Elisa Facio's "Gender and the Life Course: A Case Study of Chicana Elderly," which portrays social interaction in a senior center. As in other phases of the human life cycle, the search for self-esteem is an important feature of the aging process. Traditional Chicano family structures, in which the elderly play an important role, are not readily available to many of the center's participants. Through an analysis of social life in the center, Facio illustrates how notions of self-worth linked to women's domestic sphere are reproduced. She also notes, however, that the Chicanas in her study retained a measure of control over their lives, which enhanced their self-esteem.

NOTES

1. The ethnic label *Chicana* refers to women of Mexican descent residing in the United States. *Mexicana* specifically refers to Mexican immigrant women. See "A Note on Ethnic Labels," p. xiii above.

2. In addition to the contributors to this anthology, we interviewed Norma Alarcón, Assistant Professor, Chicano Studies Program, University of California, Berkeley, because she provided valuable editorial comments on the manuscript and has made important contributions to publishing Chicana/Latina scholarship through Third Woman Press. Adaljisa Sosa Riddell (whose interview appears in our concluding chapter) has been a leading force in the development of Mujeres Activas en Letras y Cambio Social (MALCS) and directed the Chicano Studies Program at Davis, which for three years sponsored the Chicana/Latina Summer Institute. Because of their contributions to the development of Chicano studies, we wanted to include their voices.

3. For a detailed analysis of Chicana feminist writings of this period, see Alma Garcia, "The Development of Chicana Feminist Discourse, 1970–1980," *Gender and Society* 3 (June 1989): 217–238; and D. Segura and B. Pesquera, "Beyond Indifference and Antipathy: The Chicana Movement and Chicana Feminist Discourse," *Aztlan* 2 (Fall 1988–90): 69–92.

4. At the 1990 meeting of the National Women's Studies Association, the Women of

Color Caucus voted to split from the organization and develop an organization with a focus on women of color in the United States and internationally.

5. The conference panel and discussion was prepared by Teresa Córdova and published under Mujeres en Marcha, *Chicanas in the 80's: Unsettled Issues* (Berkeley: Chicano Studies Library Publications Unit, University of California, 1983).

6. For proceedings from the conference, see Teresa Córdova et al., eds., *Chicana Voices: Intersections of Class, Race, and Gender* (Austin: Center for Mexican American Studies, University of Texas, 1986).

7. Adaljisa Sosa Riddell, ed., *Mujeres Activas en Letras y Cambio Social, Noticiera de M.A.L.C.S.* (Davis: University of California Chicano Studies Program, 1983), p. 3.

PART ONE

Acts of Domination / Acts of Resistance

TWO

Sexual Violence in the Politics and Policies of Conquest

Amerindian Women and the Spanish Conquest of Alta California

Antonia I. Castañeda

In the morning, six or seven soldiers would set out together . . . and go to the distant rancherías *[villages] even many leagues away. When both men and women at the sight of them would take off running . . . the soldiers, adept as they are at lassoing cows and mules, would lasso Indian women—who then became prey for their unbridled lust. Several Indian men who tried to defend the women were shot to death.*

JUNIPERO SERRA, 1773

In words reminiscent of sixteenth-century chroniclers Bernal Díaz del Castillo and Bartolomé de las Casas, the father president of the California missions, Junipero Serra, described the depredations of the soldiers against Indian women in his reports and letters to Viceroy Antonio María Bucareli and the father guardian of the College of San Fernando, Rafaél Verger. Sexual assaults against native women began shortly after the founding of the presidio and mission at Monterey in June 1770, wrote Serra, and continued throughout the length of California. The founding of each new mission and presidio brought new reports of sexual violence.

The despicable actions of the soldiers, Serra told Bucareli in 1773, were severely retarding the spiritual and material conquest of California. The native people were resisting missionization. Some were becoming warlike and hostile because of the soldiers' repeated outrages against the women. The assaults resulted in Amerindian attacks, which the soldiers countered with unauthorized reprisals, thereby further straining the capacity of the small military force to staff the presidios and guard the missions. Instead of pacification and order, the soldiers provoked greater conflict and thus jeopardized the position of the church in this region.[1]

Serra was particularly alarmed about occurrences at Mission San Gabriel. "Since the district is the most promising of all the missions," he wrote to Father Verger, "this mission gives me the greatest cause for anxiety; the secular arm down there was guilty of the most heinous crimes, killing the men to take their wives."[2] Father Serra related that on October 10, 1771, within a month of its having been founded, a large group of Indians suddenly attacked two soldiers who were on horseback and tried to kill the one who had outraged a woman. The soldiers retaliated. "A few days later," Serra continued, "as he went out to gather the herd of cattle . . . and [it] seems more likely to get himself a woman, a soldier, along with some others, killed the principal Chief of the gentiles; they cut off his head and brought it in triumph back to the mission."[3]

The incident prompted the Amerindians of the coast and the sierra, mortal enemies until that time, to convene a council to make peace with each other and join forces to eliminate the Spaniards. The council planned to attack the mission on October 16 but changed the plan after a new contingent of troops arrived at the mission.[4] Despite this narrowly averted disaster, the soldiers assigned to Mission San Gabriel continued their outrages.

The soldiers' behavior not only generated violence on the part of the native people as well as resistance to missionization, argued Serra; it also took its toll on the missionaries, some of whom refused to remain at their mission sites. In his 1773 memorial to Bucareli, Serra lamented the loss of one of the missionaries, who could not cope with the soldiers' disorders at San Gabriel. The priest was sick at heart, Serra stated: "He took to his bed, when he saw with his own eyes a soldier actually committing deeds of shame with an Indian who had come to the mission, and even the children who came to the mission were not safe from their baseness."[5]

Conditions at other missions were no better. Mission San Luis Obispo also lost a priest because of the assaults on Indian women. After spending two years as the sole missionary at San Luis, Father Domingo Juncosa asked for and received permission to return to Mexico because he was "shocked at the scandalous conduct of the soldiers" and could not work under such abominable conditions.[6] Even before San Luis Obispo was founded in the early fall of 1772, Tichos women had cause to fear. The most notorious molesters of non-Christian women were among the thirteen soldiers sent on a bear hunt to this area during the previous winter of starvation at Monterey.[7]

The establishment of new missions subjected the women of each new area to sexual assaults. Referring to the founding of the mission at San Juan Capistrano, Serra wrote that "it seems all the sad experiences that we went through at the beginning have come to life again. The soldiers, without any restraint or shame, have behaved like brutes toward the Indian women."[8] From this mission also, the priests reported to Serra that the soldier-guards went at night to the nearby villages to assault the women and that hiding the women did not restrain the brutes, who beat the men to force them to reveal where the women were hidden. Non-Christian Indians in the vicinity of the missions were simply not safe. They were at the mercy of soldiers with horses and guns.[9]

In 1773, a case of rape was reported at San Luis Rey, one at San Diego, and two cases at Monterey the following year.[10] Serra expressed his fears and concern to Governor Felipe de Neve, who was considering establishing a new presidio in the channel of Santa Barbara. Serra told Neve that he took it for granted that the insulting and scandalous conduct of the soldiers "would be the same as we had experienced in other places which were connected with presidios. Perhaps this one would be worse."[11]

Native women and their communities were profoundly affected by the sexual attacks and attendant violence. California Amerindians were peaceable, non-aggressive people who highly valued harmonious relationships. Physical violence and the infliction of bodily harm on one another were virtually unknown. Women did not fear men. Rape rarely, if ever, occurred. If someone stole from another or caused another's death, societal norms required that the offending party make reparations to the individual and/or the family. Appropriate channels to rectify a wrong without resorting to violence existed.[12]

Animosity, when it did surface, was often worked out ritualistically—for example, through verbal battles in the form of war songs, or song fights that lasted eight days, or encounters in which the adversaries threw stones across a river at each other with no intent actually to hit or physically injure the other party. Even among farming groups such as the Colorado River people, who practiced warfare and took women and children captive, female captives were never sexually molested. The Yumas believed that intimate contact with enemy women caused sickness.[13]

Thus, neither the women nor their people were prepared for the onslaught of aggression and violence the soldiers unleashed against them. They were horrified and terrified. One source reported that women of the San Gabriel and other southern missions raped by the soldiers were considered contaminated and obliged to undergo an extensive purification, which included a long course of sweating, the drinking of herbs, and other forms of purging. This practice was consistent with the people's belief that sickness was caused by enemies. "But their disgust and abhorrence," states the same source, "never left them till many years after."[14] Moreover, any child born as a result of these rapes, and apparently every child with white blood born among them for a very long time, was strangled and buried.[15]

Father Pedro Font, traveling overland from Tubac to Monterey with the Anza expedition between September 1775 and May 1776, recorded the impact of the violence on the native people he encountered. Font's diary verifies the terror in which native Californians, especially the women, now lived. Everybody scattered and fled at the sight of Spaniards. The women hid. They no longer moved about with freedom and ease. The people were suspicious and hostile. The priests were no longer welcome in the living quarters.

The Quabajay people of the Santa Barbara Channel, Font wrote, "appear to us to be gentle and friendly, not war-like. But it will not be easy to reduce them for they are displeased with the Spaniards for what they have done to them, now taking their fish and their food . . . now stealing their women and abusing them."[16] Upon encountering several unarmed Indians on Friday, February 23, Font commented that "the women were very cautious and hardly one left their huts, because the soldiers of Monterey . . . had offended them with various excesses."[17]

At one village, Font noted, he was unable to see the women close at hand because as soon as the Indians saw his party, "they all hastily hid in their huts, especially the girls, the men remaining outside blocking the door and taking care that nobody should go inside."[18] Font attempted to become acquainted with the people of another village on the channel. He went to the door, but "they shut the inner door on me . . . this is the result of the extortions and outrages which the soldiers have perpetrated when in their journeys they have passed along the Channel, especially at the beginning."[19] Font echoed Serra's concern that the sexual assaults and other outrages had severely retarded missionization in California.

Serra and his co-religionists had great cause for concern, because the missions were not meeting their principal objective of converting Amerindians into loyal Catholic subjects who would repel invading European forces from these shores. By the end of 1773, in the fifth year of the occupation of Alta California, fewer than five hundred baptisms and only sixty-two marriages had been performed in the five missions then existing.[20] Since the marriages probably represented the total adult converts, that meant that the remaining four hundred converts were children. These dismal statistics fueled arguments for abandoning the California missions. While various reasons may be cited for the failure to attract adult converts, certainly the sexual attacks and the impact of that violence on women and their communities were primary among them.

Few historians have recognized that the sexual extortion and abuse of native women gravely affected the political, military, religious, and social developments on this frontier. In 1943, Sherburne F. Cook commented that "the entire problem of sexual relations between whites and the natives, although one which was regarded as very serious by the founders of the province, has apparently escaped detailed consideration by later historians."[21] Cook tackled the issue in demographic terms and wrote about the catastrophic decline in the Indian population as a result of alien diseases, including venereal diseases, brought in by Europeans, as well as other maladies of the conquest.[22]

Almost thirty years later, Edwin A. Beilharz wrote that "the major causes of friction between Spaniard and Indian were the abuse of Indian women and the forced labor of Indian men. . . . Of the two, the problem of restraining the soldiers from assaulting Indian women was the more serious."[23] In his study of the administration of Governor Felipe de Neve, Beilharz notes that Neve recognized the seriousness of the problem and tried to curb the abuses.

Since the 1970s, the decade that saw both the reprinting of Cook's work and the publication of the Beilharz study, the development of gender as a category of analysis has enabled us to reexamine Spanish expansion to Alta California with new questions about sex and gender. Cook, Beilharz, and other scholars initiated but did not develop the discussion about the centrality of sex/gender issues to the politics and policies of conquest.

It is clear that the sexual exploitation of native women and related violence seriously threatened the political and military objectives of the colonial enterprise in California. Repeated attacks against women and summary reprisals against men who dared to interfere undermined the efforts of the priests to attract Amerindians to the missions and to Christianity. They also thwarted whatever attempts the military authorities might make to elicit political or military allegiance from the native peoples.[24]

From the missionaries' point of view, the attacks had more immediate, deleterious consequences for the spiritual conquest of California, because such actions belied significant principles of the Catholic moral theology they were trying to inculcate. As the primary agents of Christianization/Hispanicization, the missionaries argued that they could not teach and Amerindians could not learn and obey the moral strictures against rape, abduction, fornication, adultery, and all forms of sexual impurity while the soldiers persisted in their licentiousness and immorality. Their actions repudiated the very morality the friars were to inculcate.[25]

Early conflict between ecclesiastical and civil-military officials over deployment and discipline of the mission escort soon gave rise to constant bitter disputes centering on the question of authority and jurisdiction over the Indians in California. The conflict over control of the Indians revolved around the issue of their segregation from the non-Indian population. Rooted in the early conquest and consequent development of colonial Indian policy, the issue has been extensively discussed by other historians. The concern here is to examine it specifically from the point of view of sex/gender and to define a context for explaining why, despite strenuous efforts by church and state alike, there was little success in arresting the attacks on Indian women.[26]

Serra, for his part, blamed the military commanders and, once appointed, the governor. They were, he said, lax in enforcing military discipline and unconcerned about the moral fiber of their troops. They failed to punish immoral soldiers who assaulted native women, were flagrantly incontinent, or took Amerindian women as concubines. In California, he stated, secular authorities not only condoned the soldiers' assaults on Indian women but interfered with the missionaries' efforts to counter the abuse, and thereby exceeded their authority with respect to Amerindians.[27]

To argue his case against Lieutenant Pedro Fages, the military commander, and to muster political and economic support for the California establishments, Serra made the arduous trip to Mexico City for an audience with Viceroy Bucareli. He left California in September of 1772 and arrived in Mexico the following February. At the viceroy's request, Serra submitted a lengthy work entitled "Report on the General Conditions and Needs of the Missions and Thirty-Two Suggestions for Improving the Government of the Missions."[28] Serra addressed sex/gender issues as part of several grievances against Fages's command. His recommendations for curtailing the sexual violence and general malfeasance of the soldiers were that Fages should be removed and that Spaniards who married Indian women should be rewarded.

Once the viceroy had removed the lieutenant, Serra continued, he should give strict orders to Fages's successor that, upon the request of any missionary, "he should remove the soldier or soldiers who give bad example, especially in the matter of incontinence . . . and send, in their place, another or others who are not known as immoral or scandalous."[29]

Drawing on colonial tradition established much earlier in New Spain, wherein colonial officials encouraged intermarriage with Amerindian noblewomen in order to advance particular political, military, religious, or social interests, Serra suggested that men who married newly Christianized "daughters of the land" be rewarded.[30] In the second to last of his thirty-two suggestions, Serra asked Bucareli to "allow a bounty for those, be they soldiers or not, who enter into the state of marriage with girls of that faraway country, new Christian converts."[31]

Serra specified the three kinds of bounty to be given the individual: an animal for his own use immediately upon being married; two cows and a mule from the royal herd after he had worked the mission farms for a year or more; and, finally, allotment of a piece of land. Since soldiers were subject to being transferred from one mission or presidio to another, Serra further recommended that he who married a native woman should be allowed to remain permanently attached to his wife's mission.[32]

With this recommendation, which he discussed in more detail in a subsequent letter to the viceroy, Serra hoped to solve several related problems.[33] He sought to curb the sexual attacks on Indian women as well as to induce soldiers to remain and become permanent settlers in Alta California. Theoretically, soldiers would thereby remain on the frontier, and formal and permanent unions with Indian women would allay the natives' mistrust and help to forge a bond between them and the soldiers. These marriages would thus help to ease Indian-military tensions while also cementing Catholic family life in the region.[34]

It was equally important to remove temptation and opportunity for licentious behavior. Thus, in a second memorial to the viceroy, written in April of 1773, a little over a month after his report, Serra forcefully argued against the proposal that the annual supply ships from San Blas be replaced with mule trains coming overland. In addition to the greater expense of an overland supply line, he reasoned, the presence of one hundred guards and muleteers crossing the country would add to "the plague of immorality" running rampant in California.[35]

The document that resulted from the official review of Serra's memorial, the *Reglamento Provisional*—generally known as the *Echeveste Regulations*—was the first regulatory code drawn up for California. The *Echeveste Regulations* acted favorably on twenty-one of Serra's thirty-two original recommendations, including the removal of Fages as military commander.[36]

Implementation of the new regulations, however, did not stop the abuse of women or the immorality of the soldiers. Serra continued to blame the civil-military authorities. He charged Captain Fernando de Rivera y Moncada, who replaced Fages, with currying the soldiers' favor; and he subsequently accused the newly appointed governor, Felipe de Neve, of antireligiosity and anticlericalism. Thus, in the summary of Franciscan complaints against Neve, which Francisco Panagua, guardian of the College of San Fernando, sent Viceroy Mayorga in 1781, Father Panagua wrote that "another consequence . . . of the aversion which the said Governor [Neve] has for the religious, is that the subordinates . . . live very libidinously in unrestrained and scandalous incontinence as they use at will Indian women of every class and strata."[37] Serra further charged that Neve allowed fornication among the soldiers, "because, so I have heard him say, . . . it is winked at in Rome and tolerated in Madrid."[38]

Serra's charges against Fages, Rivera, and Neve were not well founded. As head of the California establishments, each was fully cognizant that the soldiers' excesses not only undermined military discipline, and thus their own command, but also seriously jeopardized the survival of the missions and the presidios. Fundamentally, the assaults against women were unwarranted, unprovoked, hostile acts that established conditions of war on this frontier. Although the native peoples by and large did not practice warfare, they were neither docile nor passive in the face of repeated assaults. The people of the South were especially aggressive. The country between San Diego and San Gabriel remained under Indian control for a long time.[39] It was in this region that the Indians marshaled their strongest forces and retaliated against the Spaniards. Some of the engagements, such as the one at San Gabriel in 1771, were minor skirmishes. Others were full-fledged attacks. In 1775 at Mission San Diego, for example, a force of eight hundred razed the mission, killed one priest and two artisans, and seriously wounded two soldiers. Women participated and sometimes even planned and/or led the attacks. In October 1785, Amerindians from eight *rancherías* united under the leadership of one woman and three men and launched an attack on Mission San Gabriel for the purpose of killing all the Spaniards. Toypurina, the twenty-four-year-old medicine woman of the Japchivit *ranchería,* used her considerable influence as a medicine woman to persuade six of the eight villages to join the rebellion. The attack was thwarted. Toypurina was captured and punished along with the other three leaders.[40]

Throughout their terms, Fages, Rivera, and Neve were keenly aware that Amerindians greatly outnumbered Spain's military force in the fledgling settlement and that, ultimately, the soldiers could not have staved off a prolonged Indian attack. Neve's greatest fear, expressed in his request to Bucareli for more commissioned officers, was that "if an affair of this kind [disorders caused by soldiers] ever results in a defeat of our troops, it will be irreparable if they [the Indians] come to know their power. We must prevent this with vigor."[41]

Therefore, during their respective administrations, the military authorities enforced Spain's legal codes, as well as imperial policy regarding segregation of Amerindians from non-Indians as a protective measure for the former. They prosecuted soldiers for major and minor crimes, and they issued their own edicts to curb the soldiers' abuse of Amerindians in general and women in particular. Their authority, however, was circumscribed by Spain's highly centralized form of government.[42]

While the governor of the Californias was authorized to try major criminal cases such as those involving homicide and rape, judgment and sentence were decided at the viceregal level in Mexico City. With the separation of the Interior Provinces from the kingdom of New Spain in 1776, the commandant-general, who combined in his office civil, judicial, and military powers, became the final arbiter.[43]

A 1773 case illustrates the complexity of legal procedures. This case—in which a corporal, Mateo de Soto, and two soldiers, Francisco Avila and Sebastian Alvitre, were accused of raping two young Amerindian girls and killing one of them near the mission of San Diego—dragged on for five years. Fages, Rivera, and Neve all dealt with the case, which occurred while Fages was military commander. Fages received the official complaint from Mariano Carrillo, sergeant at the San Diego presidio, who had interviewed the young survivor at that presidio in the presence of four soldiers acting as witnesses. The girl was accompanied to the presidio by two mission priests and an interpreter, who was also present at the interview.[44]

Fages forwarded the documents to Viceroy Bucareli in Mexico City and, on Bucareli's order, subsequently sent a copy to Felipe Barri, then governor of the Californias, at Loreto. When Rivera replaced Fages, he complied with the viceroy's order to bind the men for trial and to send them to Loreto, the capital of the Californias, in Baja California. By 1775, when Rivera sent Avila and Alvitre to Loreto (Soto had deserted and was never apprehended), Neve had replaced Barri as governor of the Californias. It fell to Neve to hear testimony and conduct the trial, which he opened on October 19, 1775.

The trial, including testimony from six soldiers and comments from the accused after Carrillo's charges were read to them, produced voluminous documents. Neve concluded the trial on November 22 and sent a copy of the entire proceedings to the viceroy for final disposition, along with a statement noting certain discrepancies from proscribed judicial procedure. Upon receipt of the proceedings, Bucareli turned the file over to Teodoro de Croix, recently appointed commandant-general of the Interior Provinces, which included the Californias.[45]

Almost three years elapsed before Croix called in the case.[46] On August 26, 1778, his legal adviser, Pedro Galindo Navarro, submitted his opinion to Croix. In Navarro's opinion, the accusation of rape and homicide was not proven. The dead child's body, he argued, was not examined or even seen; the identification of the soldiers accused was unsatisfactory, since it appeared to have been prompted by the interpreter; the entire charge rested on the testimony of a child, "poorly explained by an interpreter." Finally, the accused denied the charge.[47]

Navarro recommended that the penalty for Avila and Alvitre, who had been detained during the five years of the trial, be commuted to time served and that they should be sentenced to remain and become citizens of California. Croix accepted these recommendations. He issued the order, and the two discharged soldiers were enrolled in the list of settlers at the new pueblo of San José de Guadalupe.[48]

Whether local officials would have convicted the soldiers of rape and homicide must remain a matter of conjecture. In any event, despite laws and prosecutions, the sexual exploitation of Indian women did not cease. The missionaries continuously reported that soldiers "go by night to nearby villages for the purpose of raping Indian women."[49] And while some cases were recorded, many more must surely have gone unreported. Nevertheless, it is clear that the commandants and the governors did prosecute and take disciplinary action when charges were filed against individual soldiers. Contrary to Serra's charges of laxity and complicity, Fages, Rivera, and Neve did exert the full measure of their authority in this and other reported cases of sexual violence or abuse. Abundant evidence details the dual policy of prevention and punishment implemented by the three seasoned frontier administrators in their ongoing effort to check the soldiers' excesses.[50]

Ever concerned that Amerindians would discover the real weakness of the Spanish position in California, Neve sought to prevent the sexual attacks, and thereby to defuse the military and political conflicts they gave rise to, by forbidding all troops, including sergeants and corporals, from entering Indian villages. Only soldiers escorting the priests on sick calls were exempt from this order, and then the soldier was not to leave the missionary's side. Escort guards were strictly admonished against misconduct and were severely punished if they disobeyed.[51]

In the same vein, he prohibited soldiers of the mission guard from spending the night away from the mission—even if the priests demanded it. Neve emphatically repeated this same order in the instructions he left to Pedro Fages, who succeeded him as governor in September of 1782. "It is advisable," Neve further instructed Fages, "that we muzzle ourselves and not exasperate the numerous heathendom which surround us, conducting ourselves with politeness and respect. . . . It is highly useful to the service of the King and the public welfare that the heathen of these establishments do not learn to kill soldiers."[52]

Governor Fages was equally emphatic when he issued the following order in 1785: "Observing that the officers and men of these presidios are comporting and behaving themselves in the missions with a vicious license which is very prejudicial because of the scandalous disorders which they incite among the gentile and Christian women, I command you, in order to prevent the continuation of such abuses, that you circulate a prohibitory edict imposing severe penalties upon those who commit them."[53]

A decade later, Viceroy Branciforte followed up Neve's earlier order with his own decree prohibiting troops from remaining overnight away from the presidios, because among other reasons this practice was "prejudicial to good discipline and Christian morals."[54] Governor Diego de Borica, who succeeded Fages in 1794, issued a similar order the following year. These edicts had little effect.

Soldiers and civilian settlers alike disregarded the civil laws against rape as well as military orders against contact with Amerindian women outside of narrowly proscribed channels. The records verify that sexual attacks continued in areas adjacent to missions, presidios, and pueblos throughout the colonial period. Amerindian women were never free from the threat of rapacious assaults.

Why, despite strenuous efforts by officials of both church and state, did the sexual attacks persist unabated? Why, despite the obviously serious political and military conflicts the assaults ignited, did they continue? In view of extensive legislation, royal decrees, and moral prohibitions against sexual and other violence, what, in the experience of the men who came here, permitted them to objectify and dehumanize Indian women to the degree that chasing and lassoing them from mounted horses and then raping them reveals?

Until recently, scholars attributed sexual violence and other concurrent social disorders in early California to the race and culture of the mixed-blood soldier-settler population recruited or banished to this frontier. Institutional historians concluded, with Bancroft, that the "original settlers, most of them half-breeds of the least energetic classes . . . , were of a worthless character."[55] Institutional studies generally concurred with Serra's view that the soldiers were recruited from the scum of the society. Serra had repeatedly beseeched Bucareli to send "sturdy, industrious Spanish families" and asked him to advise the governor of the Californias "not to use exile to these missions as punishment for the soldier whom he may detest as insolent or perverse."[56]

In the last two decades, the conditions that shaped institutional development on this frontier have been reexamined. In addition, studies of the social history of the people recruited to Alta California have been undertaken. As a result, the earlier interpretations have been rejected. Scholars now conclude that the slow development of colonial institutions in California was attributable to limited resources, lack of uniform military codes, and other structural problems—and not to the racial or social-class origins of the soldier-settler population.[57]

Instead, the mixed-blood recruits—who themselves derived from other frontier settlements—were admirably able to survive the harsh privations and onerous conditions. In so doing, they established lasting foundations of Spanish civilization in California and the Southwest. Although the *cuera* (leather-jacket) soldiers were indeed unruly and undisciplined, their behavior reflected a particular informality and a "peculiar attitude of both officers and men."[58] According to revisionist studies, the isolation and distance from the central government, a shared life of hardship and risk, and the fact that blood and marriage ties existed among officers and common soldiers—all contributed to this attitude of informality and independence. Oakah Jones, Jr., makes essentially the same argument for contentious frontier settlers and extends the analysis. In his view, the racially mixed settlers responded to the often brutal conditions on the far northern and Pacific frontiers by creating a distinct frontier culture, characterized by self-reliance, individualism, regionalism, village orientation, resistance to outside control, innovativeness, family cohesiveness, and the preservation of Roman Catholicism as a unifying force.[59]

But these revisionists do not address sex/gender issues. The informality of disciplinary codes does not explain the origins or the continuation of sexual violence against native women. Moreover, as the documents for Alta California clearly reveal, Spanish officials enforced colonial criminal statutes and punished sexual crimes to the extent of their authority. However, neither the highly regulatory Laws of the Indies (the extensive legislation enacted to protect the rights of Amerindians), which mandated nonexploitive relations with Amerindians, nor punishment for breaking the laws arrested the violence.[60]

To begin to understand the soldier-settler violence toward native women, we must examine the stratified, patriarchal colonial society that conditioned relationships between the sexes and races in New Spain; the contemporary ideologies of sex/gender and race; and the relations and structures of conquest imposed on this frontier. While rape and other acts of sexual brutality did not represent official policy on this or any other Spanish frontier, these acts were nevertheless firmly fixed in the history and politics of expansion, war, and conquest. In the history of Western civilization writ large, rape is an act of domination, an act of power.[61] As such, it is a violent political act committed through sexual aggression against women.

"The practice of raping the women of a conquered group," writes historian Gerda Lerner, "has remained a feature of war and conquest from the second millennium to the present."[62] Under conditions of war or conquest, rape is a form of national terrorism, subjugation, and humiliation, wherein the sexual violation of women represents both the physical domination of women and the symbolic castration of the men of the conquered group. These concepts and symbolic meanings of rape, as discussed by Lerner, Susan Brownmiller, Anne Edwards, and others, are rooted in patriarchal Western society—in the ideology that devalues women in relation to men while it privatizes and reifies women as the symbolic capital (property) of men.[63] In this ideology, rape has historically been defined as a crime against property and thus against "territory." Therefore, in the context of war and conquest, rape has been considered a legitimate form of aggression against the opposing army—a legitimate expression of superiority that carries with it no civil penalty. In nonmilitary situations, punishment for rape and other crimes of sexual violence against women in Western civilization has, until very recently, generally been determined by the social condition or status of the women violated and by the status of the violator.[64]

In eighteenth-century California, the status of Amerindian women—as members of non-Christian, indigenous groups under military conquest on Spain's northernmost outpost of empire—made them twice subject to assault with impunity: they were the spoils of conquest, and they were Indian. In the mentality of the age, these two conditions firmly established the inferiority of the Amerindian woman and became the basis for devaluing her person beyond the devaluation based on sex that accrued to all women irrespective of their sociopolitical (race, class) status. The ferocity and longevity of the sexual assaults against the Amerindian woman are rooted in the devaluation of her person conditioned by the weaving together of the strands of the same ideological thread that demeaned her on interrelated counts: her sociopolitical status, her sex, and her gender.

From their earliest contact with Amerindian peoples, Europeans established categories of opposition, or otherness, within which they defined themselves as superior and Amerindians as inferior.[65] These categories were derived from the Aristotelian theory that some beings are inferior by nature, and therefore should be dominated by their superiors for their own welfare, and from the medieval Spanish concept of "purity of blood," which was based on religion and which informed the sense of national unity forged during the reconquest.[66] These ideas—which were fundamentally political concepts that separated human beings into opposing, hierarchical subject-object categories—prevailed during the era of first contact with Amerindians and the early conquests of the Americas.

By the late eighteenth century, a different political concept—racial origin—defined place and social value in the stratified social order of colonial New Spain. Race was inextricably linked to social origin and had long been a symbol for significant cleavages in society; it was one primary basis for valuation—and devaluation—of human beings.[67] In the contemporary ideology and society, Amerindian women were thus devalued on the basis of their social and racial origins, which placed them at the bottom of the social scale, and as members of a conquered group.

Two aspects of the devaluation of Amerindian women are especially noteworthy. First and foremost, it is a political devaluation. That is, it is rooted in and driven by political considerations and acts: by war, conquest, and the imposition of alien sociopolitical and economic structures of one group over another. Second, the devaluation rationalized by conquest cuts across sex. At this level, women and men of the conquered group are equally devalued and objectified by the conquering group. Amerindian women and men were both regarded as inferior social beings, whose inferiority justified the original conquest and continued to make them justifiably exploitable and expendable in the eyes of the conqueror. The obverse, of course, also holds in this equation: women and men of the conquering group share the characterization and privileges of their group. In this instance, the primary opposition is defined by sociopolitical status, not sex.

Although the ideological symbols of sociopolitical devaluation changed over time—from religion to socioracial origins to social class—the changing symbols intersected with a sex/gender ideology that has remained remarkably constant from the fifteenth to the twentieth century.[68] As the term implies, the sex/gender ideology defines two categories of opposition—sex and gender—within which women are characterized as superior or inferior in relation to others.

With respect to sex stratification, women are placed in opposition and in an inferior position to men, on the assumption that in the divine order of nature the male sex of the species is superior to the female. In this conception, the ascribed inferiority of females to males is biologically constructed.

The opposition centering on gender revolves around sexual morality and sexual conduct. This opposition creates a level of superior-inferior or good-bad stratification based on social and political value-centered concepts of women's sexuality. This dichotomization provides a very specific, socially constructed, "sexual morality" category for valuing or devaluing women.

Rooted in the corollary patriarchal concepts of woman as the possession of man and of woman's productive capacity as the most important source of her value, this ideology makes woman a pivotal element in the property structure and institutionalizes her importance to the society in the provisions of partible and bilateral inheritance. It also places woman's value, also termed her "honor," in her sexual accessibility—in her virginity while single and, once wed, in the fidelity of her sexual services to the husband to ensure a legitimate heir.[69]

Within this construct, women are placed in opposition to one another at two extremes of a social and moral spectrum defined by sexuality and accessibility. The good woman embodies all the sexual virtues or attributes essential to the maintenance of the patriarchal social structure: sexual purity, virginity, chastity, and fidelity. Historically, the norms of sexual morality and sexual conduct that patriarchal society established for women of the ruling class have been the norms against which all other women have been judged. These norms are fundamentally rooted in questions of the acquisition and transference of economic and political power, and of women's relationship to that power base.

Since the linchpins of these ideological constructs are property, legitimacy, and inheritance, a woman excluded from this property/inheritance structure for sociopolitical reasons (religion, conquest, slavery, race, class), or for reasons based on sexual immorality (any form of sexual misconduct), is consequently excluded from the corresponding concepts and structures of social legitimacy. A woman so excluded cannot produce legitimate heirs because she is not a legitimate social or sexual being.

The woman who is defined out of social legitimacy because of the abrogation of her primary value to patriarchal society, that of producing heirs, is therefore without value, without honor. She becomes the other, the bad woman, the embodiment of a corrupted, inferior, unusable sex: immoral, without virtue, loose. She is common property, sexually available to any man that comes along.

A woman (women) thus devalued may not lay claim to the rights and protections the society affords to the woman who does have sociopolitical and sexual value.[70] In colonial New Spain, as in most Western societies until the very recent period, the woman so demeaned, so objectified, could be raped, beaten, worked like a beast of burden, or otherwise abused with impunity.

The soldiers, priests, and settlers who effected the conquest and colonization of Alta California in the last third of the eighteenth century perceived and acted toward Amerindians in a manner consistent with the ideology and history of conquest—regarding them as inferior, devalued, disposable beings against whom violence was not only permissible but often necessary. For, despite the Laws of the Indies, the contradictions in the ideology and corresponding historical relations of conquest were great from the very beginning. These contradictions were generally exacerbated, rather than resolved, across time, space, and expansion to new frontiers.

From the very beginning, the papal bulls and scholarly (ideological) debates that affirmed the essential humanity of Amerindians and initiated the legislation to effect their conversion and protection sanctioned violence and exploitation under certain conditions. Loopholes in the royal statutes that were technically intended to protect Amerindians and guarantee their rights, but more specifically protected the crown's interest in Indian land and labor, had permitted virulent exploitation of Indians since the laws were first passed.[71]

More contemporary military and civil laws, such as those enacted by Neve, Fages, and Borica, carried severe penalties for illegal contact with or maltreatment of Indians; but these laws were especially contradictory because they were intended to curb certain kinds of violence by soldiers who were trained to kill Indians and who were sent to California to effect the temporal (military) conquest of this region.[72] Thus, violence against Amerindians was permissible when it advanced the particular interests of the Spanish Conquest, but punishable when it did not. Since the sexual violence that occurred in this region was but the most contemporary manifestation of a national history that included the violation of enemy women as a legitimate expression of aggression during conquest, it would seem that sexual violence became a punishable offense only when it was the source of military or political problems.[73]

Finally, perhaps the greatest contradictions were those of the greatest champion of Amerindian rights—the Catholic church. On the one hand, Catholic clergy sought to remove Amerindians from contact with Spaniards, in order to protect them from the exploitation and violence of conquistadores, soldiers, and colonists; on the other hand, Jesuits, Franciscans, and other religious orders relied heavily on corporal punishment in their programs to Christianize and Hispanicize native people. While proclaiming the humanity of Amerindians, missionaries on the frontier daily acted upon a fundamental belief in the inferiority of the Indian. Their actions belied their words.

Accordingly, in his lengthy memorial of June 19, 1801, refuting the charges of excessive cruelty to Amerindians leveled against the Franciscans by one of their own, Father President Fermín Francisco de Lasuén disputed the use of extreme cruelty in the missions of the New California. Force was used only when absolutely necessary, stated Lasuén; and it was at times necessary because the native peoples of California were "untamed savages . . . people of vicious and ferocious habits who know no law but force, no superior but their own free will, and no reason but their own caprice."[74] Of the use of force against neophyte women, Lasuén wrote that women in the mission were flogged, placed in the stocks, or shackled only because they deserved it. But, he quickly added, their right to privacy was always respected—they were flogged inside the women's dormitory, called the *monjero* (nunnery). Flogging the women in private, he further argued, was part of the civilizing process because it "instilled into them the modesty, delicacy, and virtue belonging to their sex."[75]

A key element in the missionaries' program of conversion to Christianity included the restructuring of relations between the sexes to reflect gender stratification and the corollary values and structures of the patriarchal family: subservience of women to men, monogamy, marriage without divorce, and a severely repressive code of sexual norms.

In view of the fact that the ideologies, structures, and institutions of conquest imposed here were rooted in two and a half centuries of colonial rule, the sexual and other violence toward Amerindian women in California can best be understood as ideologically justified violence institutionalized in the structures and relations of conquest initiated in the fifteenth century.[76] In California as elsewhere, sexual violence functioned as an institutionalized mechanism for ensuring subordination and compliance. It was one instrument of sociopolitical terrorism and control—first of women and then of the group under conquest.

NOTES

1. Fray Junipero Serra to Antonio María de Bucareli y Ursua, Mexico City, May 21, 1773, in *Writings of Junipero Serra*, ed. Antonine Tibesar, O.F.M., 4 vols. (Washington, D.C.: Academy of Franciscan History, 1955), 1:363.

2. Serra to Father Rafaél Verger, Monterey, August 8, 1772, in *Writings*, 1:257.

3. Serra to Bucareli, Mexico City, May 21, 1773, in *Writings*, 1:361.

4. George Harwood Phillips, *Chiefs and Challengers: Indian Resistance and Cooperation in Southern California* (Berkeley: University of California Press, 1975), p. 22.

5. Serra to Bucareli, Mexico City, May 21, 1773, in *Writings*, 1:363.

6. Serra to Father Guardian [Francisco Pangua], Monterey, July 19, 1774, in *Writings*, 2:121.

7. Serra to Verger, Monterey, August 8, 1772, in *Writings*, 1:259, 261.

8. Serra to Father Francisco Pangua or his Successor, Monterey, June 6, 1777, in *Writings*, 3:159.

9. José Francisco Ortega, Diligencias Practicadas por Sargento Francisco de Aguiar, 1777, Julio 11, San Diego, *Archives of California*, 55:279, Bancroft Library, University of California, Berkeley.

10. Sherburne F. Cook, *Conflict between the California Indian and White Civilization* (Berkeley: University of California Press, 1976), p. 24. (Originally published 1943.)

11. Serra to Father Juan Figuer, Monterey, March 30, 1779, in *Writings,* 3:305.

12. Robert F. Heizer and Albert B. Elsasser, *The Natural World of the California Indians* (Berkeley: University of California Press, 1980), p. 25.

13. Hugo Reid, "Letters on the Los Angeles County Indians," in Susana Dakin, *A Scotch Paisano: Hugo Reid's Life in California, 1832–1852* (Berkeley: University of California Press, 1939), Appendix B, pp. 215–216, 240; Heizer and Elsasser, *Natural World of the California Indians,* pp. 52–53.

14. Reid, "Letters on the Los Angeles County Indians," p. 262.

15. Ibid.; see also Herbert Howe Bancroft, *History of California,* 7 vols. (San Francisco: A. L. Bancroft, 1984–1985), 1:180 and n. 29 (same page).

16. Herbert Eugene Bolton, trans. and ed., *Font's Complete Diary: A Chronicle of the Founding of San Francisco* (Berkeley: University of California Press, 1931), p. 256.

17. Ibid., p. 247.

18. Ibid.

19. Ibid., pp. 251–252.

20. Charles E. Chapman, *A History of California: The Spanish Period* (New York: Macmillan, 1930), pp. 246–247.

21. Cook, *Conflict,* p. 24.

22. Ibid., pp. 25–30, 101–134.

23. Edwin A. Beilharz, *Felipe de Neve: First Governor of California* (San Francisco: California Historical Society, 1971), pp. 72–73.

24. This argument is based on my analysis of the documents.

25. Reverend Heribert Jone, *Moral Theology, Englished and Adapted to the Laws and Customs of the United States of America by Reverend Urban Adelman* (Westminster, Md.: Newman Press, 1960), pp. 145–161.

26. The conflict between church and state in California, which Irving Richman calls the conflict between State Secular and State Sacerdotal, is extensively discussed in general histories of Spanish California. See Bancroft, *History of California,* vol. 1; Irving Berdine Richman, *California under Spain and Mexico, 1535–1847* (Boston: Houghton Mifflin, 1911), pp. 142–158.

27. Serra to Father Fermín Francisco de Lasuén, Monterey, January 8, 1781, in *Writings,* 4:63; Beilharz, *Felipe de Neve,* p. 77; Richman, *California under Spain and Mexico,* pp. 116–337.

28. Serra to Bucareli, Mexico City, March 13, 1773, in *Writings,* 1:295–329; see also Bernard E. Bobb, *The Viceregency of Antonio María Bucareli in New Spain, 1771–1779* (Austin: University of Texas Press, 1962), p. 163.

29. Serra to Bucareli, Mexico City, March 13, 1773, in *Writings,* 1:299, 301, 305, 307; Serra to Teodoro de Croix, Santa Barbara, April 28, 1782, in *Writings,* 4:129.

30. Magnus Morner (*Race Mixture in the History of Latin America* [Boston: Little, Brown, 1967], pp. 35–37) discusses interracial marriage in the early colonial period as part of the early social experiments of the sixteenth century. I discuss the promotion of intermarriage more specifically as an instrument of conquest in chapter 5 of "Presidarias y Pobladoras: Spanish-Mexican Women in Frontier Monterey, California, 1770–1821," Ph.D. diss., Stanford University, 1990.

31. Serra to Bucareli, Mexico City, March 13, 1773, in *Writings,* 1:325.

32. Ibid.

33. Serra to Bucareli, Monterey, August 24, 1775, in *Writings,* 2:149, 151, 153.

34. This is my interpretation of the documents.

35. Serra to Bucareli, Mexico City, April 22, 1773, in *Writings,* 1:341.

36. Bancroft, *History of California,* 1:206–219; Bobb, *Viceregency of Bucareli,* pp. 162–163; Chapman, *History of California: The Spanish Period,* pp. 289–291.

37. As quoted in Beilharz, *Felipe de Neve,* p. 77.

38. Serra to Lasuén, Monterey, January 8, 1781, in *Writings,* 4:63.

39. Bancroft, *History of California,* 1:546–549; Phillips, *Chiefs and Challengers,* p. 23.

40. Fages al Comandante General, 7 de noviembre de 1785, Monterey; 30 de deciembre de 1785, San Gabriel; 5 de enero de 1786, San Gabriel— all in *Archives of California,* 22:348–349. For the interrogation of Toypurina and her coleaders of the rebellion at Mission San Gabriel, see Diligencias que del órden del Gobernador practicó el Sargento Joseph Francisco Olivera . . . , *Archivos general de la nación: Provincias Internas,* vol. 120, microfilm, Bancroft Library, University of California, Berkeley. For a popular account of Toypurina's leadership role in the rebellion, see Thomas Workman Temple II, "Toypurina the Witch and the Indian Uprising at San Gabriel," *Masterkey* 32 (September–October 1958): 136–152. For a discussion of Amerindian rebellions in California, see Bancroft, *History of California,* 1:249–256; Cook, *Conflict,* pp. 65–90; Phillips, *Chiefs and Challengers.*

41. As quoted in Beilharz, *Felipe de Neve,* p. 83.

42. Bobb, *Viceregency of Bucareli;* Alfred Barnaby Thomas, *Teodoro de Croix and the Northern Frontier of New Spain, 1776–1783* (Norman: University of Oklahoma Press, 1941).

43. Thomas, *Teodoro de Croix,* pp. 16–57, 230–246; Max L. Moorhead, *The Presidio: Bastion of the Spanish Borderlands* (Norman: University of Oklahoma Press, 1975), pp. 27–160; Sidney B. Brinckerhoff and Odie B. Faulk, *Lancers for the King: A Study of the Frontier Military System of Northern New Spain, with a Translation of the Royal Regulations of 1772* (Phoenix: Arizona Historical Foundation, 1965), p. 7.

44. Representación de Don Pedro Fages sobre el estupro violento que cometerión los tres soldados que espresa, ano de 1774, Californias, *Archivos general de la nación: Californias,* vol. 2, Part 1, microfilm. The five-year chronology of this case is from Beilharz, *Felipe de Neve,* pp. 27–30.

45. Beilharz, *Felipe de Neve,* p. 29.

46. Bobb, *Viceregency of Bucareli,* pp. 128–171; Thomas, *Teodoro de Croix,* pp. 17–57, 230–246; Beilharz, *Felipe de Neve,* p. 29.

47. Beilharz, *Felipe de Neve,* pp. 29–30.

48. Ibid.

49. Ortega, Diligencias, 1777, Julio 11, San Diego, *Archives of California,* 55:258–279; Cook, *Conflict,* pp. 106–107.

50. Beilharz, *Felipe de Neve,* pp. 67–84, 160–162.

51. Pedro Fages to Diego Gonzales, Monterey, July 1, 1785, *Archives of California,* 54:175; Cook, *Conflict,* p. 106.

52. As quoted in Beilharz, *Felipe de Neve,* p. 73; see also Neve's instructions to Fages, his successor, in Appendices, same source, pp. 161–162.

53. Fages to Gonzales, July 1, 1785, *Archives of California,* 54:175.

54. Branciforte al Gobernador de California, "Sobre escoltas a los religiosos . . . ," 5

de octubre de 1795, México, *Archives of California,* 7:256; Gobernador a Comandantes de Presidios, "Excesos de la tropa con las indias, su corrección . . . ," 11 de abril de 1796, Monterey, *Archives of California,* 23:421–422.

55. Bancroft, *History of California,* 1:601.

56. Serra to Bucareli, Mexico City, June 11, 1773; Serra to Pangua, Monterey, June 6, 1777, in *Writings,* 1:383, 3:159.

57. Oakah L. Jones, Jr., *Los Paisanos: Spanish Settlers on the Northern Frontier of New Spain* (Norman: University of Oklahoma Press, 1979); Brinckerhoff and Faulk, *Lancers for the King;* Max L. Moorhead, "The Soldado de Cuera: Stalwart of the Spanish Borderlands," and Leon G. Campbell, "The First Californios: Presidial Society in Spanish California, 1760–1822," in *The Spanish Borderlands: A First Reader,* ed. Oakah L. Jones, Jr. (Los Angeles: Lorrin L. Morrison, 1974), pp. 87–105 and 106–118, respectively. Moorhead's essay was originally published in the *Journal of the West* in January 1969, and Campbell's first appeared in the *Journal of the West* in October 1972.

58. Moorhead, "The Soldado de Cuera," p. 91.

59. Jones, *Los Paisanos,* pp. 252–253.

60. Juan de Solórzano y Pereyra, *Política indiana,* 5 vols. (Buenos Aires: Compañía Ibero-Americana de Publicaciones, 1972); José María Ots y Capdequi, *Instituciones* (Barcelona: Salvat Editores, S.A., 1959), and *Historia del derecho español en América y del derecho indiano* (Madrid: Ediciones S.A. de Aguilar, 1967).

61. The discussion about rape and other forms of sexual violence against women is based on the following sources: Gerda Lerner, *The Creation of Patriarchy* (New York: Oxford University Press, 1986); Susan Brownmiller, *Against Our Will: Men, Women and Rape* (New York: Bantam Books, 1976); Christine Ward Gailey, "Evolutionary Perspectives on Gender Hierarchy," in *Analyzing Gender: A Handbook of Social Science Research,* ed. Beth B. Hess and Myra Marx Ferree (Newbury Park, Calif.: Sage, 1987), pp. 32–67; Carole J. Sheffield, "Sexual Terrorism: The Social Control of Women," in *Analyzing Gender,* pp. 171–189; Jalna Hanmer and Mary Maynard, "Introduction: Violence and Gender Stratification," in *Women, Violence and Social Control,* ed. Jalna Hanmer and Mary Maynard (Atlantic Highlands, N.J.: Humanities Press International, 1987), pp. 1–12; Anne Edwards, "Male Violence in Feminist Theory: An Analysis of the Changing Conceptions of Sex/Gender Violence and Male Dominance," and David H. J. Morgan, "Masculinity and Violence," in *Women, Violence and Social Control,* pp. 13–29 and 180–192, respectively.

62. Lerner, *Patriarchy,* p. 80.

63. Lerner, *Patriarchy,* p. 80; Brownmiller, *Against Our Will,* pp. 23–24; Edwards, "Male Violence in Feminist Theory," p. 19; Ramón Arturo Gutiérrez, "Marriage, Sex, and the Family: Social Change in Colonial New Mexico, 1690–1846," Ph.D. diss., University of Wisconsin–Madison, 1980, p. 15.

64. Lerner, *Patriarchy,* p. 96; Brownmiller, *Against Our Will,* pp. 18–20; Sheffield, "Sexual Terrorism," pp. 173–174.

65. Tzvetan Todorov, *The Conquest of America: The Question of the Other,* trans. Richard Howard (New York: Harper and Row, 1982).

66. Lewis Hanke, *The Spanish Struggle for Justice in the Conquest of America* (Philadelphia: University of Pennsylvania Press, 1949), pp. 111–132; Verena Martínez-Alier, *Marriage, Class, and Color in Nineteenth-Century Cuba: A Study of Racial Attitudes and Sexual Values in a Slave Society* (Cambridge, England: Cambridge University Press, 1974), p. 76; Morner, *Race*

Mixture, pp. 3–5, 36; Health Dillard, "Women in Reconquest Castile: The Fueros of Sepulveda and Cuenca," in *Women in Medieval Society,* ed. Susan Mosher Stuard (Philadelphia: University of Pennsylvania Press, 1976), p. 86.

67. Martínez-Alier, *Marriage, Class, and Color in Nineteenth-Century Cuba,* p. 76.

68. Edwards, "Male Violence in Feminist Theory," p. 28, n. 4. Although some feminist scholars prefer not to make an analytical distinction between sex (biological) and gender (sociocultural) categories, I believe that the distinction is important because of the distinct oppositions within which each category places women. The biological distinction of sex places women in opposition and in a subordinate position relative to men; the sociocultural distinction of gender places women in opposition and in an inferior position to other women. This sociocultural distinction is based on concepts of sexual morality and conduct that are informed by political and economic values. With few exceptions, however, the sociocultural construction of gender has not accounted for the political and economic dimensions that historically related (if not defined) a woman's sexual morality and gender value to her sociopolitical (religion, race, class) status—and vice versa.

69. Lerner, *Patriarchy,* pp. 80–88; Sylvia Marina Arrom, *The Women of Mexico City, 1790–1850* (Stanford, Calif.: Stanford University Press, 1985), p. 71; Health Dillard, *Daughters of the Reconquest: Women in Castillian Town Society, 1100–1300* (Cambridge, England: Cambridge University Press, 1984), pp. 12–35, see especially pp. 30–32, and "Women in Reconquest Castile," pp. 86, 91.

70. For a discussion of the concept of women's honor and dishonor drawn from codes of sexual conduct and used as a basis for devaluation of women in medieval Spain, see Dillard, *Daughters of the Reconquest,* pp. 168–212; for a discussion of the concept of family honor and the political issues inherent in the devaluation of women on the basis of class and race, see Martínez-Alier, *Marriage, Class, and Color in Nineteenth-Century Cuba,* pp. 11–41, 71–81; for a discussion of these issues in the northern frontier of colonial New Spain, see Ramón A. Gutiérrez, "From Honor to Love: Transformations of the Meaning of Sexuality in Colonial New Mexico," in *Kinship Ideology and Practice in Latin America,* ed. Raymond T. Smith (Chapel Hill: University of North Carolina Press, 1984), pp. 237–263; see also Gutiérrez, "Marriage, Sex, and the Family."

71. Hanke, *The Spanish Struggle for Justice,* pp. 133–146.

72. Moorhead, "The Soldado de Cuera," p. 102.

73. For discussions of sexual violence in the national history of Spain, first during the reconquest and then during the conquest of Mexico, see Dillard, *Daughters of the Reconquest,* pp. 206–207, and "Women in Reconquest Castile," pp. 85–89; Todorov, *Conquest of America,* pp. 48–49, 59, 139, 175.

74. Refutation of Charges, Mission of San Carlos of Monterey, June 19, 1801, in *Writings of Fermín Francisco de Lasuén,* 2 vols., trans. and ed. Finbar Kenneally, O.F.M. (Washington, D.C.: Academy of American Franciscan History, 1965), 2:194–234; quotes are from 2:220.

75. Ibid., 2:217.

76. Sheffield, "Sexual Terrorism," pp. 171–189.

THREE

And, Yes . . . The Earth Did Part
On the Splitting of Chicana/o Subjectivity

Angie Chabram Dernersesian

IDENTIFYING THE CHICANA SUBJECT(S): POETIC EXCERPTS

The following excerpts, from poems written by Chicanas of different ages between the late 1960s and the early 1980s, all enlist forms of self-representation commonly found within Chicana/o discourse.[1]

1

Yo soy Chicano, tengo color
Americano pero con honor.
Cuando me dicen que hay revolución
Defiendo mi raza con mucho valor.
. . . . .
Tengo mi orgullo, tengo mi fé
Soy diferente, soy color café
Tengo cultura, tengo corazón
Y no me los quita, a mí ni un cabrón.

[I am a Chicano, brownskinned,
an American but with honor.
When they tell me the revolution has started,
I will defend my people with all my courage.
. . . . .
I have my pride. I have my faith.
I'm different, my skin is brown.

I have a culture, I have a heart,
And no one can take them from me, no not any bastard.]
Juanita Domínguez, "Yo soy Chicano"

2

Last week,
I had been white
. . . we were friends.

Yesterday,
I was Spanish
. . . we talked . . .
once in a while.

Today
I am a Chicano
. . . you do not know me.

Tomorrow,
I rise to fight
. . . and we are enemies.
Margarita Virginia Sánchez, "Escape"

3

Yo soy Chicana
de las montañas de Nuevo Mexico
My skin is dark. My hair black.
. . . . .
My heart cries for Reís López Tijerina
. . . . .
My hopes exalted with the triumph of la huelga
Dorinda Moreno, "My Sons, My Daughters"

4

. . . . .
CHICANA
. . . . .
dáte tu propio valor
eres tú MUJER
tú sola

en tus orgasmos
en tus partos y
en tu muerte
¿y en tu palabra?
. . . . .
haz lo que tus hermanos
. . . . .
CHICANA HERMANA MUJER
ahora actúa por
TI
[. . . . .
CHICANA
. . . . .
give yourself your own value
it is you woman
you alone
in your orgasms
in your childbirths
in your death
and in your word?
. . . . .
do what your brothers did
. . . . .
CHICANA SISTER WOMAN
now act for
YOURSELF]

Margarita Cota-Cárdenas, "Manifestación Tardía" (Late Declaration)

In their complete renditions, these four poems foreground the identity of a self-conscious, speaking subject, appeal to mimetic modes of representation, offer the poetic subject a collective base and an ethnic identity, evoke cultural pride, inscribe a new semantic universe, and reaffirm the partnership between identity, cultural discourse, and political struggle. Thus, the revolutionary impulse of Chicana/o cultural production is manifest: content as well as form must be transformed, re-created, if Chicana/o subjects are to speak with their own accents and populate language with their own vernacular.[2]

The plethora of forms that Chicanas/os have invented to speak themselves in poetic discourse testifies to their creative and successful manipulation of language. This manipulation is evident in the multiple forms of self-representation that the poetic subjects above employ to define themselves and their constituencies. But the excerpts also suggest that, aside from being rich in verbal expression, this self-descriptive Chicana language is also the site of violent and contradictory positionings, which evoke contrary reactions, communicate a strategic struggle and a relationship to power, enlist competing alliances, and discard identities as well as assuming them.

Thus, all these Chicana poems record the passage of an empowered ethnic subject from complacency to action, from social dislocation to political groundedness, and from individual oblivion to collective memory. They also illustrate that Chicana identity is something to be discovered rather than passively inherited. Important differences do surface, however, in the manner in which these Chicana poets author themselves into the cultural text. In poem 1, "Yo soy Chicano," the speaking subject constructs herself through terms traditionally used in the Chicano movement, such as color, militancy, ethnic awareness, and cultural pride. In addition, she marks the male gender by equating these features of Chicano identity with manliness.

In poem 2, written by a thirteen-year-old from California, self-identification is achieved through the link made between ethnic self-consciousness and the enunciation of the term *Chicano.* Within this context, "Chicano" incorporates a rejection of external definitions, such as "white" or "Spanish," that would identify the Chicano as the "other." Identity is thus described as a space of self-creation and active struggle against preconceived ethnic modalities that are more acceptable to the dominant culture.

Poem 3 foregrounds ethnicity as a central category for Chicana and/or group identity. However, this excerpt offers a more elaborate construction, following the pattern of Chicano identity set forth by artistic narratives such as "El Plan Espiritual de Aztlán" and "I Am Joaquín," which construct the ethnic subject in relation to race, origin, language, culture, a historical legacy of conquest, a political affiliation with La Causa and the socially dispossessed, and harmony with the land and one's family.[3] As in these examples, the poetic subject distinguishes herself from other ethnic groups: Spanish and Anglo. Yet she breaks with these classical models by identifying herself as both a Chicana and a daughter and by inscribing not only gender and ethnicity but her own female body onto nationalism's largely male-centered narrative.[4]

It is not until poem 4, however, that a new subjectivity is prefigured within the semantic universe of "Chicana," a universe which, the poet explains, narrates the Chicana's self-directed actions, life stages, and existential concerns and her rejection of all forms of external subjection.

Taken as a whole, these excerpts suggest that Chicana identity is not fixed "once and for all." Instead, they propose that its axis, terms of discourse, and points of contention change in accordance with the ways in which Chicana subjects are positioned and, in turn, position themselves within the discourses of history, culture, and society.[5] In addition, these poetic voices—some identifying themselves as Chicanas, others as Chicanos—inscribe the competing modes of self-representation available to Chicana subjectivity. If this were not enough, the term *Chicana* itself is a field for multiple cultural critiques (inside and outside the Chicano community) that unsettle previously conferred identities: Anglo, Hispanic, Pocho, Mexican American, Spanish, and Chicano. As Norma Alarcón suggests, the story of Chicanas/os has not turned out to be definitive; for, as she elaborates, even the term *Chicana/o* "has become a critical site of political, ideological and discursive struggle."[6]

Quite a different picture emerges, however, when we step back and read these excerpts from within the still widespread codes of cultural nationalism's preferred cultural-ideological aesthetic. From this perspective, these excerpts foreground harmony and continuity amidst fragmentation and alienation. Differences between competing identities are thus erased or contained under the influence of a universal Chicano subject, which is entrusted with providing an antidote to these social conditions. In this context, a poem such as "Manifestación Tardía," which proposes a new poetic universe for Chicanas, can be read as a simple outgrowth of familiar positions taken in the Chicano movement—as just another example of brown militancy, this time à la Chicana.

But this reading produces tensions rather than glossing over them, especially if "Manifestación Tardía" is positioned alongside counterparts: earlier *manifestaciones* such as Sor Juana's much-loved "Hombres Necios" (Foolish Men)[7] or contemporary *manifestaciones* authored by bold-spirited Chicanas such as Marcelina Trujillo, who was inspired by the Mexican muse and irreverently versed:

> Your culture emanates
> from Raza posters on your walls
> . . . . .
> Chicanismo through osmosis
> . . . . .
> to remind me
> that machi-machi-machismo
> is part of our culture.[8]

Once allowed to surface, the tensions contained in the nationalist reading explode, creating discordant notes and redirecting us toward a new form of self-definition, to be spoken, not by all but by some of us: *tú* (you); the generic Chicana, La Mujer (woman); or *hermana* (sister). Other types of intervention are inscribed as well by Trujillo's poem. Here the Chicana speaking subject does the unthinkable from the perspective of conventions popularized by nationalist discourse. She subverts the authoritative movement discourse, which posits a shared cultural legacy equally representative of all Chicanos. Further, she names her displacement from Chicano cultural production (i.e., La Raza posters), identifies herself as a gendered subject (the implicit I), and exposes La Raza cultural production as a "male" domain ("your walls"). Finally, she reminds us, as the legendary poet José Montoya once did, that "los they are us"—for Trujillo, "los they," the oppressors, are you, Chicano male. In this way, the Chicana speaking subject positions herself in a discursive space once reserved for *los poetas del movimiento* and launches her own "war of positions" on *machismo* and male privilege within "alternative" cultural productions.

TO SPLIT AZTLÁN: WRITING CHICANA SUBJECTIVITY

And thus, not long after Tomás Rivera published his now classic . . . *Y no se lo tragó la tierra,* his boy protagonist's greatest fear, that the earth would part,[9] has materialized under the pens of not one but many Chicana poets and cultural practitioners. Yes, the earth (here understood as the symbolic rendition of Chicano/a subjectivity, Aztlán) has parted, and it has parted not once but twice—this second time self-consciously along gender lines that deconstruct sexism from within the arena of Chicana/o cultural production itself. With this parting, singular constructions of idealized, homogeneous subjects of Chicano political identity have given way to a plurality of competing identities, whose differences are being consciously marked within cultural discourse in the tradition of many early Mujeres de la Raza.[10]

This essay examines the ideological formations that led to the splitting of Chicana/o subjectivity, focusing primarily on cultural productions of the 1970s and soon thereafter, in which Chicanas consciously disassociated themselves from male hegemonic constructions of group identity. This splitting of Chicana/o subjectivity has taken place in two stages. In the first stage, Chicana subjects are either displaced from group characterizations or mediated by systems of differentiation that privileged male forms of identity and subjectivity.[11] In the second stage, these forms are either subverted or displaced by alternate definitions, which foreground Chicanas as individual speaking subjects and in group characterizations; entrust them with their own self-definitions and subject positions; and combat male-oriented figurations of Chicanas.[12]

In the contemporary period, this second type of self-definition has increasingly given rise to substitutions for the word *Chicano*—namely, *Chicanas and Chicanos, Chicano/a,* or *Chicana/o.* The markers *o/a, a/o* announce the end of the nongendered Mexican American subject of cultural and political identity; they reinscribe the Chicana presence, which had been subsumed under the universal ethnic denomination *Chicano.* However, there are differences inscribed within these markers. Whereas *Chicano/a* consciously reinstates the Chicana subject within the ethnic discourse of Chicano, *Chicana/o* privileges the female subject within group characterizations that mark distinctions, giving the Chicana her own independent trajectory as well as a collective one. Yet both *Chicana/o* and *Chicano/a* are different from earlier forms of self-definition in Chicano discourse, because those who use these expressions are deliberately imposing their own selective processes onto the cultural subject being represented. Thus, they subvert the silences that have marked nationalism's cloaked splitting of Chicana/o subjectivity under the image of the Chicano male—the essential subject for group identity.

The splitting of Chicana/o subjectivity along these dimensions has an added social function. This configuration purports to emphasize the particular social distinctions that have promoted Chicana inequality in society, following the same type of logic that Carmen Tafolla enlists when asked "Why look at Chicanos separately from Anglos, women separately from men, and now, to further complicate it all, at Chicanas as a separate group?" Tafolla's reply: "It is not we who separate people off into groups—our society has already done that for us. . . . If it were not for the different treatment of ethnic and sex groups in our country, there would be no need for one book to be written about the Chicana, or about the Anglo, or about the Black."[13]

For Tafolla as for other contemporary cultural critics, visualizing the distinctions between Chicanas and Chicanos, and Chicanas/os and other groups, allows readers to encounter an oppressive differential treatment of Chicana women and to equalize cultural discourse by highlighting the particularities of the excluded element: Chicanas. However, Tafolla's rationale is also important because it responds to the question: Who split the Chicano subject? This question was routinely posed by authoritative discourses that faulted Chicanas for dividing and splitting the Chicano movement when they sought to foment Chicana-centered discourses and practices of resistance. While Tafolla does in fact call for a *Chicana* representation, thus splitting the Chicana subject away from a purportedly undifferentiated fold, her purpose is not to subvert or divide the movement but, rather, to combat exclusion. Ultimately, her aim is to incorporate Chicanas into cultural discourses that mark their distinctions as women as well as their similarities with Chicanas/os at large. However, quite another scenario emerges with the predominant male-centered authoritative discourses, which promised to include Chicanas in the cultural record of the practices of ethnic resistance if they accepted their exclusion as female subjects and dwelled only on their ethnic similarities with Chicano males. Along with nationalism's self-deceptive mirror, which promised Chicana women a transparent reflection of themselves through the images of others, these promises rarely materialized.

Round One: Rendón's Manifest Chicano

The best example of these types of male-centered discourses of exclusion can be found in Armando Rendón's *Chicano Manifesto,* published in 1971. In his description of the Chicana/o revolt, Rendón polarizes the forces of contention into the mutually exclusive categories of *machismo* (male) and *malinchismo* (female). Whereas, for Rendón, the former is synonymous with revolutionary struggle, commitment, and progress, the latter is synonymous with retrocession, betrayal, and conquest. By his pen, (Chicana) female *malinches* are in effect banished from the political movement itself, cast over to the other side with the heinous Tío Tacos (Chicano Uncle Toms) and Anglo oppressors. But female betrayal is much worse than the male version, since *malinches* betray not only a political principle but male dignity and manhood as well.[14] Ultimately, for Rendón, (Chicanas) *malinches* obstruct social progress, collective identity, and reconciliation with oneself, the family, and the nation.

Rendón's objectification of political forces in the categories of *machismo* and *malinchismo* at no point escapes its gendered focus. As he himself confessed after describing the Chicano revolt: "It may seem that when reference is made to Chicano activism, the emphasis is on the masculine alone. That tendency is mainly attributable to my being macho (male) and naturally viewing the Chicano revolt as a male-dominated phenomenon."[15] Since *macho* is not only male but a specific Chicano male (Rendón), it follows that *malinche* is also a particular Chicana female, who remains generic in his essay. Rendón also associates Chicano male with *macho* and the purportedly generic Chicano. And he implies that if Chicanas (*malinches*) want to be Chicano (the generic term) and fight oppression, they have to embrace Chicano manhood as a political and personal objective. He explains: "The essence of machismo, of being macho, is as much a symbolic principle for the Chicano revolt as it is a guideline for family life. . . . Macho, in other words, can no longer relate merely to manhood but must relate to nationhood as well. . . . The word Chicano in many ways embodies the revolt itself."[16]

Following Foucault's logic, it could be said that Rendón sets into motion a system of gender differentiation designed to maintain a form of (male) power—patriarchy, which "subjugates" the Chicana by "imposing a law of truth" upon her (*machismo*) and by making her subject to someone else (Chicano males) "by control and/or dependence."[17] Thus, Chicana subjectivity, as elaborated in Rendón's *Chicano Manifesto,* is equivalent to subjection: Chican*o*.[18] However, even with his devastating portrait of Chicanas and Malintzín Tenépal (Cortés's mistress), Rendón could not alter the onslaught of Chicana activism. As he admitted upon paying lip service to the contradictions in his text and to the virtues of some Chicanas, Chicanas weren't ready to take a back seat to anyone. And many of them didn't: they contested their negative figuration in stories of *macho* liberation and manifest Chicanos by creating their own productions of cultural and political struggle.

Round Two: Reclaiming the Chicana Subject

Given the ideological constraints that Chicanas faced, reclaiming a subject position meant parting with male-centered ethnic qualifiers that inscribed Chicana subjection; relocating Chicanas within Aztlán, the political struggle, and nationalist discourse; transforming Malinche into Malintzín;[19] rejecting the unequal and divisive practices of sexism in the struggle against domination; textualizing Chicana militancy; visualizing the experiences of Chicana women in mainstream Anglo-Saxon and alternative feminist discourses; contesting Chicano male dominance at home and at work; and providing Chicana perspectives as a means of evoking cultural pride among all people—particularly Chicanas. In brief, intervening into Chicana/o subjectivity within the context of the prevailing discourses of exclusion necessarily meant reconnecting Chicanas to themselves, to each other, and to others.

Many Chicanas boldly accepted this challenge,[20] changing the word *Chicano* to *Chicana* in order to define themselves, assuming the most progressive elements of *Chicano*, and giving Chicana/o subjectivity a female body and condition. But these Chicanas not only changed the word; they literally changed the subject, populating culture with Chicanas, often replacing the discourses of *carnalismo* and *compadres* (brotherhood and brothers) with the discourses of *feminismo* and *comadres* (sisterhood and sisters), and problematizing the domain of feminism itself.[21] Most important, they altered the subject position of Chicanas in cultural productions, taking them from subjection to subjectivity, from entrapment to liberation, and from distortion and/or censure to self-awareness and definition.[22]

In order to do all this, they enlisted more complex modes of representation, which could better accommodate multiple subjects, competing discourses, and contrary self-images. While it would be a mistake to attribute this type of oppositional stance to all Chicanas or Chicana cultural productions, these features were commonly found in the works of many Chicana cultural practitioners from the early 1970s onward. Chicanas such as Yolanda López, Ana Nieto-Gómez, Dorinda Moreno, and Bernice Zamora—whose work will be examined in the following sections—altered Chicano cultural production by interrogating, modifying, and displacing images of Chicana subjects from within different practices of resistance and ideological and cultural formations.[23]

IMAGING THE SPLIT CHICANA SUBJECT: LÓPEZ'S (FALLEN) GUADALUPE

To date, one of the best and most controversial Chicana artists is Yolanda López. The force of López's artistic production arises from her successful and repeated modification of traditional portraits of Chicanas/Mexicanas. Her most renowned work is contained in the *Serie Guadalupe* (Guadalupe series).[24] As could be expected, the target here is the stoic Christian Guadalupe, who in López's practice is frequently displaced by modern-day Chicanas in motion: militant Chicanas, fun-loving Chicanas dressed in shorts for summer, hard-working Chicana mothers breast-feeding their babes, and warm Chicana daughters and grandmothers openly expressing their affection for one another in joyful embraces.[25] Unlike the original Guadalupe, who first images herself to Juan Diego and the church, López reimages Guadalupe for contemporary Chicanas/Mexicanas seeking liberation from oppressive male-oriented images of Chicana women and from the debilitating influences of social institutions and beliefs.

Perhaps the best example of López's splitting of Chicana/o subjectivity can be found in a work depicting a fallen portrait of the traditional Guadalupe (Figure 3.1).[26] As normally occurs in the work of López, the artistic border (this time an indigenous rim that serves as the internal frame) encircling Guadalupe remains intact. However, the privileged space reserved for the traditional Guadalupe image is intentionally subverted, virtually left blank in the center of the page, where the eyes of the well-trained Chicano/Latino public fix their gaze in confirmation of the image of the Christian Virgin. Attention is drawn instead to the right, to a contemporary Chicana who jogs away toward the corner of the external frame, and to the left, to a modern-day Guadalupe feeding her child, located halfway outside of the Guadalupe border. And as a sign of its displacement, the traditional image of Guadalupe appears at the bottom of the external frame.

Thus, López's artistic text is literally split between two Chicana doubles: one set consisting of the young Chicana and her duplicate image; the other set consisting of disparate Guadalupes—the universally recognizable Virgen and the lifelike modern Guadalupe, dressed partly in the robe of the Blessed Virgin and partly in street clothes. The contrasting vertical and horizontal movements associated with these artistic subjects militate against the static quality and closure of the traditional Guadalupe portrait, and they chart new passages away from the immortal, supernatural past and toward the Chicana's worldly present. Similarly, the multiplication of Chicana subjects by doubles militates against the existence of a singular universal woman, imaged within the Chicano/Latino tradition of North America as the *mestiza* Christian mother. López also contests this singular woman by deliberately counterposing the eternal Virgin with two very different types of Chicanas/Mexicanas: a mother and a young Chicana, both of whom are consciously embodied. That is, their physical attributes are foregrounded in the text, not hidden as the cloaked Virgin's are. And López draws important distinctions between these Chicana subjects, not only in their embodiment but also in their divergent activities and social attitudes. Thus, while one of these Chicana subjects assumes the role of motherhood, and her affiliation with the saintly Guadalupe is marked by her posture, limited insertion into the privileged Guadalupe space, and support by the familiar roses, the other runs away from the Guadalupe portrait, divested of traditional imagery, unfettered by robe or child, physical or emotional stagnation, or artificial roses, perhaps toward a third image of the Chicana, yet to be constructed within another textual border.

By relegating the notably artificial, statuesque portrait of the Chicana/Mexicana Virgen to the bottom of the page, López discards this image as a viable one for contemporary Chicanas/Mexicanas, and she invites the reformulation and/or displacement of this reified female icon by new images, inspired in everyday work and play. Liberation from further subjection is inscribed in many forms within

Figure 3.1. Yolanda López, from *Serie Guadalupe*, 1978.

López's fallen Guadalupe: in the rejection of images that promote submission of Chicanas to existing power relations through the diffusion of universal "female" truths; in the lifelike images of Chicanas; and, finally, in the empty spaces, which provide an opening for future constructions of Chicanas that can assist in their self-knowledge.

While López successfully redefines one of the most traditional images of the Chicana/Mexicana, thus redefining Chicanas/Mexicanas themselves, she does not lose sight of the tensions that frame Chicana subjectivity in real life. In fact, she invites these competing images into her text at the same time that she invites her Chicana spectators outside, to contemplate their own self images and the degree to which her reformulation of the Guadalupe image approaches theirs. López also involves her viewing public in a series of intertextual dialogues with other traditional variants of Guadalupe in Chicano cultural productions—variants such as "La Familia de la Raza" (the Chicano Holy Family), "La Jefita," "I Am Joaquín," or *Bless Me, Ultima,* all of which reify Chicana subjects, extolling the virtues associated with motherhood.[27] With this dialogue, López underscores the limited artistic images available to Chicana subjects, and she extends her cultural critique to a wider range of cultural productions, interfacing as well with other Chicana texts that offer alternative visions of Chicana subjects. Thus, López's new Chicana subjects exist tensely on the border between tradition and modernity.

CHANGING THE SUBJECT(S): THE COUNTER DISCOURSES OF CHICANA FEMINIST WRITINGS

The dialogical quality featured in López's work is not unique to her particular brand of cultural production. It is commonly found in the works of other Chicana cultural practitioners, whose entrance into textual representation is marked by the appearance of a wide range of counter discourses. At their best, these counter discourses populate language with the interests and vernacular of Chicanas, subordinated within the cultural conversations of race, class, and gender oppression. The bold-spirited nature of this revisionist movement is best illustrated by the Chicana feminist writings of the early 1970s, which denounced the contradictions of the Chicano political movement and sang the virtues of La Mujer and the heroines of La Causa. Unlike early Chicano movement discourses, which privileged issues of general interest to the group, these Chicana feminist discourses reinscribed the condition of Chicanas onto the political text.[28] Ana Nieto-Gómez's "La Chicana," a political article written at a time when strenuous efforts were being made to integrate Chicanas into the curriculum, provides an illustration of these early Chicana feminist counter discourses.[29]

In this essay, Nieto-Gómez proposes that Chicana feminism "is the recognition that women are oppressed as a group and are exploited as part of la raza people" under the imperatives of a racist capitalist system. While foregrounding her discussion of the particular nature of Chicana oppression within the parameters of the group, she also emphasizes that proponents of feminism should identify and act upon the needs of Chicana women—needs such as "child care reproduction, economic stability, welfare rights, forced sterilization and prostitution." Nonetheless, she qualifies this statement by adding that "all interests must be eradicated," including female interests. Thus, she draws a clear distinction between her brand of Chicana feminism and mainstream variants, which would be content to substitute male oppressors with female ones.

With her particular construction of Chicana feminism, Nieto-Gómez deliberately and successfully contains the male-centered discourse on Chicano oppression, formulated in response to an unwarranted fear of Chicana activism. As previously suggested, these types of discourses often accused Chicanas of dividing the Chicano movement and of aligning themselves with mainstream feminists, who allegedly plotted to reinstate even more oppressive regimes. In turn, Nieto-Gómez's counter discourse challenges each of these assumptions and provides a more equitable representation of male and female interests. And she avoids the closure of Chicano movement discourse, soliciting feedback from a mixed public and calling for a more integrated approach, which addresses the very contradictions that have separated Chicana women from Chicano males. Finally, like many of her contemporaries, she argues that this approach, if it is to be successful, must aim toward transforming the entire fabric of social relationships.

Nieto-Gómez's reformulation of Chicano movement narratives shares many affinities with López's Guadalupe. The fallen Guadalupe images new interpretations of Chicana subjects; "La Mujer" offers Chicanas new subject positions within political discourse and practice. The fallen Guadalupe invites more complex forms of artistic representation of Chicana subjects; "La Mujer" invites a more complex understanding of the nature of Chicana/o oppression. The fallen Guadalupe counters competing male and female narratives of Guadalupe; Nieto-Gómez's text counters the narratives of Chicano nationalism with those of Chicana feminism. Finally, the Guadalupe portrait invites its spectators to reflect critically on the unsuitability of the traditional Christian Guadalupe for representing contemporary Chicana subjects, while the essay "La Mujer" challenges its readers to reflect on the limitations of early Chicano movement discourses for representing the interests of Chicanas in the political arena. Together, these Chicana texts successfully countered the male-centered nationalist text, which frequently laced its exclusion of active Chicana subjects with idealized archetypes that were of little value in the political struggle for self-affirmation.

Yet liberating Chicanas from their subjection entailed much more than refiguring their images and condition within contemporary cultural and political discourse. A step had to be taken toward Chicana activism. That is, discourses of liberation had to be formulated—discourses that championed Chicana militancy, consciousness, and self-empowerment. Clear distinctions had to be made between these discourses of liberation and the authoritative discourses of the Chicano movement, which favored male models of resistance (Ché, Villa, and Zapata, for instance) and were often contextualized by the exploitation of Chicanas at home and at work.[30] Once again, poetry furnished a useful medium for imagining a new type of Mujer de la Raza, a Mujer who could lead her people into liberation, textualize the passage to militancy through a new artistic sensibility, and raise awareness about her unique burden through her own counter discourses of Chicana/o liberation.

LIBERATING THE SUBJECT: SHOUT OUT, MUJER DE LA RAZA

The passage to Chicana militancy is best captured in Dorinda Moreno's "Mujer de la Raza."[31] Here Moreno urges the Mujeres de la Raza to "shout out" the anger in their souls as well as their newly found freedoms, and she predicts that today the Mujer de la Raza will "nullify her past subserviency," "activate her convictions," and "organize her liberation," "forging the direction for tomorrow." Yet her affirmation of collective liberation is but the culmination of a poetic reflection that documents the many facets of Raza women's passage to militancy: recognition of their oppression; denunciation of the pain and wrongs endured; faith in the transformative potential and leadership of Raza women; protest against oppression through political discourse and consciousness raising; and, finally, a call to action and involvement in the business of transforming the future.

The unyielding power of the Chicana's consciousness enables her to pass from one state of being, where she is "caged" in society's "concrete jungles," to another state, where she is outside its grip. According to the poetic subject, this consciousness kindles not only militancy (the renunciation of wrongs endured and the rejection of unfulfilled promises) but also a contagious appreciation for liberation of all subjects. Economic and social oppression, mental and urban ghettos—all of which have been nourished by the larger social order—are not, however, the only evils to be countered with this newly discovered Raza women's consciousness. This consciousness is also to be enlisted against the "false pride" of Raza men, who "wrongfully" believe that the place of Raza women is "only in the home." The antidote to the Raza women's triple oppression is thus to be found in their "spectacular awareness" and "perceptive insights." The power of their consciousness is so great that it can alter all aspects of their existence and can influence those who are exposed to it, regardless of gender or place of origin. By likening Raza women's consciousness to a tropical storm, Moreno captures its explosive potential:

> Our ideas like thunder
> overtake our lives

like lightning across the skies
reaching minds opening eyes.[32]

Because this political consciousness can transform the consciousness of others, Moreno concludes that Raza women and men will prevail in their united struggle against the multiple forms of Chicana subjection. In retrospect, Moreno's formulas for liberation may seem extremely naive, particularly to contemporary Mujeres de la Raza, who have militated in the presence of less than sympathetic Chicano cohorts. Nonetheless, Moreno is aware that much groundwork must be laid for building the consciousness of La Mujer. For Moreno, this type of effort demands not only militancy but the purposeful creation of a liberating discourse; thus, "reflective change" can come about only if Raza women "SHOUT OUT" the deep-seated resentment in their souls about the conditions that have subordinated them and depleted their energies. Such a political discourse, once framed in the experiences of Raza women, will, according to Moreno, then provide the base necessary for "activating" their conviction and "organizing" their liberation through strategic ventures that will enable them to meet the challenge of the day and forge the direction of tomorrow.

Although Moreno's poem ends by appealing to the collective nature of her enterprise—that is, the participation of Raza men—it is clear that the primary struggle of consciousness building and organization of Chicanas lies in the hands of the Mujer de la Raza herself; for it is she who must confront the anger and hostility that have ensued from her exploitation, just as she must savor the heart-throbbing euphoria evoked by her own self-styled *canto y grito de liberación* (song and cry of liberation).[33] And it is she who must extend her testimony and message of social reform to those who surround her. Finally, it is the Chicana subject who, in Moreno's poem, breaks out of the jail cells of economic, racial, and gender oppression, assisted by the "brotherly" support that is optimistically enlisted in such an endeavor. It goes without saying that Moreno's all-inclusive brand of Raza women's feminism is an attempt to involve Chicano males in the unique struggles of Chicanas—a strategy no doubt enlisted as a deterrent to the continued subjugation of Chicanas in the household, the factories, the fields, and the Chicano movement. Yet these tensions continue to surface in the poem, which, after all, foregrounds Chicana *women*'s struggles and experiences and does not mention the Chicano male subject until the final verses, where a course of action for the future is outlined.

Re-imaging the Female Grito (Scream) through Art

These tensions are also foregrounded from another perspective in an illustration accompanying Moreno's poem. In this anonymous black-and-white sketch, the Mujer de la Raza's passage to liberation is depicted in three scenes that progressively document her release from a jail cell containing the multiple agents and facets of oppression (Figure 3.2).[34] Unlike the poetic version of this narrative of Chicana liberation, the first scene of the triptych captures the subordination of the Mujer de la Raza in society by focusing on her entrapment in the concrete jungles of urban life, where she is accompanied by husband and daughter.[35] In this scene, she is a victim of her circumstance, a spectator who caresses the bars of her cell and assumes the posture and appearance of a passive woman. As a sign of her complacency, her lips are sealed, and she hides behind her man and her daughter, who are also subjected to society's concrete jungles.

Scene two, which marks a dramatic change in the composure and the physical appearance of the Mujer de la Raza, illustrates the crucial passage to Chicana consciousness. It is significant that in this scene the Mujer de la Raza is presented alone, her figure magnified to fill the entire artistic space of the center of the triptych, from where she shouts the anger in her soul, the resentment at her condition. Here she has shed the braids and the maidenly bun of the Spanish señorita, and her mouth is open wide, her hair free. This Mujer is clearly reminiscent of the "Militant Chicana," who was widely featured in movement publications that either captured her alone or placed her in front of Lady Liberty. The now fragmented urban structure, which formerly had caged her and her family in dilapidated housing projects, is cast off into the background: it no longer towers over the family's portrait but is lodged in her wild tresses, confined to her memory. In marked contrast stands the artistic rendition of a spectacular Chicana militancy, guaranteed (as Moreno had predicted) "to reach minds and open eyes." The power of its rage is channeled through the figure of a Chicana who assumes the features of an enraged animal and will not be deterred in her quest for freedom.

In scene three, the Mujer de la Raza begins her escape from the prison cell that continues to engulf her husband, now reinstated in the background, behind the

Figure 3.2. Irene del Rosario, *Mujer de la Raza,* c. 1975.

bars, alongside her enlarged face. Here an end to entrapment is prefigured: the head of the Mujer de la Raza, who has shouted out, already protrudes outside the bars, although her body is still trapped inside. The full and successful liberation of the Mujer de la Raza is reflected in the figure of the other Mujer de la Raza, perhaps the daughter, who appears in miniature at the bottom right of the scene. With her mouth opened in protest, and fist clenched in defiance, she leads the other Mujer (perhaps her mother) out of incarceration. The male remains in the background, not at the side of the Mujer, as Moreno had initially proposed. He neither obstructs nor aids the process of liberation, while the Chicana figure, who is prominently displayed in the center of the portrait, provides the impetus and the support for this transition from oppression to liberation. Her opened mouth, which is duplicated in the face of the Mujer de la Raza in scene two and in the face of the Mujer who has escaped incarceration, provides the necessary discourse for consciousness raising. Her long, disheveled hair, which envelops scenes one and three, sustains the human figures in these scenes, providing the bridge from subjugation to liberation.

It is significant that the Chicana who has made her way out of the cell, marking the passage to liberation, continues to display the farmworker's eagle on her chest; thus, in her person, the struggle against economic, racial, and gender oppression is fused at the symbolic level in the female body. Even with this fusion, the artist of this tripytch appears to suggest that escape from incarceration is an arduous process requiring a painful struggle with multiple antagonists as well as a supportive network. Perhaps that is why the artist chose to privilege the process leading up to liberation (as represented by the figures who are still partially entrapped in the cell) rather than its end product: the young Chicana who has escaped bondage. By privileging the process by which the Chicana is liberated (her militancy and rejection of social and domestic oppression) with an expansive spatial representation, the artist echoes Moreno's message that liberation will require various stages of political consciousness and activism on many fronts. However, here as well the seeds of liberation are to be found in the Chicana's own analytical and verbal capabilities. She must "SHOUT OUT" her condition if liberation is to be achieved, fusing the symbolism of her struggle with that of her people.

Combating Sexism: Referencing "Notes from a Chicana Coed"

In contrast to "Mujeres de la Raza," which textualizes the passage to Chicana militancy through consciousness raising without giving much attention to the internal contradictions of the Chicano movement's ideology, "Notes from a Chicana Coed" by Bernice Zamora foregrounds these contradictions, drawing attention to movement discourses that were preoccupied with issues of racial oppression.[36] Through the demystifying critique of a bold-spirited Chicana coed, Zamora deconstructs these largely nationalist analyses, which targeted the *gabacho* (the Anglo) as the sole agent of Chicano/a oppression. In her scathing and ironic critique of the movement's reductionism, she juxtaposes the nationalistic discourse of a *carnal* (male) with that of his Chicana mate, who is beginning to display a feminist consciousness. Whereas his discourse is marked by abstract expressions of national oppression, hers is marked by her own female testimonial of concrete, lived experiences of gender oppression. However, her/story prevails as the dominant one. She questions his boisterous yet rhetorical commitment to their "collective" liberation from a "foreign" enemy; and she repudiates the universal truths transmitted through authoritative movement discourses, which proposed that as Chicanos we "are oppressed first because . . . our skin is dark," and "we are exploited as workers by a system which feeds like a vulture off the work of our people,"[37] without attending to gender.

By naming her *carnal*'s (brother's) privilege—his three *gabacha guisas* (white girlfriends), use of his wife's free intellectual labor, and failure to provide for his family—Zamora foregrounds Chicanas' issues within movement discourses in much the same way that her contemporaries, such as Enriqueta Vásquez, did in the face of denial, censure, and opposition on the part of many segments of the Chicano community. As Vásquez explained: "When she [the Chicana] tries to speak of Machismo, she is immediately put down and told 'We know about it. . . .' She receives nothing but censorship again. She tries hard to say, 'Yes, there is much on Machismo, but can't you Machos look at the women and children who are the victims of your Machismo?' She tries so much to speak up and instead finds herself speaking to deaf ears and a completely closed mind."[38]

Zamora reenacts this type of discursive encounter with a "closed-minded male" in order to make him see "the victims of his machismo." She also reminds her readers, as Vásquez did earlier, that "When we talk of equality in the Mexican-American movement, we better be talking about TOTAL equality, beginning right where it all starts, At Home."[39] Thus, the Chicana subject obliges her *carnal* to see himself as an agent of oppression. More important, her active participation in this discourse serves as testimony to the fact that Chicanas themselves must lead the way toward educating others about their condition as it is represented in the political life of the community and at home. "Notes from a Chicana Coed" in fact exemplifies this type of consciousness raising as its speaking subject instructs the Chicano male about the theoretical and practical contradictions of "Chicano heavies," who promoted exploitation of women in the household while enjoying sexual privileges and leadership positions outside the home. The political lesson encapsulated within these notes is scathing. The *carnal*'s repetitive assertion that "the gabacho is oppressing us" is countered with the young poet's sarcastic assertion:

> Oye carnal, you may as well
> tell me that the moon water

cures constipation
that penguin soup prevents crudas
or that the Arctic Ocean is menudo.[40]

This defiant answer, which closes the poem, underscores the fact that there is no turning back to racial utopias which polarize the forces of oppression along ethnic lines and create fictitious narratives of domestic bliss with the concept of a male-centered familialism. The speaking subject also invites the very real possibility that other young Chicana coeds will refuse to be brainwashed or intimidated into believing rhetorical statements that run counter to their own interests and have no concrete expression in their daily lives. The poem ends in a stalemate between nationalist and feminist discourses, with no inkling of the male's response to this second alternative discourse on Chicana/o oppression. Yet, like the other cultural texts examined in this essay, "Notes from a Chicana Coed" skillfully weaves together the competing tensions that led to Chicana-centered cultural productions. Like these texts, "Notes" marks a definitive break with the Chicano discourses of exclusion, which would deprive Chicanas of a place in the political movement for self-determination and a voice in the struggle for equality.

RENAMING THE CHICANA AUTHOR(S): BORDERS, BRIDGES, AND TRAVELING THROUGH THE 1990S

Bernice Zamora, Margarita Cota-Cárdenas, Dorinda Moreno, Yolanda López, Ana Nieto-Gómez, Carmen Tafolla, Enriqueta Vásquez, Marcelina Trujillo, Martha Cotera. The contributions of these and other Chicana cultural practitioners who are not named in this essay are best summarized by the title of a collection of poems, *Puentes y fronteras* (Bridges and Borders).

Chicana cultural producers of the 1970s and early 1980s crossed the seemingly impenetrable borders of Chicano subjectivity. They transformed the language of self-representation, visualized new ethnic configurations and subject positions, and paved the way for contemporary Chicanas to explore other dimensions of the Chicana experience. Had it not been for the pioneering efforts of early Chicana cultural practitioners, who were often unjustly divorced by their own Raza, these developments would have been hampered. And of course new roads need to be traveled in the 1990s if the constantly changing panorama of an ever-growing Chicana population is to gain entrance into cultural discourse in a manner that dignifies this population and privileges its own self-constructions and the rhythms and intentions of its own vernacular. Thanks to the efforts of Mujeres de la Raza, who had the *coraje* (anger/courage) and political foresight to say "Yo soy" and mean "Chican-a," this journey toward new Chicana subjectivities in the year 2000 is facilitated.[41]

NOTES

1. Juanita Domínguez, "Yo soy Chicano," in Armando Rendón, *The Chicano Manifesto* (New York: Collier, 1971), p. 182; Margarita Virginia Sánchez, "Escape," in *We Are Chicanos,* ed. Phillip Ortego (New York: Washington Square Press, 1973), p. 208; Dorinda Moreno, "My Son, My Daughters," in *La Mujer es la tierra/La tierra da vida* (Berkeley, Calif.: Casa Editorial, 1975), n. p.; Margarita Cota-Cárdenas, "Manifestación Tardía" (Late Declaration), *La Palabra* 2, no. 2 (Fall 1980): 37. *Note:* In these poems, five spaced dots indicate omissions from the original text.

2. Following Michel Foucault, I view subjectivity as an effect, as something produced by the power of discourse and social relations. Foucault's project of examining subjectivity through "the history of the modes by which, in our culture, human beings are made subjects" is also useful here, because it allows for understanding the interrelatedness of different forms of ethnic subjectivities as they are constructed from within different historical periods. For a more complete discussion of this project, see his "The Subject and Power," *Critical Inquiry* 8, no. 4 (Summer 1982): 777.

3. The "Plan Espiritual de Aztlán (Spiritual Manifesto of Aztlán) is a declaration put forth at the Denver Conference, March 1969. This declaration identifies Aztlán as the place of the Chicano/*mestizo* nation, promotes *carnalismo* (brotherhood) as a collective value, stipulates that the "calling of our blood" is the basis for Chicano power, and establishes a link between the nations of the "bronze continent": North, South, and Central America. "I Am Joaquín" (1967) purported to be an "epic of the Chicano people." The poem follows the spiritual journey of a Chicano male protagonist who alleviates his personal and social alienation by reaffirming his ties with Mexican culture, history, and identity. The poem also prefigures the coming of a Chicano revolution, traces a racial ethnic ancestry, and militates against assimilation, passivity, and cultural genocide. "El Plan" and "Yo soy Joaquín" appeared in the popular anthology *Literatura Chicana: Texto y contexto,* ed. Joseph Sommers, Antonia Castañeda Schular, and Tomás Ybarra Frausto (Englewood Cliffs, N.J.: Prentice-Hall, 1972), pp. 93–94, 89–90.

4. After describing her dark skin and her black hair, the poetic voice brings them together in the phrase "My nipples are dark brown" (Moreno, "My Son, My Daughters," p. 6).

5. I have adopted Stuart Hall's notion of "identity as positionality" as a way of establishing connections between different forms of Chicana/o identity and subjectivity. In describing identity as positionality, Hall notes: "Identities are the names we give to the different ways we are positioned by, and position ourselves within, the narratives of the past." See his "Cultural Identity and Cinematic Representation," *Framework,* no. 36 (1988): 68–81. Stuart Hall is considered to be a leading exponent in the field of cultural studies. For an example of his influence in this respect, see *Cultural Studies,* ed. Lawrence Grossberg, Cary Nelson, and Paula Treichler (New York: Routledge, 1992).

6. Norma Alarcón, "In the Tracks of the Native Woman," *Cultural Studies* 4, no. 3 (1990): 248.

7. Sor Juana Inés de la Cruz was a famous Mexican poet. She is known for her poem "Hombres Necios," written in the late seventeenth century and considered by many to be a precursor of feminist thought because of its scathing exposition and critique of the paradoxes of male arrogance toward women.

8. Marcelina Trujillo, "Machismo Is Part of Our Culture," in *The Third Woman: Minority Woman Writers of the United States,* ed. Dexter Fisher (Boston: Houghton Mifflin, 1980), pp. 401–402.

9. . . . *And the Earth Did Not Part* (Berkeley, Calif.: Quinto Sol, 1971).

10. "Women of the Race," a term commonly used in alternative productions to refer to Chicanas.

11. I am referring to the systems of signification within nationalist discourse which effected the displacement of Chicana subjectivity. In language, for example, the universal ethnic subject often was treated as masculine (Chicano) instead of feminine (Chicana) even when fully embodied Chicanas were represented. A case in point is the volume *We Are Chicanos* (see note 1 above), which greets the reader with the image of a young Chicana representing the passage to "modern Chicano expression." Chicana subjectivity is thus overridden at the linguistic level by a gender referent that centers a Chicano masculinity and denies the Chicana an independent subjectivity as well as a separate literary trajectory. Phillip Ortego (the editor of *We Are Chicanos*) was not alone in this portrayal; similar examples abound in early Chicano productions.

12. The splitting of Chicana/o subjectivity could also be examined from the outside, through a critique of the dominant culture's figurations of Chicana/o identity and subjectivity or a critique of alternative feminist representations of Chicanas. I have elected to examine the splitting of Chicana/o subjectivity from inside the Chicana's own cultural production, in order to foreground the tensions between masculinist and feminist constructions.

Alternate definitions that foreground Chicanas as (individual) speaking subjects include those that follow the pattern found in excerpt 3, which begins "Yo soy Chicana." Group characterizations include those that appeal directly to a collective female identity without individual distinction, such as "Mujer" or "Chicana." Examples include excerpt 4 and the poem "Mujer de la Raza," analyzed later in this essay. For an analysis of these forms of Chicana identity, see my essay "I Throw Punches for My Race, but I Don't Want to Be a Man," in *Cultural Studies,* pp. 81–95.

13. Carmen Tafolla, *To Split a Human* (San Antonio: Mexican American Cultural Center, 1985), p. 1.

14. As Rendón notes: "We Chicanos have our share of malinches, which is what we call traitors to la raza who are of la raza, after the example of an Aztec woman of that name who became Cortez' concubine under the name of Doña Marina, and served him also as an interpreter and informer against her own people. The malinches are worse characters and more dangerous than the Tío Tacos, the Chicanismo euphemism for an Uncle Tom. The Tío Taco may stand in the way of progress only out of fear or misplaced self-importance. In the service of the gringo, malinches attack [their] own brothers, betray our dignity and manhood, cause jealousies and misunderstandings among us, and actually seek to retard the advance of the Chicanos, if it benefits themselves—while the gringo watches" (pp. 96–97).

15. Ibid., p. 183.

16. Ibid., p. 105.

17. Foucault, "The Subject and Power," p. 781.

18. Unarguably, Rendón's *Chicano Manifesto* is an extreme illustration; other cultural practitioners were less offensive when splitting Chicana/o subjectivity under the gaze of

ideal male figures or female figures imaged with male eyes. Yet his essay provides us with a perfect example of the contradictions of Chicano movement discourses and practices. While he castigates *malinches* for dividing the movement, and opposes the subjection of ethnic groups to immutable Anglo truths (stereotypes such as the Frito Bandito, for instance), he nonetheless activates systems of differentiation that duplicate rather than contest the subjection of Chicanas/os within the dominant social formation.

19. This renaming was conscious, and it represented another interpretation of the historical figure Malintzín Tenépal, who was said to be born around the year 1505 and who was dubbed a traitor because of her relationship with Cortés. The term *Malinche* is now synonymous with traitor, and Chicanas wish to reclaim Malintzín as a historical precursor of Chicanas and a victim of male chauvinist attitudes, which often culminated in holding her almost single-handedly responsible for the conquest of Mexico. Chicanas generally offer positive depictions of Malintzín. For an example, see Adelaida del Castillo's "Malintzín Tenépal: A Preliminary Look into a New Perspective," in *Essays on La Mujer,* ed. Rosaura Sánchez and Rosa Martínez Cruz (Los Angeles: Chicano Studies Research Center, 1977), pp. 124–149.

20. For a bibliographical sampling of some of their texts, see Elizabeth Ordóñez, "Sexual Politics and the Theme of Sexuality in Chicana Poetry," in *Women in Hispanic Literature: Icons and Fallen Idols,* ed. Beth Miller (Berkeley: University of California Press, 1983), pp. 316–337.

21. See Martha Cotera, "Feminism: The Chicana and the Anglo Versions," in *Twice a Minority: Mexican American Women,* ed. Margarita Melville (St. Louis: Mosby, 1980), pp. 217–234.

22. There were many Chicanas who of course mimicked male-oriented versions of female subjects in their cultural productions. These types of female-authored productions logically belong to the first stage of the splitting of Chicana/o subjectivity.

23. These Chicanas have been selected because of their convergence with one or more of the features listed above, and in order to give a sampling of Chicana cultural production in different domains.

24. Yolanda López, *Serie Guadalupe* (Guadalupe series), *Maize* 1, no. 4 (Spring 1978): 55–59 and front and back covers.

25. These observations are applicable to contemporary Mexicanas as well.

26. I refer to this image as the fallen Guadalupe, but this portrait is not distinguished in *Serie Guadalupe,* p. 55.

27. "La Familia de la Raza" is the name of an illustration done by the muralist Walter Baka. Significantly, *La Familia de la Raza* was also the name of a publication that stressed the principle of unity through the family as well as nationalist renditions of Chicano identity. The illustration that I am referring to recalls representations of "the holy family." Baka's illustration centers a male protagonist and a child, who engage the spectator's gaze directly through frontal portraits. The veiled woman, who is reminiscent of the Virgin, is captured by her profile, which prevents this type of definition and engagement. In addition, her body becomes an extension of the male's, as his arm extends around her, once again recentering his representation and role as "protector." For an example of this portrait, see *De Colores* 1, no. 2 (Spring 1974): 65. *Bless Me, Ultima* is the title of a novel by Rudolfo Anaya (Berkeley, Calif.: Quinto Sol, 1974). The novel is replete with traditional representations of women. These representations come together in the character of Ultima, the most

important female character, who is defined by her relationship to Antonio. "La Jefita" was published in a seminal anthology entitled *El Espejo* (Berkeley, Calif.: Quinto Sol, 1972), p. 233. "La Jefita" is intended to be a tribute to a Chicana mother who works all day and most of the night and "only complains in her sleep."

28. I am referring to Chicanas such as Martha Cotera, Enriqueta Vásquez, Francisca Rincón, and Rosa E. Domínguez, to cite a few.

29. Ana Nieto-Gómez, "La Chicana," *Women Struggle,* 1975, p. 9.

30. For an account of these contradictions, see Soñía López, "The Role of the Chicana within the Student Movement," in *Essays on La Mujer,* pp. 16–29.

31. Dorinda Moreno, "Mujer de la Raza," in *La Mujer es la tierra,* p. 27.

32. Ibid.

33. I am paraphrasing Ricardo Sánchez's *Canto y grito mi liberación* (New York: Doubleday, 1971). This title significantly carried the subheading *The Liberation of a Chicano Mind.*

34. This illustration, which I believe to be by Irene del Rosario of Vallejo, California, accompanies Moreno's "Mujer de la Raza," p. 27.

35. In Moreno's poem, this type of victimization is seen to be a thing of the past, at least for the poetic subject, who recounts her successful movement toward self-determination.

36. Bernice Zamora, "Notes from a Chicana Coed," *Caracol* 3 (1977): 19.

37. Rendón, *Chicano Manifesto,* p. 159.

38. Enriqueta Longauex y Vásquez, "The Woman of La Raza," in *Aztlan: An Anthology of Mexican-American Literature,* ed. Luis Valdez and Stan Steiner (New York: Vintage Books, 1972), p. 277.

39. Vásquez, "Woman of La Raza," p. 278.

40. Zamora, "Notes from a Chicana Coed," p. 19.

41. Le dedico este trabajo a Sylvia Lizárraga de San Diego, por el gran ejemplo que nos dio al haberse doctorado y convertido en crítica astuta de nuestra cultura. Por supuesto, me hago responsable por las limitaciones que habrán aquí. También le agradezco a Zare Dernersesian la gran ayuda que me proporcionó en la preparación de este ensayo.

FOUR

Speaking from the Margin

Uninvited Discourse on Sexuality and Power

Emma Pérez

Don't remain within the psychoanalytic closure. Take a look, then cut through.
HÉLÈNE CIXOUS, "THE LAUGH OF THE MEDUSA"

My socialist-feminist position has pushed me toward a psychoanalytic end, if only momentarily. When I was a budding graduate student in Chicana/o history and women's history, I tried stubbornly to show that a class-based movement subsumed gender.[1] While Chicano scholars argue that race must be integrated into a class-based revolution, many Chicana scholars defend the premise that the secondary status given to women's issues in a race- and class-based revolution cheats the revolution.[2]

The "unhappy marriage" between Marxism and feminism, however, remains the chosen marriage, because the alternative for feminists is capitalism—a deadly, destructive husband.[3] As socialist feminists, we opt for the man who, as our mothers point out, "sí toma hija, pero no te golpea" (yes, he drinks, but he doesn't batter you). He is far from perfect, but we tenaciously hitch ourselves to the man we are desperate to change in order to improve the marriage. This "husband" has potential if he abandons the ego-driven anxiety that defines his world on his terms. With him, at least, there is a potential for equality and freedom.[4] With the capitalist, we are battered, raped, and left to die in factories, fields, bedrooms, and boardrooms. The Marxist tells us that "women are oppressed," as he gathers with his male cohorts, then yells to you, "Oye corazón, are you finished typing my manuscript?" Lip service is worth something, whether it's in the boardroom or the bedroom, but it is not a revolution.[5]

I want to take us beyond the antiquated Marxist-feminist debate, assuming we agree that class struggle is unavoidable and that race/gender analysis and sexual autonomy must be the vanguard of a victorious revolution.[6] The question is: How are we going to achieve such a revolution given the strength and persistence of the patriarchy—a political, social, and economic system that has bound women historically to an inferior status? I analyze the patriarchy by invoking Freud, Jacques Lacan, and Michel Foucault, if only briefly, in terms of the French feminist analysis of Luce Irigaray, which deconstructs male-centered psychoanalysis. Admittedly, deconstructing white European feminism in order to reconstruct Chicana feminism is inorganic, but no more so than taking from Marx—the quintessential white, middle-class, German man—to explain the exploitation of a Chicana in the cotton fields of Texas. Consciousness—whether of race, class, gender, or sexuality—is born from one's intimate awareness of one's oppression. Theoretical models provide shortcuts to dissect exploitation.[7] Just as Marx provided a general paradigm for grasping the relationship between worker and capitalist, I claim that Luce Irigaray suggests models that interpret social and sexual relationships and hierarchical structures between and among heterosexuals, lesbians, and gay men beyond the borders of France.[8]

But where do culture, race, and colonization fit into these paradigms? Marx's theories on colonization were ethnocentric and male-centered; and Freud, Lacan, and Irigaray do not even mention colonization and its consequences for people of color. I hope to raise questions about how sexuality is expressed for colonized people, especially women. How do we, as women of color, analyze the intersection of sexism with racism in order to deconstruct the pervasive ideology based on them? How do we liberate ourselves from the sexism, heterosexism, and homophobia in our Chicano community while we combat the insipid racism in Anglo society, given that men of color experience racial oppression and displace their frustration onto women of color? I cannot answer these rhetorical questions, but I articulate them in order to acknowledge the complexities we face as women of color and to place the argument back upon sexuality, because sexuality remains an obscure controversy in our Chicana/o academic community.

As a historian trained in the Western European tradition, I ardently question white male ideology and white women's assumptions about women of color. Hence, I turn to European feminists with ambivalence and criticism. Theirs is not my language or my history, imbued as theirs is with conquest and colonization. Indeed, Europeans acted their history as conquerors and colonizers. French feminist discourse deconstructs white male language; but one of the pitfalls of deconstruction is that the method builds upon what it calls into question.[9] These feminists argue for women's method and culture yet ignore racial memory. Some, however, rebel against that which I as a Chicana historical materialist also resist—the male symbolic order. The way the French school dismembers male dominion is what intrigues me. By scrutinizing their offerings, I attempt to supplement an analysis for Chicanas that chiefly summons sexuality and embraces sexuality's relationship to race, class, and gender within our culture.[10]

EXALTING MALE BEHAVIOR: FREUD, LACAN, AND FOUCAULT

Men must cease to be theoretical imbeciles.
MARGUERITE DURAS,
IN *New French Feminisms*

To address sexuality, discourse, and power, I digress briefly to Freud, Lucan, and Foucault, the male theoreticians who, I believe, best define, classify, and—whether deliberately or not—exalt male behavior.[11] But where women are concerned, these men deserve to be labeled "theoretical imbeciles."

Let me begin with Freud, the omnipotent father. The Oedipal moment is basic to his discourse: the moment when a boy realizes he cannot have his first love object, his mother, because she belongs to his powerful father. His fear of this man, whose penis looms larger than his, increases when he realizes that his mother does not have one at all and that he, too, could lack one. Hence, castration anxiety is linked to a dread of women. Although the son repudiates the mother and allies himself with the father because they both have penises, he still competes with this powerful figure, spending his life proving that his is "bigger" and "more powerful" than any symbolic father's.[12]

He also persists in simultaneously renouncing and searching for his mother. In Luce Irigaray's words, "The little boy will never cease to desire his mother."[13] His Oedipus complex is never resolved; therefore, he acts out against women through his fear and anxiety, making a society where the laws, ideas, and customs permit him to reenact the Oedipus complex. All he has to do, he believes, is give up his desire for one woman: "Thus the—fictional—disappearance of the Oedipus complex would resolve itself into the individual's ability to make capital out of ideals and [thereby also] out of mothers, wives-mothers, laws, gazes. . . . Oedipus will have all the mothers he wants, all laws in his favor, and the right to look at anything . . . all, or most, mothers, laws, views (or at any rate points of view). Oedipus will be rich and have no complexes about it. All he has given up is the desire for a woman, for a woman's sex/organ because in any case *that had no value.*"[14]

Irigaray links capital to the Oedipus complex. Men must reify their desire for their mothers in rules, laws, and social constructs that deny women their existence. Pornography, which results from a man's "gaze," helps him swear that he no longer suffers from Oedipal anxiety. Women become his idea—castrated, passive, and eternally feminine in his eyes, in his gaze. As long as he can "gaze," as long as his "love of looking is satisfied, his domination is secure."[15]

Lacan employs Freudian theory to explain the "symbolic law of the father" entrenched in language.[16] Language, he argues, is imbued with symbols that dictate patriarchal power. But in his discussion, he, like Freud, dismisses women's subjectivity and exalts the phallus, again because women do not have one.

The French feminists argue that Freud and Lacan place woman "outside the Symbolic," outside language, the law, culture, and society, because she "does not enjoy what orders masculinity—the castration complex."[17] To French feminists, patriarchy is a law of death, of destruction, of violence. Maleness is socially constructed to be competitive, maniacal, and violent—all qualities rooted in the castration complex and evident in war, violence against women and children, the violent conquest of Third World people, rape, battering, sexual molestation, sexual harassment, and nuclear weapons shaped like penises that ejaculate death. Femaleness, on the other hand, is socially constructed to be collective, intuitive, creative, life-affirming—the other.[18] But women who accept the symbolic law of the father perpetuate it and, in essence, are male-identified women denying a bond with women and affirming men's superiority.[19] Even when women accept the law of the father, however, they do not rape, batter, and sexually molest children in the horrendous numbers that men do. The symbolic phallus, the tool of oppression, reified in guns and bombs, reduces men to dangerous imbeciles attesting to their death drive.

Foucault transcribes historical documents to ventilate "the power of discourse." He argues that "through discourse power/knowledge is realized."[20] Language, after all, is power. Third World people know that to learn the colonizer's language gives one access to power and privilege—albeit controlled, qualified power. As a historian, I have explored Foucault's writings because he surveys the history of discourse on sexuality. I read the first volume of *The History of Sexuality* with curiosity but soon discovered that Foucault, like Freud and Lacan, speaks to men, about men, and for men in male language. In a single paragraph, Foucault "thrust," "penetrated," "rigidified," and "extended" power.[21] By the end of the page, I felt violated. The imagery of "seminal" ideas "ejaculated" onto paper made reading painful at first and then comically apparent. Are these male theoreticians so pained with castration anxiety that they must spurt on paper at every opportunity? It is precisely this kind of male writing and language that rapes, numbs, and dismisses female experience at every stage.[22]

Because Foucault limits his study to the history of male discourse, he restricts himself to male-defined arenas, where women are either absent or silenced. When he argues that the discourse changes through the centuries, I am suspicious, because he reveals how men's language about sexuality and power has changed without acknowledging his bias. Like Freud and Lacan, he would have women indulge in patriarchal interpretations, at the expense of women's sanity, to reconfirm male notions of hysteria. As the other, not the subject, women remain objectified in Foucault's discourse.

I am most impatient with Foucault, however, because of what he neglects to say in this volume.[23] In the last chapter, he discusses power and its relationship to sexuality, but he overlooks the obvious. Like male theoreticians who build abstractions to mask the simple, he does not say: men, especially white men from the middle and upper classes, hold political, social, racial, and sexual power over women, but especially women of color, and these men have used that power throughout history to control women and to sustain patriarchal power. *Punto.* Is this premise transhistorical? Is it cross-cultural? Yes and no. Every aberration of sexual abuse against women and children of all races and against men of color has its historical antecedents.[24] This, I believe, is a point of departure for women historians.[25] But Chicana historians must begin with what Foucault neglects to say.[26]

Why can't Foucault declare the obvious? Because he is blinded by his privilege, his male prerogative? Surely it's not that simple. I cannot spurn Foucault so easily. As a historian, I appreciate his historical specificity, because within his constructs he forces me to ask whether patriarchal power is indeed transhistorical and whether the Oedipus complex is transhistorical and transcultural. Is an understanding of the Oedipus complex useful to Chicanas writing our history, which is inextricably enmeshed with conquest and colonization?[27]

"EL CHINGÓN": OCTAVIO PAZ AND THE OEDIPAL-CONQUEST COMPLEX

The worst kind of betrayal lies in making us believe that the Indian woman in us is the betrayer.
GLORIA ANZALDUA, *Borderlands (La Frontera)*

Perhaps Lacan is for French feminists what Octavio Paz is for Chicanas. Inevitably, we invoke Paz's *Labyrinth of Solitude,* where he unites us metaphorically with La Chingada, or La Malinche.[28] We react, we respond repeatedly to his misogyny. But misogyny alone is not what we contest. We dispute a historically specific moment that denigrates us, immortalizes us as "the betrayer" for all time, eternally stuck in an image, *la puta* (the whore). Long before the arrival of the Virgen de Guadalupe, we were La Chingada. The metaphor cuts to the core of each Chicana; each *mestiza* is flouted as *la india*/whore. Worse yet is that *la india* is our mother, and Paz slashes away at her beauty. He subordinates our first love object by violently raping her in historical text, in male language.

To Paz, the Aztec princess Malintzín, also called Malinche, "gave" herself to Hernán Cortés, the symbol of the Spanish Conquest; therefore, Paz charges her with the downfall of Mexico. In Paz, we have the symbolic son, the *mestizo,* repudiating the symbolic father, Cortés. The Oedipal triangle is completed by *la india,* whom they raped and tamed, literally and metaphorically. Malintzín, the "other," the inferior, disdained female, was not worthy of marrying, so Cortés passed her down to a soldier. With the soldier Jaramaillo, Malinche bore the first *mestizos.* For Paz, *la india* personifies the passive whore who acquiesced to the Spaniard, the conqueror, his symbolic father—the father he despises for choosing an inferior woman who begat an inferior race and the father he fears for his powerful phallus.

Paz's essay reveals more about his own castration complex than about Malinche. Obsessed with *chingar,* he expounds a theory to explain the inferiority complex of *mestizos/as.* But self-hate, the internalized racism with which Paz must contend, emanates from his text. After all, the mighty Cortés was the white Western European male conqueror, the symbol of power that Paz was a step away from, not just as the son but, more important, as the bastard Mexicano. Paz exhibits his own internalized racial inferiority. He is far less powerful than his symbolic white father, the conquistador. On the other hand, his hatred of *las chingadas* (women) and all that is female symbolically begins with this Oedipal-conquest triangle. Here the sexual, political, social, and psychological violence against *la india*—the core of the Chicana—is born. This core has been plundered through conquest and colonization. We reclaim the core for our women-tempered *sitios y lenguas* (spaces and languages).

Lacan's symbolic order of "language and meaning"[29] is epitomized in the Oedipal-conquest triangle when the *mestizo* enters the pained moment of castration anxiety; for the *mestizo* male, the entry into the symbolic order is even more confusing, because he does not know the white father's language. He cannot even guess at the meaning of symbols between himself and his conquering/colonizing father. Cultural differences divided *el español y el indio,* who were thrown together at the moment of Spanish Conquest and who misunderstood each other's symbols and language.[30]

Mestizos/as master the conqueror's language as the language of survival, but it never completely belongs to the conquered. People whose language has been swindled twice, first the native tongue, then the appropriated tongue, are forced to stumble over colonizer language. As an adult, the Chicano male is perceived as the powerless son of the white Oedipal father who makes laws in his language. An African-American man called "boy" by white men and women is reduced to this symbolic son, but African-American history of conquest and enslavement is unlike ours, and I am in no position to conjecture about this similarity. In a racist society, the *mestizo* male is a castrated man in relation to the white male colonizer-father. His anxiety encompasses not only the fear of castration but also the fear that his power will never match the supreme power of the white man. Whereas the white son has the promise of becoming the father, the *mestizo,* even when he becomes the father, is set apart by his skin color and by a lack of language, the dominant language of the colonizer. Moreover, he must repudiate *la india y la mestiza* for fear that he also could be a weak, castrated betrayer of his people. He colludes with the white colonizer-father as they both condemn the Chicana.

The Oedipal-conquest triangle dictates the sexual politics of miscegenation in the twentieth century. Although Chicanos are usually incensed when Chicanas marry the "enemy," white men, they exercise male prerogative by marrying white women to both defy and collaborate with the white father. In having half-white children, they move their sons a step closer to the nexus of power—the white colonizer-father. The Chicana who marries a white male, by contrast, embraces the white Oedipal-colonizer ambivalently, because—although theoretically she gains access to power—realistically she is still perceived as *la india* by a white dominant culture that disapproves of miscegenation. She is not her half-white children, nor will she ever be; her half-white sons will always have more social, political, and sexual power than she could imagine. (Certainly, the same principle applies to the Chicano with a white wife, but his male privilege has already granted him rank that a Chicana cannot earn.) The daughter of a white male and a Chicana has the father's white name to carry her through racist institutions, placing her closer to power relations in society.[31]

Paz's phallocratic discourse reflects the Oedipal-conquest triangle, which symbolizes social-sexual-racial relations between Chicanos and Chicanas and among the white women and white men who oversee the dilemma. It is a metaphor that dictates social-sexual-racial relations. That the Oedipal moment is historically or culturally inaccurate is not the issue. The point is that it is a symbol unconsciously perceived by Paz, who imposed the psychodrama of conquest upon the Chicano, who in turn inflicts misogyny in the image of La Malinche upon Chicanas/Mexicanas. Paz cannot be held responsible for the conquest; he merely interprets history from a masculinist ideology.

The law of the white colonizer-father conditions our world in the late twentieth century. Our challenge is to rebel against the symbol of the white father and affirm our separation from the destructive ideology to create life-affirming *sitios*. But before defying the law of the father, we must understand why we are so stuck and so addicted to the perpetrator of destruction. Why do we uphold the law of the white European colonizer father when we know the extent of damage and pain for Chicanas and Chicanos? Chicanos who absorb the white colonizer-father's ways hierarchically impose them on Chicanas, becoming caricatures of the white colonizer-father. One has only to look at any institution where Chicanos have been integrated to see how they emulate the white father to exclude women, especially women of color.[32]

BREAKING THE ADDICTIVE/DEPENDENT CYCLE OF POWER

> *He has no desire for woman to upset him in his sexual habits . . . his rather suspect respect for law and order. He does not want her to be anything but his daughter, whose gratifying fantasies of seduction it is his task to interpret, and who must be initiated into, and curbed by, the "reasonable" discourse of his [sexual] law. Or else he wants her to be his mother, whose erotic reveries he would finally gain access to. Unless again some very "unconscious" homosexual transference is tied in there, sotto voce.*
>
> LUCE IRIGARAY, *Speculum of the Other Woman*

In his theater production *Corridos,* Luis Valdez reenacts a provocative *corrido* about father-daughter incest.[33] Both Valdez's choice and his presentation of the *corrido* intrigue me. He seems titillated by and almost condones the arrangement. Valdez's "Delgadina" provides insight into the patriarchy, revealing the dynamic between perpetrators and victims who create an addictive cycle of dependence between the powerful and the powerless.[34] Like the preceding works by male centralist theorists, the production exposes Valdez's castration anxiety through his "gaze," his male definition and interpretation of what is feminine.

I use the *corrido* to critique Freud's "Electra complex," the inverse of the Oedipus complex. Freud hypothesized the Electra complex to explain a daughter's recognition that she cannot have her father. But he cannot establish just how a daughter transfers desire for her mother as her first love object to the father, so that she can embrace heterosexuality. I believe, like many feminists, that he invokes patriarchal law to put an end to the daughter's wavering transference, thereby rationalizing his own desire for the daughter to transfer her desire from the mother to the father.

Patriarchal law dictates the tacit language and behavior of incest, which place fear in the daughter's psyche. At some point, she unconsciously recognizes the supreme phallus's potential to harm her psyche. Freud does not speculate that the remotest possibility of incest victimizes the daughter. According to Freud, the questions to ask about a daughter are: Does she repudiate her mother to embrace the father and to be impregnated by him, producing a baby as a substitute for the penis she was not born with? Does she turn to the father to embrace "normal" femininity? Freud, however, refuses to ask whether the daughter can remain attached to her first love object, her mother. If so, the questions change: Wouldn't a daughter's attachment to her mother lead to a woman-loving culture? Or to lesbianism? Wouldn't the mother-daughter relationship press heterosexual women to examine their bisexual ambivalence—their occasional desire for women even while gripping the law of the father?[35]

The "Delgadina" *corrido* represents a daughter's painful entrance into the law of the father. The first part of her name—*De,* meaning "belonging to," "a man's possession"—is worth noting.

Briefly, the *corrido* tells the story of a beautiful young woman whose father watches her dance by moonlight, craves her, and then decides to pounce. As they walk home from church one day, he commands her to be his lover. When she refuses, he jails her in a tower (phallic), waiting for her to succumb. While in the tower, she is denied food and water as punishment for disobeying her father. She begs her mother, her brother, and her sister for food, water, and release. Each one fears violating the father's order, his sexual laws; so each ostracizes Delgadina. Her mother and her sister, who are "an integral part of a phallic masculine economy," betray her.[36] And yet, what is their alternative? For women need a moment, a specific moment of consciousness, when they can separate from the law of the father into their own space and language. Delgadina has nowhere to turn and eventually dies from hunger for nourishment, for freedom. Her father, a broken man, is left with the memory of never having consummated sex with the young, alluring love object—his daughter.

Unlike La Malinche, Delgadina does not succumb. Indeed, she dies a virgin. A patriarchal society betrays her by blinding itself and keeping a secret in disbelief that the father could rape his daughter or desire to rape her. But behavior and language are basic to sexual molestation. A sign, a word, a gesture can be as damaging as penetration by the penis. But patriarchal laws ignore behavior and language in cases of molestation. According to these male-defined laws, the penis must penetrate; otherwise, these laws will not consider that harm was done. For Delgadina, a patriarch's peremptory laws penetrate "only" her psyche.

Valdez chose to tell us this story to peer into the "secret" of a father's sexual arousal by his daughter. This is voyeurism, the male gaze asserted. Like Hollywood's pornographic filmmakers, Valdez eroticizes women's victimization to appeal to his male audience. All this is not beside the point. To eroticize the father-daughter incestuous relationship implicitly grants permission to older men who seek young women as lovers and marriage partners. The relationship asserts male sexual power over a younger woman who could very likely be a daughter. Patriarchal society condones the older man–young woman relationship; in fact, it envies the man who successfully catches a young woman. Such a woman, after all, gives complete adoration—at first. Indeed, there are historical roots to arrangements between older men and younger women. In colonial California, the Catholic church and the Spanish-Mexican settlers colluded when the church condoned marriages between older men and young women, often nieces, to keep property within the family. Older Spanish-Mexican soldiers also married young women to be assured that the women were virgins.[37]

But there is another implicit message in the *corrido*. That is, although the *corrido* warns against incest, it also communicates the danger to a young woman when she challenges the sexual law of the father. She cannot break that law, happy and free to join women who believe her or a community who will allow her to be herself. There is no such community. Instead, a male-centered society with male-identified women cannot even hear her language, her pain. They only know that they cannot defy the father.

But Delgadina does not have an opportunity to resist her father, because—even before he commands her to be his lover—he has already employed incestuous language and behavior. The "molestation" parodied in his behavior creates her "memory of molestation," which by social definition has not taken place because physical touch and penetration by the penis never occur. But in her memory, it did take place. The behavior, inappropriate for a father, to say the least, is not confronted by her mother, her sister, or her brother. Not by anyone.

The addictive/dependent cycle has begun for both of them.[38] When she tries to break from it, however, she finds no support. Like Delgadina, women live in a cycle of addiction/dependency to the patriarchy that has ruled them since the precise historical moment in which they became aware that women's bodies are sexually desired and/or overpowered by the penis. A young girl fears its power and tries to tame it, manipulate it, adore it, loathe it, or ignore it. She may feel any variety of emotions toward the tool of oppression, but envy is not one of them. Why should she envy that which symbolically destroys?

This reminder, this memory of molestation, a memory of origin, haunts the young girl through womanhood. Indeed, the memories of sexual molestation dictate sexual desire. Either women repudiate the molester/perpetrator or they embrace him. This pattern persists throughout their relationships until the addictive/dependent cycle is broken. Not until victims resist perpetrators and have the courage to abandon the pattern, not until women and men stop assigning the perpetrators power, can women and men abandon phallocratic law and order.

When will those of us making a revolution expunge the capitalist patriarchal tradition of sexual law and order that dictates the perpetrator-victim dynamic? When will we embrace the real, yet ideal, beliefs of the collective, to work together for the common good? Within capitalist patriarchal ideology, the sensitive human being who is willing to transform the world is disregarded; Marxist patriarchs are also guilty. Our personal revolutions—each member of the collective taking responsibility for her/his contradictions within the collective—are belittled in our movements. Are we willing to grapple with questions like "Am I exploiting anyone, and if I am, how can I change?" If we do not challenge our own contradictions, then we only pretend to make a revolution.

Both women and men are addicted to that which destroys them—the patriarchy within capitalist constructs in the late twentieth century. The social-sexual-racial relations between men and women condoned by the patriarchy are inherently unhealthy and destructive most of the time. The dynamic begins, I argue, in the collective memories of Western European conquerors and people of color, who are subdued by the memory of the Oedipal-conquest triangle.

How do we achieve a successful revolution/movement given the strength and persistence of the patriarchy? In one respect, the answer lies in rejecting the addictive pattern. We begin by shedding internalized sexist, homophobic, elitist, and racist behaviors. We change destructive patterns today, immediately, with the hope of raising children and teaching students who do not have to appropriate society's addictive capitalist patriarchal discourse to survive. The individual is responsible to the collective, after all. When one heals oneself within the collective, the collective is healed. But that is only one small integral step. There is much more to do.[39]

NOTES

1. In 1982, I wrote an essay on the Mexican anarchist group the Partido Liberal Mexicano. I argued that the nationalist class-based movement placed women's exploitation as workers in the forefront but dismissed their oppression in the home and in their social-sexual relationships with the male leaders of the organization. The essay should have been published years ago, but political circumstances delayed it. In light of current debates spawned by deconstruction, the essay is dated but perhaps useful because it analyzes the gender ideology within nationalist class-based movements. See Emma Pérez, " 'A La Mujer': A Critique of the Partido Liberal Mexicano's Gender Ideology on Women," in *Between Borders: Essays on Mexicana/Chicana History,* ed. Adelaida del Castillo (Encino, Calif.:

Floricanto Press, 1990), pp. 459–482. Also refer to my dissertation, " 'Through Her Love and Sweetness': Women, Revolution and Reform in Yucatán, 1910–1918," Ph.D. diss., University of California, Los Angeles, 1988. Again I point out that, in a region where socialism was attempted, women's issues were brought to the forefront only to benefit a male-defined political arena.

2. For a historical materialist analysis of Chicano/Mexicano social movements, see Mario Barrera, *Race and Class in the Southwest: A Theory of Racial Inequality* (Notre Dame, Ind.: University of Notre Dame Press, 1979). See any number of essays by Tomás Almaguer and Juan Gómez-Quiñones, and, most recently, David Montejano, *Anglos and Mexicans in the Making of Texas, 1836–1986* (Austin: University of Texas Press, 1987). For studies by Chicanas who examine the primary place of gender along with a race and class analysis, see Patricia Zavella, *Women's Work and Chicano Families: Cannery Workers of the Santa Clara Valley* (Ithaca, N.Y.: Cornell University Press, 1987); Vicki Ruiz, *Cannery Women, Cannery Lives: Mexican Women, Unionization, and the California Food Processing Industry, 1930–1950* (Albuquerque: University of New Mexico Press, 1987). Also refer to Deena González, "The Spanish-Mexican Women of Santa Fé: Patterns of Resistance and Accommodation, 1820–1880," Ph.D. diss., University of California, Berkeley, 1985; Antonia Castañeda, "Presidarias y Pobladoras: Spanish-Mexican Women in Frontier Monterey, California, 1770–1821," Ph.D. diss., Stanford University, 1990; and published and unpublished works by Lourdes Arguelles, Teresa Córdova, Elisa Facio, Clara Lomas, Beatríz Pesquera, Denise Segura, Adaljisa Sosa Riddell, and Gloria Romero, to name a few.

3. Heidi Hartmann's essay on this subject elucidates the antiquated, unresolved debate. See "The Unhappy Marriage of Marxism and Feminism: Towards a More Progressive Union," in *Women and Revolution,* ed. Lydia Sargent (Boston: South End Press, 1981), pp. 2–41. I refuse to identify myself as a "Marxist" and prefer "socialist" because Marxist identifies one with a male, Karl Marx. Although I sanction Marx's theories and writings, I prefer to call my method socialist-feminist or historical materialist.

4. I recognize that this is a heterosexist analogy; however, I employ it to ridicule the social arrangement called marriage, which imposes itself at every level of our psyche.

5. Chicano studies departments that have existed for ten years or more and still have not hired and tenured more than one Chicana are embarrassments to our community. They offer lip service about their hiring practices.

6. I owe my development of socialist-feminist theory to works by Juliet Mitchell, particularly *Woman's Estate* (New York: Random House, 1973), still an excellent book, and to Michele Barrett, *Women's Oppression Today* (New York: Schocken Books, 1981), where she discusses the significance of gender ideology. Numerous socialist-feminist writings generated my analysis; but in my Chicana community, historians Deena González, Antonia Castañeda, and the Chicana scholars of MALCS help me to imagine our specific, organic movement, especially through our organization, Mujeres Activas en Letras y Cambio Social (MALCS). MALCS was founded in 1982 in northern California by approximately ten Chicana academics eager to affirm our Chicana network within the university. The organization meets yearly and boasts a membership of over one hundred Chicana scholars from around the nation.

7. As a historical materialist, I am aware that theory follows practice, but as a socialist feminist, I probe theory to apply what is useful and disregard the rest.

8. I agree with Leslie Wahl Rabine, who argues that "Lacanian psychoanalysis is, I

think, of greater interest and use to feminist theory than Derridean deconstruction, and, not surprisingly, feminists have a much more intense relation of ambivalence and outrage to this theory" (see "A Feminist Politics of Non-Identity," *Feminist Studies* 14, no. 1 [Spring 1988]: 11–31). For me, French feminists' deconstruction of Lacanian psychoanalysis opens up feminist theory on sexuality. I also want to suggest the importance of Gayatri Chakravorty Spivak's deconstructive essays on colonialism and feminism (see *In Other Worlds: Essays in Cultural Politics* [New York: Routledge, 1987]). In this essay, I rely on theoreticians who discuss sexuality directly. For me, that is Luce Irigaray. I believe that Irigaray's probing of sexuality may provide lesbians with a language to decode our oppression and then invert the language with our command (see *This Sex Which Is Not One,* trans. Catherine Porter (Ithaca, N.Y.: Cornell University Press, 1985). One of my favorite passages by Irigaray (on page 28) reveals that women's sexuality is plural. "The pleasure of the vaginal caress does not have to be substituted for that of the clitoral caress. They each contribute, irreplaceably, to women's pleasure. . . . Fondling the breasts, touching the vulva, spreading the lips, stroking the posterior wall of the vagina, brushing against the mouth of the uterus, and so on. To evoke only a few of the most specifically female pleasures . . . woman has sex organs more or less everywhere." A beautiful example of woman-loving prose.

9. G. C. Spivak quotes Jacques Derrida, "The enterprise of deconstruction always in a certain way falls prey to its own work" (see Spivak, "Feminism and Deconstruction, Again," in *Between Feminism and Psychoanalysis,* ed. Teresa Brennan [New York: Routledge, 1989], p. 213).

10. Internalized homophobia and bisexual ambivalence frighten many heterosexual Chicanas/os into a rigid analysis of the Chicana/o family. Studies in the social sciences on the Chicana/o family that ignore nontraditional family arrangements perpetuate Anglo perceptions about our community—that is, that Latino family tradition is anchored in *machismo.* Anglo feminist accusations lead to problematic Chicana discourse within feminist constructs. When white feminists ardently insist on discussing *machismo,* they impose phallocratic discourse. By "centering" and "focusing" on the phallus, they deflect attention from their racism. The evasion, racist and heterosexist, deters the building of coalitions between white feminists and Chicana feminists.

11. I use the definition of discourse put forth by the editors Elaine Marks and Isabelle de Courtivron in *New French Feminisms* (Amherst: University of Massachusetts Press, 1980), p. 3. Discourse is "the relation between language and the object to which it apparently refers," for instance, women.

12. This is gross oversimplification, but it suits my needs. For Freud's own words, see Sigmund Freud, *Sexuality and the Psychology of Love,* ed. Philip Rieff (New York: Macmillan, 1963), pp. 176–182.

13. Luce Irigaray, *Speculum of the Other Woman,* trans. Gillian G. Gill (Ithaca, N.Y.: Cornell University Press, 1985), p. 81.

14. Ibid.

15. According to Toril Moi, "gaze," in Freud's terms, is "phallic activity linked to the anal desire for sadistic mastery of the object." The "love of looking" and the sadistic male are hence linked to violence in pornography. For her interpretation of Freud's "gaze," see Toril Moi, *Sexual/Textual Politics* (New York: Routledge, 1985), p. 134. Also see Irigaray, *Speculum,* p. 47.

16. Jacques Lacan, *Écrits: A Selection,* trans. Alan Sheridan (New York: Norton, 1977).

17. Hélène Cixous, "Castration or Decapitation?" *Signs* 7, no. 1 (Autumn 1981): 46.

18. The French feminists are not arguing that "biology is destiny," any more than Freud and Lacan are. They understand that gender is socially constructed, not biologically determined. British Marxist feminist Juliet Mitchell best argues this point in her study *Psychoanalysis and Feminism* (New York: Random House, 1975), and she was chided for her position in the 1970s. I think we are closer to accepting the value of psychoanalysis in that it does provide an understanding of the male symbolic order—the patriarchy. I argue that an examination of the Oedipal triangle can release us finally from its enslavement, from women's and men's addiction to and dependency on the patriarchy.

19. Xaviere Gauthier, "Is There Such a Thing as Women's Writing?" in *New French Feminisms*, p. 162. Gauthier argues that women accept the phallic system to "find their place in male language, law, grammar, syntax." They become "completely divorced from themselves without knowing it." They go crazy denying themselves in order to accommodate male definitions of what women should be—more like men but still unlike them. The double messages and double binds make us appear irrational and hysterical.

20. Jeffrey Weeks, *Sex, Politics and Society: The Regulation of Sexuality since 1800* (London: Longman, 1981), p. 7. I use Weeks's interpretation of Foucault lore.

21. Michel Foucault, *The History of Sexuality*, vol. 1: *An Introduction*, trans. Robert Hurley (New York: Pantheon Books, 1978), p. 48. I read the English translation; therefore, the translator may be the culprit. The original may or may not be far from its English translation, but it is disconcerting that the translation should read as such.

22. I am reminded of a male friend who asked whether I had enjoyed the film *Dangerous Liaisons*. I responded that I thought it was misogynist, to which he queried, "But didn't you enjoy it?" He might as well have asked, "Forget the fact that it was a rape; didn't you enjoy it anyway?" I refuse to indulge myself in Hollywood's interpretation of male-female sexual power relations. Even when Hollywood attempts to make a "feminist" film like *The Accused*, about a woman's brutal gang rape, the filmmakers rely on the fact that the male audience will practice their "gaze" undeterred by the weak feminist message.

23. Perhaps he clarifies this omission in the other volumes, but I doubt that he appropriates a feminist analysis.

24. The fusion of sex and power provides the basis for violence against all women and children and men of color. Lynchings, whippings, beatings, and murder of black- and brown-skinned men must also be addressed when one is discussing sexual power relations. I will not do so at any length, but I recognize the social-historical brutality against men of color and its damage to their psyches and to the psyche of our community. However, when men of color become perpetrators against women and children, and many do, I lose compassion and patience.

25. Linda Gordon has written an excellent study about child abuse in the nineteenth-century United States, a different aberration from late-twentieth-century sexual molestation cases (see *Heroes of Their Own Lives* [New York: Viking, 1988]).

26. Historian Deena González argues, "If we conceptualize most history as written by white males from a white male perspective, then we must start with the premise that it is all biased history" (quoted in Gregg Mitchell, "Barrier Crusaders," *Pomona College Today*, Summer 1989, p. 17). I agree with González's premise that Chicana historians are forced to deconstruct what has been written before we can reconstruct our own history. Small wonder that our work takes longer to produce.

27. I also address these questions in an expanded version of this essay, "Sexuality and Discourse: Notes from a Chicana Survivor," in *Chicana Lesbians: The Girls Our Mothers Warned Us About,* ed. Carla Trujillo (Berkeley, Calif.: Third Woman Press, 1991), pp. 159–184.

28. Octavio Paz, *The Labyrinth of Solitude,* trans. Lysander Kemp (New York: Grove Press, 1961), pp. 65–88. I refer of course to the chapter on "La Chingada," which denigrates the Aztec princess Malintzín Tenépal. Adelaida del Castillo's criticism of Paz's ahistorical account of Malintzín still stands up well. See "Malintzín Tenépal: A Preliminary Look into a New Perspective," in *Essays on La Mujer,* ed. Rosaura Sánchez and Rosa Martínez Cruz (Los Angeles: Chicano Studies Research Center, University of California, 1977), pp. 124–149. I will not reiterate this history. I assume that most readers already know it. Many Chicana scholars have responded to Paz's misogyny at some point. To list all the essays, publications, and private gripes is a pointless exercise. Take my word for it, or ask any Chicana about Paz's Chingada. I do recommend Norma Alarcón's essay "Chicana Feminist Literature: A Re-vision through Malintzín/or Malintzín: Putting Flesh Back on the Object," in *This Bridge Called My Back: Writings by Radical Women of Color,* ed. Cherrie Moraga and Gloria Anzaldua (Watertown, Mass.: Persephone Press, 1981), pp. 182–190. Alarcón argues, and I agree, that we must also delve into the psychosexual exploitation of women of color along with exposing economic exploitation.

29. On Lacan, see Weeks, *Sex, Politics and Society,* pp. 3–4.

30. Tzvetan Todorov explains the significance of symbols as miscommunication between Spaniards and the Aztecs. Spaniards assumed they understood Aztec symbols and actions, and, of course, they did not (see *The Conquest of America: The Question of the Other,* trans. Richard Howard [New York: Harper and Row, 1982]).

31. Skin color, however, plays an important role for half-breeds. The lighter the skin, the more possible it is to pass through doors of power and privilege. Of course, skin color does not just apply to half-breeds. But when one has the white skin and the white name of a white father and a *mestiza* for a mother, one is likely to have access to more power in a racist society. What one does with that power politically is a different issue altogether. Of course, class status is also a prominent factor to consider in these matchings.

32. For Chicanos, their maleness offers them male language and behavior since childhood. They must learn to master the colonizer male dialect, however.

33. Chicana scholars in literature and theater have criticized Valdez's negative, one-dimensional depiction of women in his productions. I am interested in examining his choice as a symbol that perpetuates the law of the father. Delgadina was one of the acts in the production *Corridos,* first staged in San Francisco in 1983. For more on Valdez, see Yolanda Broyles-González, "What Price Mainstream? Luis Valdez's *Corridos* on Stage and Film," *Cultural Studies* 4, no. 3 (October 1990): 281–293.

34. I am indebted to Helen Bauer, executive director of the Ephpheta Counseling Center in Ontario, California, for her ideas about the addiction/dependency cycle. I developed my analysis of the cycle's relationship to the patriarchy from her concept.

35. Irigaray, *Speculum,* p. 72. She discusses "the girl's turning to the father" to embrace "normal" femininity and "renounce phallic activity."

36. Antoinette Fouque, in *New French Feminisms,* p. 117.

37. Castañeda, "Presidarias y Pobladoras," chap. 5.

38. Numerous studies on sexual molestation and child abuse discuss this persistent pattern of addiction and dependency. I recommend the work by counseling psychologist

Charlotte Davis Kasl, *Women, Sex, and Addiction: A Search for Love and Power* (New York: Ticknor and Fields, 1989). I particularly like Kasl's approach because she moves beyond sexual damage to recovery and healing. For a new study on child abuse and its violent damage, see Leonard Shengold, *Soul Murder: The Effects of Childhood Abuse and Deprivation* (New Haven, Conn.: Yale University Press, 1989).

39. This essay has been adapted from papers that I presented at the National Association for Chicano Studies Conference, Albuquerque, New Mexico, April 1990; and at the MALCS Chicana/Latina Summer Institute, University of California, Los Angeles, August 1990.

PART TWO

Cultural Representations / Cultural Presentations

FIVE

La Tules of Image and Reality

Euro-American Attitudes and Legend Formation on a Spanish-Mexican Frontier

Deena J. González

In the summer of 1846, Doña Gertrudis Barceló stood at an important crossroad. Exempted from the hardships and tribulations endured by the women around her, Barceló had profited enormously from the "gringo" merchants and itinerant retailers who had arrived in Santa Fé after the conquest. The town's leading businesswoman, owner of a gambling house and saloon, and its most unusual character, Barceló exemplified an ingenious turnaround in the way she and others in her community began resolving the problem of the Euro-American, now lodged more firmly than ever in their midst. Barceló also epitomized the growing dilemma of dealing with newcomers whose culture and orientation differed from hers.

Since 1821, people like Barceló had seen traders enter their town and change it. But local shopkeepers and vendors had done more than observe the developing marketplace. They had forged ahead, establishing a partnership with the adventurers who brought manufactured items and textiles to Santa Fé while exporting the products of Nuevo México, including gold, silver, and equally valuable goods, such as Navajo blankets and handwoven rugs.[1]

Barceló's life and activities were indisputably anchored in a community shaped by a changing economy, as well as by other political, social, and cultural demands. Orthodox interpretations of her life have overlooked the primacy of the surrounding turmoil. Moreover, by 1846, she would become the female object of the easiest, most exaggerated misunderstandings bred by such complicated frontier situations. The exaggerations have been examined from several perspectives; but standard works have failed to assess the role that sex and gender played in discussions of Barceló's business and personality.[2] The outcome has been the creation of a legend around her, one directly shaped by the disruptions experienced by her generation and focused on her business and her sex.

Gertrudis Barceló was said to have controlled men and to have dabbled in local politics, but these insinuations do not form the core of her legend. Rather, reporters of her time, professional historians today, and novelists have debated her morals, arguing about her influence over political leaders and speculating about whether she was operating a brothel. These concerns are consistently revealed in early accounts of Barceló by writers and soldiers recalling their experiences in the "hinterlands" of northern Mexico. The negative images and anti-Mexican stereotypes in these works not only stigmatized Barceló but also helped legitimize the Euro-Americans' conquest of the region. Absorbed and reiterated by succeeding generations of professional historians and novelists, the legend of Barceló has obscured the complex reality of cultural accommodation and ongoing resistance.

Moreover, the legend evolving around Barceló affected the lives of other Spanish-Mexican women. Her supposed moral laxity and outrageous dress were generalized to include all the women of Santa Fé. Susan Shelby Magoffin, the first Euro-American woman to travel down the Santa Fé Trail, observed in 1846 that "These were dressed in the Mexican style; large sleeves, short waists, ruffled skirts, and no bustles—which latter looks exceedingly odd in this day of grass skirts and pillows. All danced and smoked cigarittos, from the old woman with false hair and teeth [Doña Tula], to the little child."[3]

This was not the first account of La Tules, as Barceló was affectionately called (in reference either to her slimness or to her plumpness, because *tules* means "reed").[4] Josiah Gregg, a trader during the 1830s, said that La Tules was a woman of "loose habits," who "roamed" in Taos before she came to Santa Fé.[5] In his widely read *Commerce of the Prairies,* Gregg linked local customs—smoking, gambling, and dancing—to social and moral disintegration. La Tules embodied, for him and others, the extent of Spanish-Mexican decadence.

La Tules's dilemmas predated 1846 and, at a social and economic level, portended a community's difficulties, which were not long in developing. Governing officers in Chihuahua had already sent word of a crackdown on illegal trafficking.[6] Bishop Zubiría in Durango issued a pastoral limiting church holidays and celebrations, in an effort to economize on expenses but also on priests' time. This pastoral gave added emphasis to the regulations descending on New Mexicans, who now became aware that the Catholic church, too, was reconsidering its obligations. In this period, Barceló and other Spanish-Mexicans experienced the tightening grip of the Mexican state, which was bent on rooting out uncontrolled trading; but they gained a reprieve accidentally. As orders arrived from the church concerning the condition of Christians on the northern frontier, the United States chose to invade, hurling General Stephen Kearny and his troops toward the capital city.[7]

Barceló's activities and business acumen demonstrated, despite these pressures, the *vecinos'* (residents') proven resilience and the town's characteristic adaptability. But in the 1840s Barceló also became the object of intense Euro-American scrutiny and harsh ridicule. She was an expert dealer at monte, a card game named after the *monte* (mountain) of cards that accumulated with each hand. She drew hundreds of dollars out of merchants and soldiers alike; it was the former who embellished her name and reputation, imbuing her facetiously with characteristics of superiority and eccentricity.

Josiah Gregg, the trader, first brought Barceló notoriety because his book described her as a loose woman. But Gregg also argued that money from gambling eventually helped elevate her moral character.[8] A Protestant, and a doctor in failing health, Gregg respected only her gift—the one he understood best—for making money. During her lifetime, she became extraordinarily wealthy, and for that reason as well, Gregg and others would simultaneously admire and disdain her.

In the face of such contradictory attitudes toward her, Barceló ventured down a trail of her own choosing. Not quite as rebellious as Juana Lopes, who had defied husband and judge alike, she nevertheless achieved personal autonomy. Several times, she appeared before magistrates to pay fines, testifying once against an indicted judge who had pocketed her money. She even involved her family in her pursuits, and they were fined along with her.[9] As early as 1825, she was at the mining camp outside of Santa Fé, Real del Oro, doing a brisk business at monte.[10] By the 1830s, the card dealer was back in town, enticing Euro-Americans to gamble under terms she prescribed. At her saloon, she served the men alcohol as she dealt rounds of cards. Controlling consumption as well as the games, Barceló accommodated the newcomers, but on her own terms. "Shrewd," Susan Shelby Magoffin, wife of the trader Samuel Magoffin, called Barceló in 1846.[11]

Barceló had proven her shrewdness long before that. Since the 1820s, Barceló had engaged in an extremely profitable enterprise. Gambling, dubbed by observers the national pastime, was ubiquitous, and by the mid-1830s nearly every traveler and merchant felt compelled to describe Barceló's contributions to the game.[12] Matt Field, an actor and journalist from Missouri, depicted Barceló's saloon as a place where her "calm seriousness was alone discernible, and the cards fell from her fingers as steadily as though she were handling only a knitting needle. . . . Again and again the long fingers of Señora Toulous swept off the pile of gold, and again were they replaced by the unsteady fingers of her opponent."[13] By any account, Euro-Americans could understand what drove Barceló. Because they recognized in her their own hungry search for profit, they embellished their stories and, just as frequently, maligned her.

When Barceló died in 1852, she was worth over ten thousand dollars, a sum twice as high as most wealthy Spanish-Mexican men possessed and larger than the average worth of Euro-Americans in Santa Fé.[14] Her properties were extensive: she owned the saloon, a long building with large rooms, and she had an even larger home not far from the plaza. She made enough money to give generously to the church and to her relatives, supporting families and adopting children.[15] Military officers claimed that she entertained lavishly and frequently.[16]

Dinners, dances, gambling, and assistance to the poverty-stricken elevated Barceló to a special place in New Mexican society, where she remained throughout her life. The community respected her, since it tolerated atypical behavior in others and rarely seemed preoccupied with what Barceló represented. Even her scornful critics were struck by how well received and openly admired the woman with the "red hair and heavy jewelry" was among Santa Fé's "best society."[17]

What was it about Nuevo México in the two decades before the war that allowed a woman like Barceló to step outside the accepted boundaries of normal or typical female behavior, make a huge sum of money, undergo excessive scrutiny, primarily by newcomers to Santa Fé, and yet be eulogized by her own people? Some answers lie within her Spanish-Mexican community, which, although beset by persisting problems, had flexibility and an inclination toward change. Others lie in the general position and treatment of women in that society.

Court records and other documents reveal that Santa Fé's women were expected to defer to men but did not, that they were bound by a code of honor and respectability but often manipulated it to their advantage, and that they were restrained by fathers and brothers from venturing too far out of family and household but frequently disobeyed them. One professional historian has argued that social codes in colonial New Mexican society, with their twin emphasis on honor and virtue, were primarily metaphors for expressing hierarchical relationships but also served to resolve conflict as much as to restrict women.[18] Women's behavior and the espoused social ideals of restraint, respectability, and deference were at cross-purposes, especially in a community that was supremely concerned about the appearance of honor if not its reality. Separate requirements based on gender—or what the society would label appropriate masculine and feminine virtues—occupied an equally important place in these social codes and also concerned power and the resolution of conflict.

Barceló's gambling and drinking violated the rigid codes organizing appropriate female behavior, but such behavior was not the key to her distinctiveness. Rather, her success as a businesswoman and gambler gave her a unique independence ordinarily denied women. Thus, the most hostile comments about her frequently came from Spanish-Mexican women. In particular, complaints filed against Barceló reveal the extent of other women's animosity, not men's, and were usually thinly disguised as aspersions on her honor. In 1835, Ana María Rendón remonstrated that Barceló and Lucius Thruston, a migrant from Kentucky, were cohabiting.[19] In fact, Barceló's husband lived in the same house, indicating that Thruston was probably a boarder. Honor lay in the proof, and Barceló achieved both by defending herself and her husband as well. Another time, Barceló complained about a slanderous comment made by Josefa Tenório and was also exonerated.[20] Spanish-Mexicans of Santa Fé remained a litigious people, and they waged battles on many fronts. The *alcalde* court (local court) prevailed as the best place to seek resolution. However, Catholic Spanish-Mexican *vecinos* were generally a forgiving people, especially where slander and gossip were involved. Barceló forgave Ana María Rendón's complaint when Rendón retracted it, and the records are filled with similar recantations in other cases.[21]

At issue, then, were not Barceló's violations of gender and social codes—she had in part moved beyond that—but the others' violations of her good name and reputation. On one level, their hostility and outright distrust of Barceló were vendettas directed against a neighbor on the road to wealth and prestige. On another, women upheld the gender code (albeit with some trepidation) because, in complaining about Barceló, they defended themselves and their society. Even when she was fined for gambling, the amounts were so minuscule that they neither halted Barceló's gambling nor conveyed a forceful message about modifying social behavior.[22]

Barceló, a married woman, would not have been able to step outside the boundaries of her society, nor would Manuela Baca or Juana Lopes in the previous decade, if there were no disjunction between the idealized married life and the conditions that stood in the way of its realization—conditions such as taking in boarders or having children out of wedlock. Rallitas Washington, Barceló's grandniece born out of wedlock, as well as hundreds of other women whose mothers were unmarried, formed a decidedly heterodox, yet devoutly Catholic, community.[23] In relationships as in personal behavior, these women's lack of conformity did not shake the conscience of a community as much as needle it.

Beyond cultural mores and behavioral codes, though, what might go unrecognized is that women of the Far West who defied the rules might have been viewed from the outset as marginal. When not ignored completely, women who have existed outside the boundaries of a society of community—or who have been ostracized for various reasons—have frequently been termed outlaws and burdened with characteristics obscuring their social or economic conditions. That may have been standard procedure for marginal women everywhere.[24]

But marginality signifies not only the transgression of social boundaries but also the aftermath of such transgression; it represents the fate of people who press against those boundaries and afterward must live on the edges of society. Barceló cleverly crossed social and sexual barriers to gamble, make money, buy property, and influence politicians, but she avoided marginality. She did not regard herself as a marginal woman, nor was she necessarily marginalized, except by Euro-Americans. She was unusual and she was mocked for it, but not by her own people. In fact, her life and legend are interesting precisely because, in the eyes of observers, she came to represent the worst in Spanish-Mexican culture while, as a Spanish-Mexican, she mastered the strategies and methods of the Americanizers; she achieved what they had professed in speeches and reports originally to want for all New Mexicans.[25]

Barceló's life and her legend contradict orthodox notions of marginality in a situation of conquest. In their writings, conquerors maligned and ostracized her. The opinions they expressed and the images they drew of her sealed her legend in the popular imagination, because their works were distributed throughout the United States. Translated into several languages, Gregg's *Commerce of the Prairies* was reprinted three times between 1844, when it first appeared, and 1857.

Thousands of readers learned through him of the "certain female of very loose habits, known as La Tules."[26] What Gregg and the others could not communicate to their audience was that La Tules was adaptable, and that, before their eyes, she had begun disproving their notion that Spanish-Mexicans were "lazy and indolent."[27] She contradicted James Josiah Webb's contention that all Spanish-Mexicans did was "literally dance from the cradle to the grave."[28] Barceló's busy saloon hosted nightly fandangos, or dances, and their organizer easily became the target of Webb's manipulation of stereotype. Dancing, drinking, and gambling—the order was often changed according to how much the writer wanted to emphasize licentious behavior—gave these Protestant travelers pause, and they quickly made use of the observations to fictionalize Barceló's, and all women's, lives.

But the tales about La Tules are important in another respect. Fictitious representations marginalized Barceló because they shrouded her life in mystery and called forth several stereotypes about Mexicans. Yet Barceló was hardly the excessive woman the travelers depicted. Instead, she became pivotal in the achievement of their conquest. Worth thousands of dollars, supportive of the army, friendly to accommodating politicians, Barceló was in the right place to win over Spanish-Mexicans for the intruders. Using business and political skills, she made the saloon the hub of the town's social and economic life, and at the hall she kept abreast of the latest political developments. Politicians and military officers alike went there seeking her opinion, or involved her in their discussions about trade or the army.[29] As adviser and confidante, she took on a role few other women could have filled. If she existed on the fringes of a society, it was because she chose to place herself there—a woman with enormous foresight who pushed against her own community's barriers and risked being labeled by the travelers a madam or a whore.

Such caricatures denied her contributions to the economy and the society. Had she not been a gambler, a keeper of a saloon, or a woman, she might have been praised for her industry and resourcefulness, traits that antebellum Americans valued in their own people.[30] But from the point of view of the writers, the admirable qualities of a woman who lived by gambling and who was her own proprietor would have been lost on Protestant, middle-class readers. Furthermore, they could hardly imagine, let alone tolerate, the diversity Santa Fé exhibited. It became easier to reaffirm their guiding values and walk a literary tightrope by making La Tules a symbol of Spanish-Mexican degeneracy or an outcast altogether. Barceló had exceeded their wildest expectations, and in their eyes she was an outlaw.

Yet the aspersions heaped on Barceló were not designed solely to obscure her personality and life or to make her activities legendary. They created an image that fit the Euro-Americans' preconceptions about Spanish-Mexicans. Thus described to the readers, the image of Barceló in the travel documents merely confirmed older, pernicious stereotypes. Many recalled the *leyenda negra* (black legend) of the sixteenth century, when Spaniards were objectified as a fanatical, brutal people.[31] Historians and others have traced another critical stage in the development of anti-Mexican fervor to the antebellum period, when expansionist dreams and sentiments of such politicians as Senator Thomas Hart Benton gave rise to a continued confusion about Spanish-Mexican culture.[32] Not only travelers from the United States but residents in general harbored deep prejudices toward Spanish-Mexicans.[33] The travelers of the nineteenth century thus represented broader racial attitudes and demonstrated the ethnocentrism of a population back home.

Racial slurs and derogatory comments about Mexicans appeared regularly in the *Congressional Record,* in newspapers, and, not coincidentally, in travel accounts.[34] Speeches and statements consistently equated brown skin with promiscuity, immorality, and decay. Albert Pike, who arrived in New Mexico from New England in 1831, called the area around Santa Fé "bleak, black, and barren;"[35] New Mexicans, he said, were "peculiarly blessed with ugliness."[36] The chronicler of a military expedition to New Mexico in the 1840s, Frank Edwards, said that all Mexicans were "debased in all moral sense"[37] and amounted to little more than "swarthy thieves and liars."[38] The same judgments were made later, long after the war had ended, and reflect the persistence of the same thinking. The historian Francis Parkman argued that people in the West could be "separated into three divisions, arranged in order of their merits: white men, Indians, and Mexicans; to the latter of whom the honorable title of 'whites' is by no means conceded."[39] In the same period, William H. Emory of the boundary commission declared that the "darker colored" races were inevitably "inferior and syphilitic."[40]

These select references—and there are hundreds of other comments like them—describe a set of racist attitudes and ethnocentric beliefs from the Jacksonian period that carried into Santa Fé. Travelers thus mirrored the intrinsic values of a nation encroaching on Mexican territory and were fueled by the heightened fervor over destiny and superiority.

Scholars have assessed the genre of travel guides and recollections as contributions to literature and have debated its special characteristics of construction, organization, and distortion.[41] But the books had something besides literary appeal; they sold rapidly in a country hungry for information about the West. Many planned visits and escapes to the healthier climates of the Southwest, while others intended to live in warmer areas and to find markets for their goods: such motives had inspired Gregg to leave Missouri for Santa Fé. Although he and his fellow adventurers were genuinely curious about Mexicans and about what the West had to offer, one important consequence of their visits, vacations, and reports, at least for Barceló, was that the migrants also brought capital to Santa Fé.[42] The accounts cannot, therefore, be considered only as travel literature; they do not, as some have argued, simply unveil anti-Mexican, anti-Catholic sentiment.[43] Rather, they describe—from the outside in, from the perspective of the colonizer—the systematic movement of an ethnocentric people to Santa Fé and reveal the interest in the promise of continued prosperity in the Southwest.

Travel writers of the nineteenth century, however, were also conscious of the desires and proclivities of their readers. Hence, these writers described the unsavory material culture (Matt Field gazed upon the adobe buildings and labeled Santa Fé's houses a testament to "the power of mud")[44] and the miserable conditions because they thought the objectionable portraits would suit their audience. Assessed today, the writers and their reflections continue to convey the overwhelmingly persistent attitudes, values, and ideas of a conquering group interpreting others. Except for a government official, Brantz Mayer, whose book indicted United States travelers by citing their prejudices against Mexicans, these writers mainly exhibited condescension and an implied, if not outspoken, sense of superiority.[45]

This uniformity in outlook is not the only characteristic binding these works and suggesting their significance in conquest. Many of the writers patterned their books after previously published accounts, such as Zebulon Pike's narrative of his reconnaissance trips in the early nineteenth century.[46] Imitating his organization and style, such writers as Gregg exaggerated La Tules's appearance, blamed her for the ruin of many "wayward youth," and imitated previous travelogues in other ways to portray and dismiss the wretched condition of the Spanish-Mexicans. Barceló's smoking and gambling were but two of the most widely reported vices. George Brewerton, writing for *Harper's Magazine* in the 1850s, continued the tradition. To the growing list of those at fault, he added the duplicitous New Mexican priests, for stifling individuality and stunting well-being:

> Here were the men, women, and children—the strong man, the mother, and the lisping child—all engaged in the most debasing of vices, gambling, the entire devotion to which is the besetting sin of the whole Mexican people. . . . What better could you have expected from an ignorant, priest-ridden peasantry, when those whom they are taught to reverence and respect, and who should have been their prompters to better things, not only allow, but openly practice this and all other iniquities?[47]

The popularity of gambling and drinking among all people prompted Brewerton and his predecessors to decry the pervasive debauchery—which, it seemed, only they, as Americans, could relieve. They failed to understand that Spanish-Mexicans loved celebration and socializing. The church organized parties, pageants, and social affairs on varied occasions; yet even officially sanctioned church holidays or the days when patron saints were honored did not escape Euro-American comments.[48] Brewerton found "rude engravings" of saints everywhere, among rich and poor, which he said would be "decked out by the females of the family with all sorts of tawdry ornaments."[49] He wondered about people who would use a doll to represent the Virgin Mary. Brewerton failed, in his rigid anti-Catholic viewpoint, to understand the beauty and intricacy of the *bultos* and *retablos* (icons and altarpieces). Catholicism, in Brewerton's opinion, did nothing but give Spanish-Mexicans occasion to revel in superstition, or to drink and dance. A community's way of celebrating—even the pious processions when the

Virgin and the saints were paraded through town for all to worship in the annual outpouring of public devotion—was lost on Protestants: "During this whole time the city exhibited a scene of universal carousing and revelry. All classes abandoned themselves to the most reckless dissipation and profligacy. . . . I never saw a people so infatuated with the passion for gaming."[50] Whether commemorating saints or gathering for entertainment and diversion, Spanish-Mexicans appeared lascivious.

To the Protestant mind, nothing short of the complete elimination of gambling would lift New Mexicans out of their servility and make them worthy of United States citizenship. The Jacksonian Americans wanted to replace gambling with industry and enterprise. To them, gambling stemmed from a fundamental lack of faith in the individual, and it was risky besides. Travelers called monte a game of chance; they said that it required no particular skills and brought undeserved wealth.[51] By that logic, La Tules, a dealer par excellence, was not an entrepreneur; her wealth was undeserved because it sprang from "unbridled passions."[52] Her gravest sin against Protestant ethics became not the unskilled nature of her trade or her undeserved success but her lack of restraint: her wealth was uncontrolled. Yet initial misgivings about Barceló and the games passed after many entertaining evenings at the gambling house. Once soldiers and others began going there, they lingered, and returned often.[53] Deep-seated anti-Mexican feelings and moralistic judgments gave way to the profits that awaited them if they won at monte, or the pleasures to be savored each evening in Santa Fé even if they lost.

At the numerous tables that lined Barceló's establishment, men who could not speak Spanish and people who did not understand English learned a new language. Card games required the deciphering of gestures and facial expressions but did not depend on any verbal communication. Soldiers and travelers new to Santa Fé understood easily enough what was important at the gaming table. Over cards, the men and women exchanged gold or currency in a ritual that emblazoned their meetings with new intentions. Drinking, cursing, and smoking, the soldiers and others unloaded their money at the table; if Barceló profited, they lost. But the game was such a diversion for the lonely soldiers that they hardly seemed to mind. The stakes grew larger at every turn, and many dropped away from the table to stand at the bar. Barceló's saloon took care of those who did not gamble as well as those who lost. Sometimes a group of musicians arrived and began playing. Sometimes women—who, if not gambling, had been observing the scene—cleared a space in the long room, and dancing began.[54]

Barceló did more than accommodate men by inviting them to gamble. She furthered their adjustment to Santa Fé by bringing them into a setting that required their presence and money. At the saloon, the men were introduced to Spanish-Mexican music, habits, and humor. They could judge the locals firsthand and could observe a community's values and habits through this single activity. After they had a few drinks, their initial fears and prejudices gradually yielded to the relaxed, sociable atmosphere of the gambling hall.

In the spring of 1847, Lieutenant Alexander Dyer first visited the saloon. By June, his journal listed attendance at no fewer than forty fandangos and described numerous visits to La Tules's saloon. Frequently, cryptic citations indicated his rush to abandon the journal for the card games: "at the Me. House tonight" meant a visit to the monte house, and it appeared dozens of times in any given month.[55] Dyer's "Mexican War Journal" leaves the distinct impression that a soldier's life, for those of his stripe, involved a constant round of entertainment; visits and parties at Barceló's hall were part of an officer's busy social life.

Thus, rhetoric about gambling or cavorting lessened with time. If visitors did not entirely accept the sociable atmosphere, they were sufficiently lonely for Euro-American women and companionship to go to Barceló's saloon and attend other events to which they were invited. When Kearny and his officers went to Mass on their first Sunday in town, they endeared themselves to Spanish-Mexicans.[56] Some soldiers at the fort, like Dyer, had little choice but to adapt, because they were assigned to Santa Fé for two years. Other newcomers, however, were shocked into submission.

Finding much to upset them, visitors were nevertheless impressed by the scenic grandeur of Santa Fé and the environs. James Ohio Pattie remained as awed by Taos Mountain, stretching fifteen thousand feet high, as he was intrigued by the native life below it. He puzzled over differences: "I had expected to find no difference between these people and our own, but their language. I was never so mistaken. The men and women were not clothed in our fashion."[57]

Nine days later, Pattie reached Santa Fé, and this time his tone grew prosaic:

> The town contains between four and five thousand inhabitants. It is situated on a large plain. A handsome stream runs through it, adding life and beauty to a scene striking and agreeable from the union of amenity and cultivation around, with the distant view of snow clad mountains. It is pleasant to walk on the flat roofs of the houses in the evening, and look on the town and plain spread below.[58]

In a few weeks, Pattie had reached Chihuahua City, traveling the considerable distance in a short time. He described it as the "largest and handsomest town I had ever seen."[59] The trek across treacherous deserts, the long unbroken plain, and probably the fact that Spanish-Mexicans were much friendlier to him than Indians (whom he feared and loathed) changed Pattie's original reservations.

But travel records contain an underlying difficulty: they tend to freeze their author's thoughts in time and do not reveal the extent of the adaptations or changes a writer might have experienced. Many travelers evidently did not find anything to admire or enjoy in Santa Fé, but some did. Although locked into a particular time and a special setting, the men, after consistent reflection and observation, relaxed their worst fears. Pattie's descriptions might not have been atypical in that regard.

Court cases offer other impressions of how sojourning Euro-Americans changed their organizing concepts and values. The evidence is especially suggestive for those who began making a transition to becoming settlers. In the 1820s, Julian Green was fined for gambling at monte; on the same day, the judge assessed a fine against Barceló.[60] In 1850, the census lists Green, with a woman named María, in a household containing six children; all have Spanish first names.[61] Another *vecino,* Marcelo Pacheco, sued William Messervy for slander in the 1840s, calling the merchant "a trespasser who thinks he owns everything."[62] He won his case, and Messervy had to pay a fine. Perhaps Green and Messervy were perplexed about Santa Fé's ways, as many migrants had been, but because they paid their fines and stayed in Santa Fé, they changed.

Investigations in these records delineate the onset of the newcomers' accommodation. Barceló was not the only one practicing accommodation; it worked in two directions. Whether obeying the community's laws or breaking them, new men were adjusting to life away from home. Santa Fé modified the settling Euro-Americans, at times even the sojourning ones, and Barceló had begun to socialize them in the traditions of an older settlement. The people of the Dancing Ground continued their practice of accepting newcomers, particularly those who seemed able to tolerate, if not embrace, the community's religious and secular values.

At the same time, the conquering soldiers were armed, as the merchants Gregg and Webb were, with purpose and commitment. Military men brought plans and realized them: a fort above the town was begun the day after Kearny marched into Santa Fé. Soldiers built a two-story-high flagstaff, and the imposing structure on the plaza attracted visitors from the Dancing Ground who came supposedly to admire it, but probably also were there to assess the military's strength.[63] What better symbol than a new garrison and an obtrusive monument rising high for all the people to notice? Soldiers hailed these crowning achievements as signs of blessings from God to a nation destined to control the hemisphere, but locals were not so pleased.

A new wave of resistance derailed Barceló's efforts to help resettle Euro-Americans in Santa Fé. Nevertheless, even after her death in 1852, Barceló's legend continued to indicate that her role extended beyond the immediate helping hand she had lent Euro-Americans. No documents written by her, except a will, have survived to tell whether she even recognized her accomplishment or if she read much into the assistance she had given the American cause. Her wealth would suggest that she might have harbored an understanding of her influential status in the process of colonization. One fact remains, whether she realized it or not: beginning with her, the accommodation of Euro-Americans proceeded on several levels. Barceló had inaugurated the first, at the gambling hall, and she set the stage as well for the second, when women began marrying the newcomers.

But as one retraces the original surrounding tensions—deriving from the steady and continuing presence of traders, merchants, and soldiers—and juxtaposes them against Barceló's achievement as an architect of a plan that reconciled the Euro-American to Santa Fé, the realities of displacement and encroachment must not be forgotten. Lieutenant Dyer reported problems as he observed them, and he commented a year after his arrival in Santa Fé: "Still it began to be apparent that the people generally were dissatisfied with the change."[64] In January 1847, resisters in Taos caught and scalped Governor Charles Bent, leaving him to die.[65] In the spring, a lieutenant who had been pursuing horse thieves was murdered, and forty-three Spanish-Mexicans were brought to Santa Fé to stand trial for the crime.[66] In October of the same year, some months after several revolts had been suppressed and their instigators hanged, Dyer reported "a large meeting of citizens at the Palace," where speakers expressed "disaffection at the course of the commissioned officers."[67]

Local dissatisfaction and political troubles had not subsided, in spite of Barceló's work. In the late 1840s, Navajos and Apaches stepped up their raids, and reports filtered in of surrounding mayhem.[68] The garrisoned soldiers grew impatient and acted rashly, and Dyer reported that "a Mexican was unfortunately shot last night by the sentinel at my store house. Tonight we have a rumor that the Mexicans are to rise and attack us."[69] The government in Santa Fé was being forced again to come to terms with each new case of racial and cultural conflict, because it was still charged with trying murders and treason, and it had now become the seat for initiating solutions. Problems no longer brewed outside; they had been brought home by accommodated Euro-Americans.

But Barceló should not be blamed here, as she has been by some, for so many problems. She symbolized the transformations plaguing her people. She symbolized as well how an older community had handled the arrival of men from a new, young nation still seeking to tap markets and find a route to the Pacific. Moreover, she exemplified contact and conflict between independent female Catholics and westering male Protestants. The political and social constraints within which she existed had not disappeared as a community contemplated what to do with the strangers among them.

The people of Santa Fé did not kill any newcomers as residents of Taos had. Surrounding the Dancing Ground, stories and legends of other people resisting Americanization were about to begin, and these no longer emphasized accommodation. Barceló was unusual in that way as well. She was of a particular time and a special place. The famed resister to American encroachment, Padre Antonio José Martínez of Taos, opposed (in his separatist plans and principles) all that Barceló had exemplified. A legend developed around him that stands in interesting contrast to La Tules's.[70]

Yet, in New Mexico and throughout the West, resistance was giving way to Euro-American encroachment. Richard Henry Dana, traveling in California during the 1830s, mourned the seemingly wasted opportunity presented by land still in the possession of Spanish-Mexicans: "In the hands of an enterprising people, what a country this might be!"[71] His fellow sojourners to New Mexico concurred. What Dana and the other Euro-Americans failed to see was that the land and its communities were already in the hands of such enterprising persons as Barceló. But rather than acknowledge the truth, they disparaged her; their conqueror's minds could not comprehend her intellect, enterprise, and success. Barceló, they believed, had erred. Yet in giving herself to the conquest, but not the conquerors, she survived and succeeded. She drew betting clients to her saloon; they played but lost, she gambled and won. In the end, the saloon that attracted conquerors released men who had been conquered.

NOTES

1. Josiah Gregg, *The Commerce of the Prairies*, ed. Max Moorhead (Norman: University of Oklahoma Press, 1954), pp. 105–106. (Originally published 1844.)

2. Fray Angélico Chávez, "Doña Tules: Her Fame and Her Funeral," *El Palacio* 62 (August 1950): 227–234; Janet Lecompte, "The Independent Women of Hispanic New Mexico, 1821–1846," *Western Historical Quarterly* 22 (January 1981): 25–26.

3. Stella Drumm, ed., *The Diary of Susan Shelby Magoffin, 1846–1847: Down the Santa Fe Trail and into Mexico* (Lincoln: University of Nebraska Press, 1982), p. 145.

4. Tules was the diminutive for Gertrudis. See Marc Simmons, *The Little Lion of the Southwest: A Life of Manuel Antonio Cháves* (Chicago: University of Chicago Press, 1983), p. 55.

5. Gregg, *Commerce of the Prairies,* p. 168.

6. Howard R. Lamar, *Far Southwest* (New York: Norton, 1970), p. 55.

7. On the church, see "Zubiría Pastoral," 1840, Archives of the Archdiocese of Santa Fe, Coronado Collection, University of New Mexico, microfilm, LDD, no. 2; and "Bishop Zubiría's Visitation," 1845, Archives of the Archdiocese of Santa Fe, box 4, book 89.

8. Gregg, *Commerce of the Prairies,* pp. 168–169.

9. See Trinidad Barceló, June 9, 1825, Probate Court Journals, Mexican Archives of New Mexico, New Mexico State Records Center, microfilm, roll 26, frame 187.

10. Janet Lecompte, "La Tules and the Americans," *Arizona and the West* (Autumn 1978): 220.

11. Drumm, *Diary of Susan Shelby Magoffin,* p. 120.

12. For Gregg's comments, see *Commerce of the Prairies,* pp. 168–169; for other comments, see William Clark Kennedy, *Persimmon Hill: A Narrative of St. Louis and the Far West* (Norman: University of Oklahoma Press, 1948), p. 191; and John E. Sunder, ed., *Matt Field on the Santa Fé Trail* (Norman: University of Oklahoma Press, 1960), p. 206.

13. Sunder, *Matt Field,* p. 209.

14. For comparison, see Table 6.2 in the essay by Angelina Veyna in this volume.

15. Will of Gertrudis Barceló, Santa Fe County Records, Wills and Testaments, 1848–1856, book A-1, p. 154.

16. John Galvin, ed., *Western America in 1846–1847: The Original Travel Diary of Lieutenant J. W. Abert, Who Mapped New Mexico for the United States Army* (San Francisco: J. Howell, 1966), p. 75; see Abert's report in *Senate Executive Document* no. 23, 29th Cong., 1st sess.

17. Gregg, *Commerce of the Prairies,* pp. 168–169.

18. Ramón Arturo Gutiérrez, in a paper presented at the annual meeting of the Western Historical Association, Salt Lake City, October 12, 1984.

19. See Lecompte, "La Tules," p. 222, and the source, Complaint of Ana María Rendón to the alcalde, Probate Court Journals, 1835, roll 20.

20. Complaint of Ana María Rendón.

21. Lecompte, "La Tules," p. 222; for recantations, see Complaint against José Tenório, January 15, 1828, and November 14, 1829, Probate Court Journals, roll 8, frame 310; Petition of Juan Francisco Gonzales, Probate Court Journals, 1829, roll 10, frame 177.

22. Gertrudis Barceló, June 9, 1825, Probate Court Journals, roll 26, frame 186.

23. On the issues of illegitimacy and legitimacy, see Ramón Arturo Gutiérrez, "Marriage, Sex, and the Family: Social Change in Colonial New Mexico, 1690–1846," Ph.D. diss., University of Wisconsin–Madison, 1980. For examples of the church's stance on legitimacy and baptism, see Books of Baptisms, 1826–1841, Archives of the Archdiocese of Santa Fe, New Mexico State Records Center, microfilm.

24. On the Far West, see George M. Blackburn and Sherman L. Richards, "The Prostitutes and Gamblers of Virginia City, Nevada: 1870," *Pacific Historical Review* 48, no. 2 (May 1979): 239–258; and Lawrence B. de Graaf, "Race, Sex and Region: Black Women in the American West, 1850–1920," *Pacific Historical Review* 49, no. 2 (May 1980): 285–313. For earlier periods and for women of two different worlds, see Adelaida del Castillo, "Malintzín Tenépal: A Preliminary Look into a New Perspective," in *Essays on La Mujer,* ed. Rosaura Sánchez and Rosa Martínez Cruz (Los Angeles: Chicano Studies Research Center, University of California, 1977), pp. 124–149; and Marina Warner, *Joan of Arc: The Image of Female Heroism* (New York: Knopf, 1981).

25. For speeches, see Kearny's in Ralph Emerson Twitchell, *The Story of the Conquest of Santa Fe: New Mexico and the Building of Old Fort Marcy, A.D. 1846* (Santa Fe: Historical Society of New Mexico, 1923), p. 30; for another, see *Santa Fe Republican,* January 22, 1848; and for an earlier version of the same ideas but espoused in the United States, see *Richmond Enquirer,* May 11, 1847; for a report and discussion on the benefits a railroad would bring, see the *Western Journal,* vol. 1, p. 260, and the *Richmond Daily Union,* May 13, 1847.

26. Gregg, *Commerce of the Prairies,* p. 168.

27. Waddy Thompson, *Recollections of Mexico* (New York: Wiley and Putnam, 1846), p. 23.

28. James Josiah Webb, "Memoirs, 1844–1889," Museum of New Mexico, History Library, Santa Fe, manuscript, p. 46; James Ohio Pattie, *The Personal Narrative of James O. Pattie, of Kentucky* (Ann Arbor: University of Michigan Press, 1966), p. 120 (originally published 1831).

29. Simmons, *Little Lion,* p. 55; for the officers at the game of monte, see Walter Briggs, "The Lady They Called Tules," *New Mexico Magazine* 39 (1971): 9–16.

30. For an overview, see Edward Pessen, *Jacksonian America: Society, Personality and Politics* (Homewood, Ill.: Row, Peterson, 1969). For criticism of the attendant values, see Herman Melville, *The Confidence-Man: His Masquerade* (New York: New American Library, 1964; originally published 1857); for an interpretation of the novel, see Roy Harvey Pearce, "Melville's Indian Hater: A Note on the Meaning of 'The Confidence-Man,' " *Publications of the Modern Language Association* 67 (1952): 942–948.

31. The legend's origins have been traced to several sources, among them Bartolomé de las Casas, *In Defense of the Indians,* trans. Stafford Poole (De Kalb: Northern Illinois University Press, 1974). For other arguments about the origins, see Stanley T. Williams, *The Spanish Background of American Literature* (New York: Shoe String Press, 1968), 1:3; and Philip Wayne Powell, *Tree of Hate: Propaganda and Prejudices Affecting United States Social Relations with the Hispanic World* (New York: Basic Books, 1971).

32. Thomas Hart Benton, Speech on the Oregon Question, May 28, 1846, Senate Document, *Congressional Globe,* 29th Cong., 1st sess., pp. 915, 917.

33. For earlier statements, see Joel Roberts Poinsett, *Notes on Mexico Made in the Autumn*

of 1822 (New York: Praeger, 1969), pp. 40, 120–122 (originally published 1824); for a detailed survey of attitudes toward Mexicans, see Philip Anthony Hernández, "The Other Americans: The American Image of Mexico and Mexicans, 1550–1850," Ph.D. diss., University of California, Berkeley, 1974.

34. Dr. Adolphus Wislizenus, "Memoir of a Tour to Northern Mexico," *Senate Miscellaneous Document,* 30th Cong., 1st sess., pp. 2–3. For an example of an anti-Mexican travel account in Texas, see Mary Austin Holley, *Observations, Historical, Geographical, and Descriptive* (Austin: University of Texas Press, 1935), p. 128 (originally published 1833); in California, see Alfred Robinson, *Life in California* (New York: Da Capo, 1969), p. 73 (originally published 1846).

35. Albert Pike, *Prose Sketches and Poems, Written in the Western Country with Additional Stories,* ed. David Weber (Albuquerque: University of New Mexico Press, 1967), p. 7.

36. Ibid., p. 275. For a Euro-American woman's reactions during visits to Santa Fe, see Jane Austin, Letter to her "Dear Brother," October 23, 1846, Museum of New Mexico, History Library, Santa Fe, box 4, p. 1.

37. Frank S. Edwards, *A Campaign in New Mexico with Colonel Doniphan* (Philadelphia: Carey and Hart, 1847), p. 132.

38. Ibid., p. 50.

39. Francis Parkman, *The California and Oregon Trail: Being Sketches of Prairie and Rocky Mountain Life* . . . (New York: Putnam, 1849), p. 360.

40. W. H. Emory, "Notes of a Military Reconnaissance from Fort Leavenworth, in Missouri, to San Diego, in California . . . Made in 1846–7, with the Advanced Guard of the Army of the West," *House Executive Document* no. 41, 30th Cong., 1st sess., p. 110.

41. Mabel Major, Rebecca Smith, and T. M. Pearce, *Southwest Heritage: A Literary History with Bibliography* (Albuquerque: University of New Mexico Press, 1938). For deciphering distortion, see Robert A. LeVine and Donald Campbell, *Ethnocentrism: Theories of Conflict, Ethnic Attitudes, and Group Behavior* (New York: Wiley, 1972).

42. Richard Onofre Ulibarri, "American Interest in the Spanish-Mexican Southwest, 1803–1848," Ph.D. diss., University of Utah, 1963, p. 80.

43. Ray Allen Billington, *The Protestant Crusade, 1800–1860: A Study of the Origins of American Nativism* (1938; rpt. Gloucester, Mass.: Peter Smith, 1963), pp. 75, 223–230. For a comment by Webb, see Ralph Bieber, ed., *Adventures in the Santa Fe Trade, 1844–1847, by James Josiah Webb* (Glendale, Ca.: Arthur H. Clark, 1931), p. 102.

44. Sunder, *Matt Field,* p. 194.

45. Brantz Mayer, *Mexico, as It Was and as It Is* (Philadelphia: G. B. Zieber, 1847); for an example of an observer who vacillated in his opinions about Mexicans, see Abiel Abbot Livermore, *The War with Mexico Reviewed* (Boston: American Peace Society, 1850).

46. Susan Reyner Kenneson, "Through the Looking-Glass: A History of Anglo-American Attitudes towards the Spanish-Americans and Indians of New Mexico," Ph.D. diss., Yale University, 1978, p. 130.

47. George Brewerton, "Incidents of Travel in New Mexico," *Harper's Magazine* 47 (April 1854): 589.

48. Gregg, *Commerce of the Prairies,* pp. 173, 179–180.

49. Brewerton, "Incidents," p. 578.

50. Thomas James, *Three Years among the Indians and Mexicans* (Philadelphia: Lippincott, 1962), pp. 88–89 (originally published 1916).

51. Gregg, *Commerce of the Prairies,* pp. 167–168.

52. Brewerton, "Incidents," p. 588.

53. Alexander B. Dyer, "Mexican War Journal, 1846–1848," Museum of New Mexico, History Library, manuscript, pp. 80–81, 84, 118–119.

54. "Gen. Kearny and the Army of the West: Extracts from the Journal of Lieut. Emory," *Niles National Register* 71 (November 7, 1846): 158.

55. Dyer, "Mexican War Journal," p. 96.

56. Drumm, *Diary of Susan Shelby Magoffin,* p. 138; for an example of the continuing partnership between the church and the military, see the inauguration of Governor David Meriwether in Gunther Barth, *Instant Cities: Urbanization and the Rise of San Francisco and Denver* (New York: Oxford University Press, 1975), p. 70.

57. Pattie, *Narrative,* p. 41.

58. Ibid., p. 44.

59. Ibid., p. 110.

60. Testimony of Julian Green, June 9, 1825, Probate Court Journals, roll 20, frame 188.

61. United States Bureau of the Census, Seventh Census of Population, for Santa Fe, 1850 (microfilm, New Mexico State Records Center).

62. Complaint of Marcelo Pacheco, April 11, 1846, Probate Court Journals, roll 32, frame 185. See also the Euro-Americans fined for "making fandangos without licenses," Jury Book, 1848–1856, Probate Court Journal, Santa Fe County Records, pp. 137–140.

63. James Madison Cutts, *The Conquest of California and New Mexico by the Forces of the United States in the Years 1846–1847* (Philadelphia: Carey and Hart, 1847), p. 84.

64. Alexander Dyer to Robert Johnston, February 14, 1847, Museum of New Mexico, History Library, box 4, p. 2.

65. Lamar, *Far Southwest,* p. 68.

66. Dyer to Johnston, February 14, 1847, pp. 2–3.

67. Dyer, "Mexican War Journal," p. 97.

68. Ibid., p. 62; on Navajo and Apache raids, see David J. Weber, *The Mexican Frontier, 1821–1846: The American Southwest under Mexico* (Albuquerque: University of New Mexico Press, 1982), pp. 92–93.

69. Dyer, "Mexican War Journal," p. 82.

70. On Martínez's activities, see Lamar, *Far Southwest,* p. 72; on the legend, see E. K. Francis, "Padre Martínez: A New Mexico Myth, *New Mexico Historical Review* 31 (October 1956): 265–289; for a short biography, see Pedro Sánchez, "Memorias sobre la vida del presbitero don Antonio José Martínez," in *Northern Mexico on the Eve of the United States Invasion,* ed. David Weber (New York: Arno Press, 1976); in the same collection, see "Historia consisa del cura de Taos Antonio José Martínez" (originally published in *El Historiador,* May 4, 1861).

71. Richard Henry Dana, *Two Years before the Mast* (New York: New American Library, 1864), p. 136. (Originally published 1840.)

SIX

"It Is My Last Wish That . . ."

A Look at Colonial Nuevo Mexicanas through Their Testaments

Angelina F. Veyna

Throughout the past few decades, efforts have increasingly been made to document the many and varied historical experiences of women, including those of the Chicana and her predecessor, the Mexican woman.[1] Attention has overwhelmingly been given to women who have excelled in some manner, especially in the literary arts and the political arena.[2] Unfortunately, their experiences are often taken to represent the experiences of all their contemporaries. In an effort to provide a contrasting perspective, this study will examine *ordinary* women's lives during the eighteenth century in present-day northern New Mexico. The observations presented here are based on women's testaments and related estate documentation from the Spanish Archives of New Mexico and span the years 1715–1768.[3]

The paucity of research on colonial New Mexican women has led one noted New Mexican scholar to conclude that almost nothing is known about any specific role played by women.[4] While both men and women initiated and appeared in notarial documentation of the eighteenth century, it is not always evident that women were involved, since documents are predominantly classified under men's names.[5] It thus becomes necessary for the researcher first to dissect each document, to ascertain that women appear, and then to reconstruct the roles and conditions of women during this time. Women's wills provide one of the few available direct approaches to the attainment of data concerning women.

Anderson and his colleagues' observations regarding Nahuatl testaments equally apply to the study of colonial New Mexican women's wills; that is, testaments are valuable because they provide intimate and systematic information regarding the testators, and they exist for persons of varying social levels.[6] The portrait of women that emerges from the present study is that colonial New Mexican women owned a variety of goods, disposed of them as they deemed necessary, and were neither poor, dependent, nor passive. Twelve women from

TABLE 6.1 Overview of Women Considered in This Study

Name	*Year of Document*	*Place*	*Marital Status*	*Children*	*Executor/s of Will*
María de Perea	1715	Santa Fé	First husband: Miguel Maese Second husband: Agustín Luján	1 daughter from first marriage; raising 1 other child	Husband and son-in-law
Juana Domínguez	1717	Santa Fé	First husband: Domingo Luján Second husband: Lorenzo de la Madrid	1 son, 3 daughters from first marriage	Son
María Hurtado	1725	Santa Fé	Antonio Montoya, now deceased	possibly 11	*Alcalde (mayor)*
María Calabacita	1744	Santo Domingo Pueblo	Single	3 sons, 1 daughter	—
Margarita Martín	1744	Nuestra Sra. de la Soledad (Jurisdiction of Santa Cruz de la Cañada)	First husband: don Juan de Padilla Second husband: don Bernardo Roybal	4 children from first marriage; 3 children from second marriage	—

the *villas* (towns) of Santa Fé, Santa Cruz de la Cañada, and Albuquerque and from Santo Domingo Pueblo, San Buenaventura de Cochití, and el Puesto de Nuestra Señora de la Soledad (jurisdiction of Santa Cruz) were included in this study.[7] Wills and related estate proceedings were reviewed for María de Perea, Juana Domínguez, María Hurtado, María Calabacita, Margarita Martín, Juanotilla, Lugarda Quintana, Rosa Martina Fernández, María de la Candelaria Gonzales, Chatalina Durana, Petrona de Cárdenas, and María Rosalía Durán de Armijo.[8] (Table 6.1 provides an overview of these women.) All the women identified themselves as *vecinas* (citizens) of their respective settlements.

Testaments and related estate proceedings considered for this study follow conventions known to most scholars of Hispanic America.[9] In the opening paragraphs of the documents, the testator usually invoked the Catholic church, its saints, and all its beliefs, after which the testator accepted God's will for her to pass on. The woman then noted her marital status, stated the number of children she had had, and indicated whether she wanted to be buried in the local church. For example, María de Perea indicated that she wanted to be buried in the church of

TABLE 6.1 (*continued*)

Name	*Year of Document*	*Place*	*Marital Status*	*Children*	*Executor/s of Will*
Juanotilla, *coyota*	1747	San Buenaventura de Cochití	Though mention is made that she is legally married, no data on her husband	3 daughters, 1 son	—
Lugarda Quintana	1749	Santa Cruz de la Cañada	Married to: Asencio Archuleta	3	Compadre
Rosa Martina Fernández	1750	Santa Cruz de la Cañada	Married to: Nicolás López	2	Brother
María de la Candelaria Gonzales	1750	Santa Fé	Manuel Trujillo, now deceased	2 known; possibly 4	Son
Chatalina Durana	1752	Santa Fé	Bartolomé Garduño, now deceased	4	Grandson
Petrona de Cárdenas	1767	Santa Cruz de la Cañada	Married to: Roque Jaramillo	14	Son-in-law
María Rosalía Durán de Armijo	1768	Santa Fé	Married to: Miguel Crespín Lobato	—	Husband

Santa Fé; Petrona de Cárdenas wanted to be buried in the church of Santa Cruz de la Cañada, specifically in the chapel of Nuestra Señora del Carmen; and Juana Domínguez instructed that she be buried in the chapel of Our Lady of the Rosary in the church of Santa Fé. As was typical of most Hispanic wills, the age of the testator was not given. The bulk of a testament consisted of an item-by-item list of the woman's possessions, her designated inheritors, and any other special instructions; the wealthier the woman, the more numerous the designations. The first item listed was the *mandas forzosas,* or required church donations (generally, the minimum amount was given). Subsequently, the testator designated her *albacea/s* (executor/s), and the common practice of having someone else sign on her behalf concluded the document.[10] None of the women considered in this study signed her name; Rosa Martina Fernández provided a closing similar to that of the other women: "Y no lo firmé por no saver. Lo firmó a mi ruego Salvador Varela" ("And I did not sign because I did not know how to. Salvador Varela signed at my request").

After a person's death, the *alcalde* (local chief magistrate), accompanied by two witnesses,[11] went to the home of the woman to inventory her belongings and ascribe to them a monetary value.[12] Once this list was compiled, proceedings were then formally undertaken to deliver to each person what he or she was bequeathed. In legal, written form, the inheritors then acknowledged receipt of their share. (It was not infrequent for relatives and others to contest the wills, but such proceedings are outside the scope of this chapter.)

Monies also were set aside for funerary costs—for example, for the burial mass and the internment box—and for the local civil and church officials involved in the estate proceedings. In the proceedings of Margarita Martín, 5 percent of the estate went to the commissioner who oversaw the settlement. The commissioner stated: "Mando se separen doscientos sesenta y cinco pesos que me corresponden a mí de los derechos del cinco por ciento." ("I order that 265 pesos be separated [from the estate] because of the 5 percent fee to which I am entitled.")

It was also a common practice for the testators to list debts they still owed, debts owed to them, and outstanding debts owed to their deceased husbands. For example, María de Perea clarified that she did not owe anyone, nor did anyone owe her anything. In 1717, Juana Domínguez recalled that she had owed eight pesos to two persons since her childhood, but because she could not recall their names and did not know whether they were still living, she instructed her son to have four masses said in lieu of payment.

A detailed examination of Juanotilla's estate settlement should convey the flavor of this genre and the data it yields.[13] (An itemization and distribution list of Juanotilla's possessions are provided in Table 6.2.) The proceedings were initiated in San Buenaventura Cochití in 1747, and were carried out by the *alcalde mayor* and two witnesses, who went to Juanotilla's home to inventory her belongings. When they arrived at Cochití, they discovered that Juanotilla had previously executed a will in 1731, and they proceeded to recognize it. Juanotilla had four legitimate children; at the time of her death, two were living (Diego and Micaela) and two were deceased (Sebastiana and Ysabel). In her will, Juanotilla instructed that Sebastiana and Ysabel's inheritance was to pass on to their children. The citations in Juanotilla's will are similar to the following: "a Micaela [doy] dos hachas, un azadón, una reja, una coa, una jícara, tres cueros de cíbolo" ("to Micaela [I bequeath] two axes, one hoe, one steel point, one digging stick, one gourd, three buffalo hides"). Besides leaving possessions to her children and grandchildren, Juanotilla also bequeathed goods to two servants, Cristóbal and Joaquín. Each was bequeathed one horse, one saddle with stirrups, one small sword, one bridle, one cow, and one bull. The servants were to receive these items in appreciation for care rendered to her until her time of death.

The possessions listed in these eighteenth-century women's testaments and settlements can be divided into the following categories: property and structures, livestock, farming tools, domestic wares, clothing, and other personal belongings. Eleven of the twelve women owned property, though the amount varied. Land was generally described in *pedazos* (pieces), and only in two instances were mea-

TABLE 6.2 Itemization and Distribution of Juanotilla's Possessions to Family Members[a]

Item	*(Spanish)*	*Micaela*	*Diego*	*Regina*[b]	*Rosa*[c]
Axes	hachas	2	1	3	1
Hoe	azadón	1	1	—	—
Steel plow point	reja	1	—	1	1
Adze	azuela	1	—	—	—
Digging stick	coa	1	—	1	1
Gourd	jícara	1	—	1	1
Buffalo hide	cuero de cíbolo	3	—	3	3
Iron digging point	cavador	—	—	—	1
Elk hide	antagorda	1	—	1	1
Horses	caballos	"some"	4	3	3
Mare	yegua	1	1	1	1
Cows	vacas	11	11	11	12
Oxen	bueyes	1	2	1	1
Bulls	toros	7	7	7	1
Goats	cabras	10	10	—	5
Sheep	ovejas	5	5	—	4
House/property[d]	casa y tierras	portion	portion	portion	portion
Vest	cuera	—	1	—	—
Chisel	escoplo	—	1	—	—
Gauge	gurbia	—	1	—	—
Wooden plow point	punta	—	1	—	—
Small sword	espadín	—	1	—	—
Shotgun	escopeta	—	1	—	—
Stirrups	estribos	—	"some"	—	—

[a] Juanotilla had four children: Diego, Sebastiana, Micaela, and Ysabel. At the time Juanotilla executed her will, Ysabel and Sebastiana were deceased. In addition to family members, Juanotilla also left goods to two servants.

[b] Juanotilla's daughter Ysabel had two daughters of her own, Regina and Ysabel. Regina is supposed to share her inheritance with her two nephews, since her sister is deceased.

[c] Rosa was to receive her deceased mother's (Sebastiana's) inheritance; she was to share her portion with two other brothers.

[d] Property and houses were to be divided equally among the four inheritors.

surements of the property actually provided. Testators for the most part offered a description of the whereabouts of the land they were bequeathing. For example, Margarita Martín owned property in Taos "between two rivers," and María de Perea owned a house and adjacent property that "ran from the Camino Real [the main road] to the property of Benito Domínguez." While such descriptions might seem vague by present-day standards, they were well understood by local settlers. Some of the women bequeathed specific pieces of property to specific inheritors; others, such as Juanotilla, simply noted that their property was to be equally divided among their heirs.

Property mentioned in these wills included *solar* (residential property) and *caballería* (agricultural land). These women owned, for example, "una casa y la tierra que linda" (a house and nearby land) and "tierras bajo de riego" (irrigated lands). In a society largely based on farming, access to water was of prime importance, and thus irrigated lands were of utmost value. Wheat was one of the crops grown, as illustrated by María Hurtado's will. Other citations indicate that women owned fruit orchards; and cultivation of corn was alluded to in one will, in which a "milpita de maíz" was designated.[14] It also became apparent that the property owned by these women was spread out in various locations. For example, Margarita Martín lived near Santa Cruz de la Cañada but had land near Taos, and Rosa Fernández lived in Santa Cruz but owned land in Chimayó. The distribution patterns and quantity of other pieces of land listed in these papers indicate that personal property did not have to be—and often was not—close or adjacent to the owner's place of residence.

Structures often accompanied the property that was bequeathed.[15] To avoid confusion, testators would distinguish similar types of structures when bequeathing them. For example, Margarita Martín distinguished "one house" she owned from another "old house." Sometimes a general description of the house also was provided. Again, Margarita Martín differentiated between "a house with a living room, a kitchen, a pantry, and two bedrooms" and "another with two living rooms and three additional rooms." Living quarters were identified in terms of *cuartos,* which could describe an individual structure or specific rooms in a house; different rooms in a single residence were often bequeathed to different members of the family. Among the structures bequeathed by Rosa Fernández were "dos cuartos de vivienda" (one dwelling with two rooms) and another consisting of "tres cuartos de vivienda con patio" (three rooms and a patio). Lugarda Quintana additionally delineated a room she bequeathed by providing its measurements.

Livestock comprised the largest category of goods bequeathed or mentioned in these testaments. Juanotilla's sample testament listed cows, bulls, sheep, horses, calves, mares, and goats. There was a tendency by colonial settlers to distinguish between *ganado mayor* (horses and cattle) and *ganado menor* (sheep and goats) and between *caballos de rienda* (riding horses) and *caballos de carga* (work horses). The livestock inventoried in these women's estate documents seemed to be divided equally between male and female heirs. The estate proceedings especially indicate that some of the women's livestock were out grazing; for example, the local magistrate instructed the Indians from nearby pueblos to round up María Calabacita's livestock so that it could be inventoried efficiently.

Of the occupational implements itemized in these documents, almost all were agriculturally related; these included digging sticks, steel and wooden plow points (*rejas* and *puntas*), and hoes. All the women in this study owned only one or two of each item. Perhaps these limited amounts of tools were all they needed to cultivate their personal land, but most likely, given the distance from central

Mexico, such tools were in short supply. It is also possible that agricultural implements were bequeathed mainly by men and therefore do not appear in larger quantities in these women's wills.

Juanotilla's testament is noteworthy for two reasons. First, she seems to have owned a larger collection of tools than the rest of the women—seven axes, two hoes, and three steel points (*rejas*), as opposed to the single items generally listed for the other women. Second, the presence of *rejas* among her possessions is significant. The three that were listed in Juanotilla's testament were all bequeathed to females (her daughter and granddaughters). In a previous study, I found that when tools were distributed to settlers of Santa Cruz de la Cañada in 1712, only women were allotted *rejas*.[16] These steel plow points may have been considered such a valuable commodity in this agricultural society that they were distributed only to women, with the expectation that they would safely guard them. One fact supporting this contention is that steel was a scarce metal at the time.[17] The possibility also exists that women were primarily responsible for making furrows as part of their daily farming activities. Implements associated with carpentry and woodworking—for instance, *escoplos* (chisels) and *azuelas* (adzes)—were also included in the wills, but to a lesser degree.

Domestic wares owned and designated by these women predominantly centered on food preparation. These included *cazos* (caldrons), *jarros* (jugs), *metates* (grinding stones), *cedazos* (sieves), and *comales* (heating griddles); Juana Domínguez listed a "jarro chocolatero" (pitcher for chocolate) among her goods, and Margarita Martín listed a "jarro de cobre viejo para beber agua" (an old copper jug for drinking water). Also included were a few serving utensils, such as spoons and knives, and gourds to store foods and liquids; Lugarda Quintana even had serving linens, such as a tablecloth and napkins. Besides the normal kitchen goods, Margarita Martín, unlike the rest of the women, owned six china plates. Margarita was also the only woman who owned a wooden cabinet for storing her wares.

Furniture items found in the homes of these women included stools, tables, benches, chairs, beds, mattresses, and blankets (*frezadas*). Most of the women also owned wooden chests, probably for storing their clothing or prized possessions. References to "cajas mechoacanas" (chests made in Michoacán, Mexico) indicate that some of these chests were imported.

A fourth category, composed of personal goods, was dominated by women's clothing and fabrics;[18] only two citations enumerated men's articles of clothing: a pair of men's shoes and a man's vest. Clothing articles bequeathed by these women included a variety of skirts, capes, mantillas, handkerchiefs, stockings, slips, and blankets. Stockings were apparently of special importance to Juana Domínguez; numerous citations note that she both owed and was owed pairs of stockings. The variety of available fabrics—linen, silk, cotton, serge, and wool—is interesting to observe (for example, "a blue satin mantilla" and a set of "French sleeves embroidered with silk" were bequeathed by one woman). Juana Domínguez's testament also listed a "manta de la tierra" (locally produced cloth). Decorative items such as ribbon, lace, and fringe were also important to these women. Almost all of them bequeathed some form of clothing or fabric; the following sample citations taken from the wills of Lugarda Quintana and Margarita Martín illustrate the variety of textures and designs:

Four *varas* of fine lace
Four *varas* of ribbon
Wool stockings
One piece of fringe
Ten *varas* of fabric with silver flowers
One long skirt with silver fringe
One scarlet-colored skirt
One foot-blanket

Among what might be considered luxury goods were jewelry and musical instruments; in one will, a harp was listed; in another, a guitar was bequeathed. Several of the women owned jewelry. María de Perea owned several coral bracelets; Margarita Martín owned seven strands of dark pearls; and Lugarda Quintana owned a coral and silver choker, some blue enamel bracelets, and some "fine" pearl earrings. María de Perea was also the only woman to have owned a mirror. A musket and a small sword, necessary weapons of the time, also formed part of Juanotilla's list; she bequeathed both of these items to her son. Unique among the items bequeathed by the women were several candles, several strands of chile, and, in the case of Margarita Martín, a *carreta* and a *carretón* (carts), which she left to two of her daughters.

This estate documentation also tells us something about the Christian beliefs and practices of settlers in New Mexico at this time. Among the religious articles owned by the women were crucifixes, pictures of saints (*retablos* or *cuadros*), and statues (*bultos*). The saints enumerated by these women included Santa Isabel, San José, San Antonio, Nuestra Señora del Pilar, and Nuestra Señora de los Remedios. It is interesting to note that the Virgen de Guadalupe was part of the religious beliefs of Nuevo Mexicanas. María Calabacita bequeathed a picture of the Virgen de Guadalupe in 1744, and in 1767 Petrona de Cárdenas left some of her forced donation money to the cult of the Virgen de Guadalupe. Lugarda Quintana bequeathed one bronze crucifix, an old prayer book of San Antonio, and fourteen effigies of saints (not specified). María Hurtado bequeathed a statue of Christ and a framed picture of Nuestra Señora de la Soledad to the local church in Santa Fé; María explicitly requested that the picture should help decorate the altar of San Antonio. Interestingly, of all the women who bequeathed religious articles, the woman with the most was María Calabacita, the Indian woman from Santo Domingo. Listed in the inventory of her belongings were a small statue of the baby Jesus, a picture of San José and the Virgen Mary, another picture of Our Lady of Guadalupe, a glass-bead rosary, two small silver Christs, one small religious medal, a "large" silver shrine with its saints, and an "ordinary" shrine made of tin.

What are we to conclude from these bequests? At the outset, we can say that women maintained their own goods, which apparently were kept separate from those commonly held with their husbands. In their wills, they consistently made distinctions between *their* personal belongings and those that were *bienes gananciales,* possessions acquired after marriage. Two examples of this separation of goods appear in this corpus. As part of Margarita Martín's testament papers, don Bernardo Roybal presented a petition to separate his goods from those of his wife, to ensure that his belongings were not bequeathed to her inheritors. Also, when the division of Lugarda Quintana's possessions was carried out, she noted that the property at a given location was her husband's but that the structure on it was hers. These eighteenth-century Nuevo Mexicanas were well aware of what and how much they owned and clearly made personal decisions about how they wanted their belongings to be distributed.

With the exception of María Calabacita, all these Nuevo Mexicanas owned property, though to varying degrees. Work by Jenkins and my own research suggest that women, throughout the colonial period, were actively engaged in various facets of buying, selling, and managing property.[19] Jenkins has also observed: "A widow had greater freedom, to be sure, but even if there was a husband whose consent had to be secured in the signing of a property conveyance, the evidence indicates that it was the woman who made the decision." This sample documentation also alludes to the assertiveness of these women in securing debts owed to them and to their deceased husbands, and also in trying to settle their own accounts. For example, Juana Domínguez listed stockings and various amounts of money owed to her.

These documents portray the women of New Mexico as active participants in the two primary livelihoods of this geographical area: agriculture and stock raising. Agriculture was the most basic and prevalent economic activity involving the most people; that these women were involved in or closely allied with these endeavors is illustrated by the numerous references in their wills to agricultural implements. In fact, women may have possessed one of the most valuable instruments of the farming trade—the steel plow point. The enumeration of the different varieties of livestock in these wills also gives some indication of the role of women in this occupation. Gómez-Quiñones summarizes the relationship between these daily endeavors: "Although agriculture and livestock work were different, both activities were integrated, often involving the same people and occurring at the same place."[20] This observation seems to be confirmed by the wills, since both livestock and agricultural implements were listed in the same testament as personal belongings and both types of implements were bequeathed to members of both sexes. Yet to be documented is the degree to which women were involved in each of these spheres and the specific activities they undertook.

Of the twelve women considered for this study, eight were married at the time they made their wills or at the time of death; three of them were in their second marriage. Three other women were widows: María Hurtado, María de la Candelaria Gonzales, and Chatalina Durana. Research by others indicates that there was a large widow element in New Mexican colonial society.[21] The present research suggests that these same widows, under special circumstances, felt free to request the assistance of male family members, *compadres,* or even local officials.

Three of the women had different marital circumstances. María Calabacita of Santo Domingo Pueblo was described as a *soltera* (single woman) with four "natural" children. Juanotilla, though described in the document as being "legally" married (and also with four children), had no reference made to her husband at any time during her settlement. Lugarda Quintana noted that she was married to Ascencio Archuleta but did not know his whereabouts (perhaps out on a military campaign). For this reason apparently, she selected her *compadre* as her executor. Without doubt, widowed women and other single women functioned as individual heads of household, thoroughly responsible for the welfare of their family members and the supervision of their property and belongings. The fact that several women were on their second marriages indicates a higher mortality rate for men[22] and a social acceptance of remarriage in colonial New Mexican society.

The number of children in a family varied. Most of the women had two to four children; Petrona de Cárdenas, and possibly María Hurtado, had more than ten. Six of Petrona's children were deceased; her will indicates that younger children were often named after those who had died. Initial observations regarding patterns of inheritance indicate that the women attempted to divide their goods equally among their children. María Calabacita, unique for not bequeathing any property, noted that all her goods should be equally divided among her children. Petrona de Cárdenas also said in her will that her husband had transferred some property to her, and she bequeathed that property to her children, who were to divide it "por partes iguales" (equally). Livestock also seemed to be equally divided. Women's clothing and fabric bequeathed by these women almost always went to daughters or granddaughters, but if a husband was still living, he too inherited some of his wife's clothes. Domestic wares were generally assigned to female relatives, while furniture and agricultural implements seem to have been equally designated. If children were deceased, mothers tended to make sure that some of their belongings were transferred to their grandchildren. No doubt, future research will provide more clearly defined inheritance patterns for colonial New Mexico.

Women appear to have raised not only their own children but also others brought into the family under a variety of circumstances. For example, María de Perea, in addition to raising her own daughter, also helped raised a son belonging to her first husband. María stated in her testament that since the time of his birth she had raised Miguel Maese, named after his father, as if he were her own son. She also felt it necessary to clarify that he was an *español* (Spaniard); this was the only instance in which this term appeared throughout the collection of documents. Concerned for the welfare of this fifteen-year-old, María instructed that after her death he was to remain with her second husband, since he too had helped raise him. Rosa Martina Fernández also indicated in her will that she was bequeathing some goods to "mi ahijada" (my godchild), whom she had raised as an adopted daughter.

If upon her death the woman's husband was deceased, and minor children were involved, another family member would generally be assigned their guardianship. Unmarried children up to the age of twenty-five were evidently considered minors. If such children inherited goods, the guardian was responsible for their welfare and also for increasing their share of the inheritance. For example, María Calabacita's father, as guardian of her minor children, was expected to multiply the number of livestock she left behind. Margarita Martín gave her second husband the guardianship of their three children. Women's concern for rewarding family members who had cared for them is illustrated by Juanotilla, who explained that she was bequeathing goods to her grandchildren because they had watched over her. Another study also indicates that property was often given by family members and friends as a reward for personal care or services rendered.[23]

When the settlers ventured northward from Mexico, one of the social relationships they brought with them was that of the *compadrazgo* (coparenthood). Juana Domínguez of Santa Fé and Lugarda Quintana of Santa Cruz de la Cañada illustrate that this kinship was very much a part of everyday life in colonial New Mexico. In listing debts outstanding to her, Juana indicated that her *comadre* Juana Griego owed her three pairs of stockings and some gloves. As noted, Lugarda Quintana appointed her *compadre* Pedro Sánchez executor of her will. Since Lugarda did not know the whereabouts of her husband, her *compadre* was entrusted with her husband's responsibilities as an executor.

There is no question that all these women were involved in similar livelihoods. However, their wills indicate that not all of them were socially equal. Oakah L. Jones believes that class differences did not mean much in this frontier context and that, therefore, there was little hostility among members of different classes.[24] Scholes, on the other hand, contends that visible social differences did exist: "Despite the easy and free intermingling of classes, and despite the fact also that no man could attain any great measure of wealth in New Mexico, there was a fairly well defined local aristocracy based on family, service to the Crown, and worldly possessions."[25]

The inventories of goods formulated for three women in the present study shed light on existing socioeconomic differences. Since their possessions were ascribed a monetary value, we learn that Chatalina Durana's possessions in 1752 tallied 106 pesos, that María Calabacita's goods in 1744 were worth approximately 1,486 pesos, and that Margarita Martín's goods amounted to about 5,298 pesos in 1744. Not only does the value of Margarita Martín's goods allude to her higher economic level above the rest of the women in this study, but the fact that on both occasions she married men with the title of *don* also confirms her higher socioeconomic standing, though she herself did not have *doña* before her name. The titles of *don* and *doña* in earlier times connoted nobility and in this sociohistorical context most likely indicated social and economic importance.[26] Interestingly, two of Margarita Martín's daughters from her first marriage to don Juan Padilla also inherited the title of *doña,* but none of her other children did. The inventory of Margarita's goods also illustrated her preference for varied and refined clothing, as compared to the rest of the women. Lugarda Quintana also seems to have formed part of the elite of the *villa* of Santa Cruz de la Cañada; among her possessions were found jewelry, extra food-serving supplies such as a tablecloth, and the fourteen religious effigies in addition to property and numerous livestock. The rest of the women probably reflect the majority of New Mexican Hispanic women throughout the colonial period. These women on a daily basis maintained a family, were responsible for domestic chores, owned livestock, and appear to have participated in farming activities.

None of the women described themselves as belonging to a specific racial or ethnic group. In fact, as mentioned, the only reference to *español/española* was made by María de Perea, who used the term to identify her stepson. However, ethnicity was mentioned for those women who appeared to be non-Spanish and whose estates had to be inventoried by others. For example, Juanotilla's estate papers cite her as "Juanotilla, de calidad coyota." That Juanotilla was not identified with a last name suggests that she might have gone by a native Indian name within her pueblo. The phrase "de calidad coyota" served to clarify her social/ethnic status within her community; she was ethnically recognized as a *coyota* (of mixed blood). According to Adrian Bustamante, *coyote/coyota* is an ascriptive ethnic category generally used in reference to a person of mixed Spanish and Indian or black heritage. Bustamante suggests that by the 1800s this term supplanted the more widely used term *mestizo* in New Mexico.[27]

Though Juanotilla is from the pueblo of San Buenaventura de Cochití, her possessions are similar to those of nonpueblo women; in fact, she owned a more ample and varied amount of goods than most of them. Whether Juanotilla inherited her goods from her parents or acquired them individually or through marriage is not discernible from the document. It does appear that, by New Mexican standards of the time, Juanotilla was economically stable. Moreover, Juanotilla's estate settlement indicates that she personally owned two servants.

María Calabacita was the only Indian woman whose estate proceedings were reviewed for this study. At the time her estate was inventoried, she was described as an *india* (Indian woman) from Santo Domingo Pueblo. She died in 1744, leaving four minor children, three sons and one daughter. Her possessions were inventoried after the local magistrate went to Santo Domingo and met with her father via a translator. Among María Calabacita's possessions were embroidered fabric, ribbon, blankets decorated with lace and ribbon, coral and jet bracelets, Christian articles, digging sticks, axes, and numerous livestock. She had also previously owned some dishes, but these were delivered for masses to the local priest. María's father was designated the primary beneficiary and appointed guardian of his grandchildren's goods until they became of age or were married. As recognition of the guardianship, the brand on María's livestock was changed to a brand indicating ownership by her father.

Several other indigenous women were mentioned in these wills. One of them was an Indian woman named Rosa, who was listed as having been paid four pesos by Margarita Martín's estate. Another was Juana María Velásquez, also an Indian woman, who was paid two pesos from Margarita's goods. A third Indian woman was bequeathed to one of Margarita Martín's daughters; she was described as "una india de rescate" and was valued at one hundred pesos. (The words *de rescate* indicated that these women had been captured or traded for the purpose of servitude.) Lugarda Quintana also mentioned in her testament that an Indian woman named Madalena owed her a goat and that another, "Francisca, la india," owed her an amount equivalent to a mass.

Other references to Indian persons appeared in María de la Candelaria's will. As part of her testament, she freed a woman named María Jucepa and also a male Indian. The irony, though, is that, while these servants were being given their freedom, they were simultaneously being designated to remain with the testator's family members. The following directive appeared in María de la Candelaria's will: "Es mi última voluntad que una indiuela que tengo llamada María Jucepa quede libre por haberme servido con puntualidad y que se quede con mi hija María Francisca para que dicha mi hija la mire y atienda como que la hemos criado, y dicha india mire y atienda a la dicha mi hija como su madre" ("It is my last will that an Indian woman that I have by the name of Maria Jucepa be freed for having served me with punctuality and that she remain with my daughter, María Francisca, so that my daughter will watch over her as we have raised her, and the foresaid Indian watch over and assist my daughter as if she were her mother"). The term *indiuela* appeared several times in the documents, very likely connoting a young Indian girl.

Through the use of testaments and estate proceedings, the present study has been able to shed light on the lives of eighteenth-century Nuevo Mexicanas. Without doubt, such primary sources serve as one of the few direct approaches available for the study of women of past centuries. The notarial documentation used in this study illustrates that New Mexican women, similar to women in other parts of Latin America at this time,[28] were making wills and having their estates settled by other family members. Moreover, we know that women who lived in pueblos and appear to have been Hispanicized were also using Spanish practices to bequeath their goods. Goods bequeathed by all the women were similar: houses or rooms, property, livestock, domestic wares, agricultural implements, and religious articles and jewelry. What set some women apart from others was the amount of goods owned. Life for eighteenth-century New Mexican women also included the loss of husbands, second marriages, death at childbirth, and the presence of extended and other family members—such as adopted children, godchildren, and Indian servants—in their households. Daily activities related to stock raising and crop cultivation were just as important as developing religiosity and bonding with others—for example, through *compadrazgo.*

Although the present study documents ordinary life in colonial New Mexico, much more research is necessary on related themes. Hernández, for example, has been able to describe the first female settlers who ventured north from Mexico;[29] however, we still need to describe the process whereby they adapted to a new geographical and cultural environment. Also, while the present study describes women and family members and some of their daily activities, we still need to understand the relationships between women and their family members and between women and other women, both Spanish and Indian. A study comparing and contrasting women from the various *villas,* outlying settlements, and pueblos might also help identify the social, occupational, and cultural differences among them. Early Nuevo Mexicanas largely contributed to the importation, adaptation, and continuity of cultural beliefs and practices, and these beliefs and practices also merit attention. Finally, the present research has, I hope, increased our understanding of women's lives during the eighteenth century and will contribute to a more realistic interpretation of the role of women of Mexican origin throughout the colonial Southwest.[30]

NOTES

1. General works analyzing the historical experiences of Chicana and Mexicana women include the following: *Frontiers: A Journal of Women's Studies,* special issue entitled "Chicanas en el ambiente nacional" (Chicanas in the national landscape) 5, no. 2 (Summer 1980); and special issue entitled "Las Chicanas" 11, no. 1 (1990); Teresa Córdova et al., eds., *Chicana Voices: Intersections of Class, Race, and Gender* (Austin: Center for Mexican American Studies, University of Texas, 1986); Martha P. Cotera, *Diosa y Hembra: The History and Heritage of Chicanas in the United States* (Austin: Information Systems Development, 1976); Adelaida del Castillo, ed., *Between Borders: Essays on Mexicana/Chicana History* (Encino, Calif.: Floricanto Press, 1990); Nan Elsasser, Kyle MacKenzie, and Yvonne Tixier y Vigil, *Las Mujeres: Conversations from a Hispanic Community* (Old Westbury, N.Y.: Feminist Press, 1980); Margarita Melville, ed., *Twice a Minority: Mexican American Women* (St. Louis: Mosby, 1980), and *Mexicanas at Work in the United States* (Houston: Mexican American Studies Program, University of Houston, 1989); Alfredo Mirandé and Evangelina Enríquez, *La Chicana: The Mexican American Woman* (Chicago: University of Chicago Press, 1979); Magdalena Mora and Adelaida R. del Castillo, eds., *Mexican Women in the United States: Struggles Past and Present* (Los Angeles: Chicano Studies Research Center, University of California, 1980); Vicki L. Ruiz, *Cannery Women, Cannery Lives: Mexican Women, Unionization, and the California Food Processing Industry, 1930–1950* (Albuquerque: University of New Mexico Press, 1987); Vicki L. Ruiz and Susan Tiano, eds., *Women on the United States–Mexico Border: Responses to Change* (Boston: Allen and Unwin, 1987); Rosaura Sánchez and Rosa Martínez Cruz, eds., *Essays on La*

Mujer (Los Angeles: Chicano Studies Research Center, University of California, 1977); Patricia Zavella, *Women's Work and Chicano Families: Cannery Workers of the Santa Clara Valley* (Ithaca, N.Y.: Cornell University Press, 1987).

2. Sor Juana Inés de la Cruz is one woman who frequently appears in anthologies describing the Mexicana historical experience and in those describing the Chicana historical experience. For a discussion of the "great women" approach, see Alma M. Garcia, "Studying Chicanas: Bringing Women into the Frame of Chicano Studies," in *Chicana Voices,* pp. 20–21.

3. In 1932, Louis H. Warner published the first study that used estate documentation for New Mexico (see "Wills and Hijuelas," *New Mexican Historical Review* 7, no. 1 [January 1932]: 75–89). In 1970, Carmen Espinosa used wills to reconstruct clothing for early colonial New Mexican women (see *Shawls, Crinolines, Filigree: The Dress and Adornment of the Women of New Mexico, 1739 to 1900* [El Paso: Texas Western Press, University of Texas, 1970]). More recently, Richard Eighme Ahlborn has provided an in-depth study of one will ("The Will of a Woman in 1762," *New Mexico Historical Review* 65, no. 3 [July 1990]: 319–355).

Other Latin American scholars who have utilized wills and estate documentation include Arthur J. O. Anderson, Frances Berdan, and James Lockhart, eds., *Beyond the Codices: The Nahua View of Colonial Mexico* (Berkeley: University of California Press, 1976); Asunción Lavrin and Edith Couturier, "Dowries and Wills: A View of Women's Socioeconomic Role in Colonial Guadalajara and Puebla, 1640–1790," *Hispanic American Historical Review* 59, no. 2 (May 1979): 280–304; S. L. Cline, *Colonial Culhuacan, 1580–1600* (Albuquerque: University of New Mexico Press, 1986); and Frank Solomon, "Indian Women of Early Colonial Quito as Seen through Their Testaments," *The Americas* 44, no. 3 (January 1988): 325–342.

The Spanish Archives of New Mexico, housed at the State of New Mexico Records Center and Archives in Santa Fe, consist of administrative records and land records encompassing the years 1621–1821. Among the various documents in this collection are military records, litigation proceedings of civil and criminal cases, and auxiliary documents such as petitions and estate papers. For a history and an explanation of these records, see Myra Ellen Jenkins et al., *Guide to the Microfilm Edition of the Spanish Archives of New Mexico, 1621–1821,* 2nd ed. (Santa Fe: State of New Mexico Records Center and Archives, 1975). The notarial sources reviewed for this study follow the classification of the Spanish Archives of New Mexico (SANM) as listed in the above guide and as noted in Ralph Emerson Twitchell, *The Spanish Archives of New Mexico,* 2 vols. (New York: Arno Press, 1976; reprint of 1914 edition).

4. Myra Ellen Jenkins, "Some Eighteenth-Century New Mexico Women of Property," in *Hispanic Arts and Ethnohistory in the Southwest,* ed. Marta Weigle (Santa Fe: Ancient City Press, 1983), p. 335. Recent efforts to fill this void on early colonial New Mexican women include Angelina F. Veyna, "Women in Early New Mexico: A Preliminary View," in *Chicana Voices,* pp. 120–135; Salomé Hernández, "Nueva Mexicanas as Refugees and Reconquest Settlers, 1680–1696," in *New Mexico Women: Intercultural Perspectives,* ed. Joan M. Jensen and Darlis A. Miller (Albuquerque: University of New Mexico Press, 1986), pp. 41–70; Rosalind Z. Rock, " 'Pido y Suplico': Women and the Law in Spanish New Mexico, 1697–1763," *New Mexico Historical Review* 65, no. 2 (April 1990): 145–159; Ramón A. Gutiérrez, *When Jesus Came, the Corn Mothers Went Away: Marriage, Sexuality, and Power in*

New Mexico, 1500–1846 (Stanford, Calif.: Stanford University Press, 1991); and Ahlborn, "The Will of a Woman in 1762."

Demographic studies of New Mexico also provide useful information on women in the late eighteenth century. See Antonio Ríos-Bustamante, "New Mexico in the Eighteenth Century: Life, Labor and Trade in La Villa de San Felipe de Albuquerque, 1706–1790," *Aztlan* 7, no. 3 (Fall 1976): 357–389; Janie Louise Aragón, "The People of Santa Fe in the 1790's," *Aztlan* 7, no. 3 (Fall 1976): 391–417; Alicia Vidaurreta Tjarks, "Demographic, Ethnic and Occupational Structure of New Mexico, 1790," *The Americas* 35, no. 1 (July 1978): 45–88; and Angelina F. Veyna, "A Look at New Mexican Society in the 1790's: The Case of Santa Cruz de la Cañada," unpublished manuscript, 1984.

5. For example, a document listed as "Criminal Proceedings against Diego Martín Moraga of Santa Cruz" (SANM, Twitchell 2, item 228) conceals the fact that these proceedings came about as a result of a brother fighting with a neighbor over his sister's honor. It further conceals the fact that a woman served as one of the case witnesses.

6. Anderson, Berdan, and Lockhart, *Beyond the Codices,* p. 23.

7. These women's documents are referenced according to the *Calendar of the Microfilm Edition of the Spanish Archives of New Mexico, 1621–1821* (Santa Fe: State of New Mexico Records Center, 1968). Eight wills and four estate settlements were reviewed for the present study. Additional comments in note 8 have been taken from Fray Angélico Chávez to provide background data for some of the women. See *Origins of New Mexico Families* (Santa Fe: William Ganon Publishers, 1975; originally published 1954 by Fray Angélico Chávez in conjunction with the Historical Society of New Mexico).

8. Because women are so often erased by such collective terms as *settlers, colonizers, citizens,* and *New Mexicans,* I think it especially important that the women of these documents be identified by name throughout this study. The present chapter is based on the following sources:

María de Perea, will, Santa Fé, 1715, SANM, Twitchell 1, item 680. María was the daughter of Juan de Perea, a soldier, and Alonza Varela de Losada.

Juana Domínguez, will, Santa Fé, 1717, SANM, Twitchell 1, item 235. Juana had three daughters and one son from her first marriage to Domingo Luján, and no children from her second marriage to Lorenzo de la Madrid.

María Hurtado, will, Santa Fé, 1725, SANM, Twitchell 1, item 405. María was a widow at the time she executed her will. She seems to have been married for forty-six years to Antonio Montoya, during which time they had eleven children.

Codallos y Rabal, Santa Fé, settlement of estate of María Calacacita, Indian of Santo Domingo, 1744, SANM, Twitchell 2, item 452. During indexing of this document, María's last name appears to have been mistakenly transcribed; the original estate proceedings indicate that her last name was *Calabacita.* At the time of her death, she was survived by her father and four "natural" children; no reference was made to their father in the document.

Margarita Martín, settlement of estate, Río Arriba, 1744, SANM, Twitchell 1, item 530. Margarita married don Juan de Padilla early in the 1700s; in 1731, she married don Bernardo Roybal. Her father served as *alcalde* of Santa Cruz in 1714 and also built a chapel at La Soledad. In 1730, her father was forced to vacate lands that were too close to Taos Pueblo (see Chávez, *Origins,* pp. 224–225). The present estate proceedings were initiated by her son-in-law, husband of her only married daughter.

Juanotilla, coyota, settlement of estate, Cochití, 1747, SANM, Twitchell 1, item 185. No last name was provided for Juanotilla; she was identified only as "Juanotilla, de calidad coyota." Of four children, two were deceased at the time of her death.

Lugarda Quintana, will, Santa Cruz, 1749, SANM, Twitchell 1, item 968. Lugarda appears to have been the daughter of Miguel de Quintana, one of the founding colonists of the Villa of Santa Cruz de la Cañada (Chávez, *Origins,* p. 261).

Rosa Martín, will, Santa Cruz, 1750, SANM, Twitchell 1, item 536. According to the original document, this woman's full name was Rosa Martina Fernández; this is the name by which she will be referred to in this study. Rosa may have been Margarita Martín's sister (Chávez, *Origins,* pp. 224–225).

María de la Candelaria Gonzales, will, Santa Fé, 1750, SANM, Twitchell 1, item 344; and *Partition of lands to the heirs of Manuel Truxillo and María de la Candelaria Gonzales, 1751,* SANM, Twitchell 1, item 970.

Settlement of estate of Chatalina Durana, Santa Fé, 1752, SANM, Twitchell 1, item 243. The index of the SANM identifies this woman as Chatalina "Durán"; the text of her papers indicates that her name was *Durana.* Chatalina appears to have married Bartolomé Garduño, a native of Querétaro, Mexico, in 1695 (Chávez, *Origins,* p. 184).

Petrona de Cárdenas, will, Santa Cruz, 1767, SANM, Twitchell 1, item 198. Petrona was the daughter of Andrés de Cárdenas and Juana de Abalos, and wife of Roque Jaramillo, a native of Mexico City. She and her husband were among the first colonists who settled in the area of Santa Cruz de la Cañada in 1693 (Chávez, *Origins,* p. 199). Her parents were originally from Puebla, and they migrated north in 1693; Petrona was apparently born in Mexico City (Chávez, *Origins,* p. 156).

María Rosalía Durán de Armijo, will, Santa Fé, 1768, SANM, Twitchell 1, item 1237. María was the daughter of Salvador Martín de la Cruz Durán de Armijo and María Rosalía Romero. According to this will, she and her husband had been married for twelve years and did not have any children.

9. See Anderson, Berdan, and Lockhart, *Beyond the Codices,* pp. 23–27; Thomas C. Barnes, Thomas H. Naylor, and Charles W. Polzer, *Northern New Spain: A Research Guide* (Tucson: University of Arizona Press, 1981), p. 15; and S. L. Cline and Miguel León-Portilla, *The Testaments of Culhuacan,* Nahuatl Studies Series, vol. 1 (Los Angeles: Latin American Center, University of California, 1984).

10. For a discussion of illiteracy among women in early colonial New Mexico, see France V. Scholes, "Civil Government and Society in New Mexico in the Seventeenth Century," *New Mexico Historical Review* 10, no. 2 (April 1935): 100. Scholes notes that between 1626 and 1680 more than 90 percent of the women could not sign Inquisition depositions.

11. All the witnesses were men. It is interesting to note that several of these witnesses were referred to as men of *ciencia* (science), *conciencia* (conscience), and *inteligensia* (intelligence) (SANM, Twitchell 1, items 530 and 185). These terms were likely used to identify these assistants as trustworthy and impartial individuals.

12. For a general overview of equivalency of goods, see Louis H. Warner, "Conveyance of Property: The Spanish and Mexican Way," *New Mexico Historical Review* 6, no. 4 (October 1931): 334–359; and Manuel Carrera Stampa, "The Evolution of Weights and Measures in New Spain," *Hispanic American Historical Review* 29 (1949): 2–24.

13. *Juanotilla, coyota, settlement of estate, Cochití, 1747,* SANM, Twitchell 1, item 185, Roll 1, frames 1332–1338.

14. For an overview of agricultural practices and products in colonial New Mexico, see Marc Simmons, "New Mexico's Colonial Agriculture," *El Palacio* 89, no. 1 (Spring 1983): 3–10.

15. The term *casa*, as used in these documents, can describe a single room or a house with an indefinite number of rooms. It might also designate a structure occupied by a single nuclear family, or it might include extended family members. Generally, the context in which the term appears suggests the number of persons living together.

16. Veyna, "Women in Early New Mexico."

17. Simmons, "New Mexico's Colonial Agriculture," p. 9.

18. For an overview of women's clothing in New Mexican history, see Espinosa, *Shawls, Crinolines, Filigree.* Clothing and accessories belonging to Margarita Martín, one of the women in this study, are described on pp. 12–13. For a description of the stockings used during this time, see Marc Simmons, *Coronado's Land: Essays on Daily Life in Colonial New Mexico* (Albuquerque: University of New Mexico Press, 1991), pp. 8–11.

19. Jenkins, "New Mexico Women of Property," p. 335; Angelina F. Veyna, "Women and Property in Colonial New Mexico: Issues and Perspectives," unpublished manuscript, 1991.

20. Juan Gómez-Quiñones, *Development of the Mexican Working Class North of the Río Bravo: Work and Culture among Laborers and Artisans, 1600–1900,* Popular Series No. 2 (Los Angeles: Chicano Studies Research Center, University of California, 1982), p. 18.

21. Aragón, "People of Santa Fe in the 1790's"; Veyna, "New Mexican Society in the 1790's."

22. Aragón, "People of Santa Fe in the 1790's," p. 409.

23. "Veyna, "Women and Property in Colonial New Mexico."

24. Oakah L. Jones, Jr., *Los Paisanos: Spanish Settlers on the Northern Frontier of New Spain* (Norman: University of Oklahoma Press, 1979), p. 164.

25. Scholes, "Civil Government and Society in New Mexico," p. 98.

26. Aragón, "People of Santa Fe in the 1790's," p. 397.

27. For a discussion of the significance of *calidad,* see Gutiérrez, *When Jesus Came, the Corn Mothers Went Away,* pp. 190–191. For a discussion of the term *coyote/a* and other ethnic/caste labels, see Adrian Bustamante, " 'The Matter Was Never Resolved': The *Casta* System in Colonial New Mexico, 1693–1823," *New Mexico Historical Review* 66, no. 2 (April 1991): 143–163.

28. Lavrín and Couturier, "Dowries and Wills."

29. Hernández, "Nueva Mexicanas as Refugees."

30. An earlier version of this chapter appeared as "A View of the Past: Women in Colonial New Mexico, 1744–1767," *Trabajos Monográficos: Studies in Chicana/Latina Research* 1, no. 1 (1985): 28–42.

SEVEN

"Star Struck"
Acculturation, Adolescence, and the Mexican American Woman, 1920–1950

Vicki L. Ruiz

Siga Las Estrellas (Follow the Stars)
MAX FACTOR COSMETIC AD, *La Opinión*, JUNE 5, 1927

Ethnic identity, Americanization, and generational tension first captured the historical imagination during the 1950s with the publication of Oscar Handlin's *The Uprooted* and Alfred Kazin's *A Walker in the City*.[1] These issues continue to provoke discussion among both humanists and social scientists. Within the last decade, feminist scholars have expanded and enriched our knowledge of acculturation through the study of immigrant daughters. Cross-class analysis of adolescent culture provides another window into the world of ethnic youth.[2] This vibrant discourse on generation, gender, and U.S. popular culture has a decidedly East Coast orientation. Are patterns typical of working-class immigrants in New York City applicable to those in Los Angeles?

This essay discusses the forces of Americanization and the extent to which they influenced a generation of Mexican American women coming of age during the 1920s and 1930s. The adoption of new cultural forms, however, did not take place in a vacuum. The political and economic environment surrounding Mexican immigrants and their children would color their responses to mainstream U.S. society. The Spanish-speaking population in the United States soared between 1910 and 1930 as over one million Mexicanos migrated northward. Pushed by the economic and political chaos generated by the Mexican Revolution and lured by jobs in U.S. agribusiness and industry, they settled into existing barrios and forged new communities both in the Southwest and the Midwest, in small towns and cities. For example, in 1900 only 3,000 to 5,000 Mexicans lived in Los Angeles, but by 1930 approximately 150,000 persons of Mexican birth or heritage had settled into the city's expanding barrios.[3] On a national level, by 1930 Mexicans, outnumbered only by Anglos and blacks, formed the "third largest 'racial' group."[4]

Pioneering social scientists, particularly Manuel Gamio, Paul Taylor, and Emory Bogardus, examined the lives of these Mexican immigrants, but their materials on women are sprinkled here and there and at times are hidden in unpublished field notes. Among Chicano historians and writers, there appears a fascination with second-generation Mexican American men, especially as *pachucos*.[5] The life-styles and attitudes of their female counterparts have gone largely unnoticed, even though women may have experienced deeper generational tensions.[6] "Walking in two worlds," they blended elements of Americanization with Mexican expectations and values.[7] To set the context, I will look at education, employment, and media as agents of Americanization and assess the ways in which Mexican American women incorporated their messages. Drawing on social science fieldwork and oral interviews, I will discuss also the sources of conflict between adolescent women and their parents as well as the contradictions between the promise of the American dream and the reality of restricted mobility and ethnic prejudice.

This study relies extensively on oral history. The memories of thirteen women serve as the basis for my reconstruction of adolescent aspirations and experiences (or dreams and routines). Of the thirteen full-blown life histories, ten are housed in university archives, eight as part of the *Rosie the Riveter* collection at California State University, Long Beach. I became familiar with most of these interviews during the course of my research for *Cannery Women, Cannery Lives,* and two surfaced as student oral history projects. I personally interviewed three of the informants.

The women themselves are fairly homogeneous by nativity, class, residence, and family structure. With one exception, all are U.S. citizens by birth and attended southwestern schools. Ten of the interviewees were born between 1913 and 1929.[8] Although two came from families once considered middle class in Mexico, all can be considered working class in the United States. Their fathers' typical occupations included farm worker, day laborer, and busboy. Two women had fathers with skilled blue-collar jobs (butcher and surveyor), and two were the daughters of small family farmers. The informants usually characterized their mothers as homemakers, although several remembered that their mothers took seasonal jobs in area factories and fields. The mother of the youngest interviewee (Rosa Guerrero) supported her family through domestic labor and fortune-telling. Eleven grew up in urban barrios, ten in Los Angeles. Most families were nuclear, rather than extended, although kin usually (but not always) resided nearby. Rich in detail, these interviews reveal the complex negotiations across generation and across culture.

Education and employment were the most significant agents of Americanization. Educators generally relied on an immersion method in teaching the English language to their Mexican pupils. In other words, Spanish-speaking children had to sink or swim in an English-only environment. Even on the playground, students were enjoined from conversing in their native Spanish. Admonishments such as "Don't speak that ugly language, you are an American now," not only reflected a strong belief in Anglo conformity but denigrated the self-esteem of Mexican

American children and dampened their enthusiasm for education.[9] Ruby Estrada remembered that corporal punishment was a popular method for teaching English. "The teacher was mean and the kids got mean."[10] At times children internalized these lessons, as Mary Luna reflected: "It was rough because I didn't know English. The teacher wouldn't let us talk Spanish. How can you talk to anybody? If you can't talk Spanish and you can't talk English, what are you going to do? . . . It wasn't until maybe the fourth or fifth grade that I started catching up. And all along that time I just felt I was stupid."[11]

Students also became familiar with U.S. history and holidays (e.g., Thanksgiving). In recounting her childhood, Rosa Guerrero elaborated on how, in her own mind, she reconciled the history lessons at school with her own heritage. "The school system would teach everything about American history, the colonists and all of that," she explained. "Then I would do a comparison in my mind of where my grandparents came from, what they did, and wonder how I was to be evolved and educated."[12]

Schools, in some instances, raised expectations. Imbued with the American dream, young women (and men) believed that hard work would bring material rewards and social acceptance. In fact, a California grower disdained education for Mexicans because it would give them "tastes for things they can't acquire."[13] Some teenage women aspired to college while others planned careers as secretaries. "I want to study science or be a stenographer," one Colorado adolescent informed Paul Taylor. "I thinned beets this spring, but I believe it is the last time. The girls who don't go to school will continue to top beets the rest of their lives."[14]

Courses in typing and shorthand were popular among Mexican American women, even though few southwestern businesses hired Spanish-surnamed office workers. In 1930, only 2.6 percent of all Mexican women wage earners held clerical jobs. Anthropologist Ruth Tuck noted the contradiction between training and placement. When she asked one teacher why Mexican women were being trained for clerical positions largely closed to them, the educator replied, " 'To teach them respect for the white collar job.' " Skin color also played a role in obtaining office work. As one typing teacher pointed out to young Julia Luna, " 'Who's going to hire you. You're so dark.' "[15]

Many young Mexican women never attended high school but took industrial or service-sector jobs directly after the completion of the eighth grade. Like the Eastern European and French Canadian workers studied by John Bodnar and Tamara Hareven, they gave family needs priority over individual goals. Family obligations and economic necessity propelled Mexican women into the labor force. One government study appearing in a 1931 issue of *Monthly Labor Review* revealed that in Los Angeles over 35 percent of the Mexican families surveyed had wage-earning children.[16] By 1930, approximately one-quarter of Mexicana and Mexican American female wage earners in the Southwest obtained employment as industrial workers. In California, they labored principally in canneries and garment firms.[17] Like many female factory workers in the United States, most

Mexican operatives were young, unmarried daughters whose wage labor was essential to the economic survival of their families. As members of a "family wage economy," they relinquished all or part of their wages to their elders. According to a 1933 University of California study, of the Mexican families surveyed with working children, the children's monetary contributions comprised 35 percent of total household income.[18]

At times working for wages gave women a feeling of independence. Historian Douglas Monroy asserted that outside employment "facilitated greater freedom of activity and more assertiveness in the family for Mexicanas." Some young women went a step further and used their earnings to leave the family home. Facing family disapproval, even ostracism, they defied parental authority by sharing an apartment with female friends.[19] Conversely, kin networks, particularly in canneries and packing houses, reinforced a sense of family. Working alongside female kin, adolescents found employment less than liberating. At the same time, the work environment did give women an opportunity to develop friendships with other Spanish-surnamed operatives and occasionally with their ethnic immigrant peers. They began to discuss with one another their problems and concerns, finding common ground both as factory workers and as second-generation ethnic women. Teenagers chatted about fads, fashions, and celebrities.[20]

Along with outside employment, the media also influenced the acculturation of Mexican women. Movie and romance magazines enabled adolescents (and older women as well) to experience vicariously the middle-class and affluent life-styles heralded in these publications and thus could nurture a desire for consumer goods. Radios, motion pictures, and Madison Avenue advertising had a profound impact on America's cultural landscape. According to historians John D'Emilio and Estelle Freedman, "corporate leaders needed consumers . . . who were ready to spend their earnings to purchase a growing array of goods designed for personal use." They continue: "Americans did not automatically respond to factory output by multiplying their desire for material goods; an ethic of consumption had to be sold."[21] The Mexican community was not immune to this orchestration of desire, and there appeared a propensity toward consumerism among second-generation women. In his 1928 study on Mexican women in Los Angeles industry, Paul Taylor contended that, second to economic need, the prevalent motive for employment among single women was a desire to buy the "extras"—a radio, a phonograph, jazz records, fashionable clothes. As Carmen Escobar revealed, "After I started working, I liked the money. I love clothes—I used to buy myself beautiful clothes."[22] As members of a "consumer wage economy," daughters also worked in order to purchase items for their families' comfort, such as furniture, draperies, and area rugs.[23] Other teenagers had more modest goals. After giving most of her wages to her mother, Rosa Guerrero reserved a portion to buy peanut butter and shampoo. "Shampoo to me was a luxury. I had to buy shampoo so I wouldn't have to wash my hair with the dirty old Oxydol. I used to wash my hair with the soap for the clothes."[24]

The American cinema also made an impression. Although times were lean, many southern California women had dreams of fame and fortune, nurtured, in part, by the proximity to Hollywood. Movies, both Mexican and American, provided a popular form of entertainment for barrio residents. It was not uncommon on Saturday mornings to see children and young adults combing the streets for bottles, so that they could afford the price of admission—ten cents for the afternoon matinee. Preteens would frequently come home and act out what they had seen on the screen. "I was going to be Clara Bow," remembered Adele Hernández Milligan. Another woman recounted that she had definitely been "star struck" as a youngster and attempted to fulfill her fantasy in junior high by "acting in plays galore." The handful of Latina actresses appearing in Hollywood films, such as Dolores Del Rio and Lupe Velez, also whetted these aspirations. Older "star-struck" adolescents enjoyed afternoon outings to Hollywood, filled with the hope of being discovered as they strolled along Hollywood and Vine with their friends.[25]

The influential Spanish-language newspaper *La Opinión* encouraged these fantasies, in part, by publishing gossipy stories about movie stars, like Charlie Chaplin and Norma Shearer, as well as up-to-the-minute reports on the private lives and careers of Latino celebrities. It also carried reviews of Spanish-language films, concerts, and plays.[26] Although promoting pride in Latino cultural events, the society pages reflected the public fascination with Hollywood. One week after its first issue, *La Opinión* featured a Spanish translation of Louella Parsons's nationally syndicated gossip column. Furthermore, the Los Angeles–based newspaper directly capitalized on the dreams of youth by sponsoring a contest with Metro-Goldwyn-Mayer. "Day by day we see how a young man or woman, winner of some contest, becomes famous overnight," reminded *La Opinión* as it publicized its efforts to offer its readers a similar chance. Touted as "the unique opportunity for all young men and women who aspire to movie stardom," this promotion held out the promise of a screen test to one lucky contestant.[27]

For many, show business had obvious appeal; it was perceived as a glamorous avenue for mobility. One could overcome poverty and prejudice as a successful entertainer. As an article on Lupe Velez optimistically claimed, "Art has neither nationalities nor borders."[28]

Americanization seemed to seep into the barrios from all directions—from schools, factories, and even their ethnic press. Parental responses to the Americanization of their children can be classified into two distinct categories: accommodation and resistance. These responses seem more rooted in class than in gender. In the sample of thirteen interviews and in my survey of early ethnographies, I can find no indicaton that integenerational tension occurred more frequently among fathers and daughters than among mothers and daughters. While parents cannot be viewed as a monolithic group, certainly both took an active interest in the socialization of their children. Although resistance was the norm, some parents encouraged attempts at acculturation, and at times entire families took adult education courses in a concerted effort to become "good Americans." Paul Taylor argues that middle-class Mexicans desiring to dissociate themselves from their working-class neighbors had the most fervent aspirations for assimilation. Once in the United States, middle-class Mexicanos found themselves subject to ethnic prejudice that did not discriminate by class. Because of restrictive real estate covenants and segregated schools, these immigrants had lived in the barrios with people they considered inferiors.[29] By passing as "Spanish," they cherished hopes of melting into the American social landscape. Sometimes mobility-minded parents sought to regulate their children's choice of friends and later marriage partners. "My folks never allowed us to go around with Mexicans," remembered Alicia Mendeola Shelit. "We went sneaking around, but my dad wouldn't allow it. We'd always be with whites." Interestingly, Shelit was married twice, both times to Anglos. As anthropologist Margarita Melville has concluded in her contemporary study of Mexican women immigrants, "aspirations for upward mobility" emerged as the most distinguishing factor in the process of acculturation.[30] Of course, it would be unfair to characterize all middle-class Mexican immigrants as repudiating their *mestizo* identity. As one young woman cleverly remarked, "Listen, I may be a Mexican in a fur coat, but I'm still a Mexican."[31]

Although enjoying the creature comforts afforded by life in the United States, Mexican immigrants retained their cultural traditions, and parents developed strategies to counteract the alarming acculturation of their young. Required to speak only English at school, Mexican youngsters were then instructed to speak only Spanish at home. Even when they permitted the use of English, parents took steps to ensure the retention of Spanish among their children. Rosa Guerrero fondly remembered sitting with her father and conjugating verbs in Spanish, "just for the love of it."[32] Proximity to Mexico also played an important role in maintaining cultural ties. Growing up in El Paso, Texas, Guerrero crossed the border into Ciudad Juárez every weekend with her family in order to attend traditional recreational events, such as the bull fights. Her family, moreover, made yearly treks to visit relatives in central Mexico. Those who lived substantial distances from the border resisted assimilation by building ethnic pride through nostalgic stories of life in Mexico.[33] As one San Jose woman related:

> My mother never . . . tired of telling us stories of her native village in Guanajuato; she never let us children forget the things that her village was noted for, its handicrafts and arts, its songs and its stories. . . . She made it all sound so beautiful with her descriptions of the mountains and the lakes, the old traditions, the happy people, and the dances and weddings and fiestas. From the time I was a small child I always wanted to go back to Mexico and see the village where my mother was born.[34]

While many youngsters relished the folk and family lore told by their parents or grandparents, others failed to appreciate their elders' efforts. "Grandmother Perez's stories about the witches and ghosts of Los Conejos get scant audience, in competition with Dick Tracy and Buck Rogers."[35]

In bolstering cultural consciousness, parents found help through youth-oriented community organizations. Church, service, and political clubs reinforced ethnic awareness. Examples included the "Logia 'Juventud Latina' " of the Alianza Hispano Americana; the Mexican American Movement, initially sponsored by the YMCA; and the youth division of El Congreso de Pueblos Que Hablan Español. Bert Corona, a leading California civil rights advocate for over four decades, began his career of activism as a leader in both the Mexican American Movement and the youth auxiliary of the Spanish-Speaking People's Congress.[36]

Interestingly, only two of the thirteen women mentioned Catholicism as an important early influence. The Catholic church played more of a social role; it organized youth clubs and dances, and it was the place for baptisms, marriages, and funerals.[37] For others, Protestant churches offered a similar sense of community. Establishing small niches in Mexican barrios, Protestant missionaries envisioned themselves as the harbingers of salvation and Americanization. Yet some converts saw their churches as reaffirming traditional Mexican values. "I was beginning to think that the Baptist church was a little too Mexican. Too much restriction," remembered Rose Escheverria Mulligan. Indeed, this woman longed to join her Catholic peers who regularly attended church-sponsored dances. "I noticed they were having a good time."[38] Whether gathering for a Baptist picnic or a Catholic dance, teenagers seemed more attracted to the social rather than the spiritual side of their religion. Certainly, more research is needed to assess the impact of Protestant social workers and missionaries on the attitudes of adolescent women. Mary Luna, for example, credited her love of reading to an Anglo educator who converted a small house in the barrio into a makeshift community center and library. The dual thrust of Americanization, education and consumerism, can be discerned in the following excerpt from Luna's oral history. "To this day I just love going to libraries. . . . There are two places that I can go in and get a real warm, happy feeling; that is, the library and Bullock's [department store] in the perfume and makeup department."[39] Blending new behavior with traditional ideals, young women also had to balance family expectations with their own need for individual expression.

Within families, young women, perhaps more than their brothers, were expected to uphold certain standards. Indeed, Chicano social scientists have generally portrayed women as "the 'glue' that keeps the Chicano family together" and as the guardians of "traditional culture."[40] Parents, therefore, often assumed what they perceived as their unquestionable prerogative to regulate the actions and attitudes of their adolescent daughters. Teenagers, on the other hand, did not always acquiesce in the boundaries set down for them by their elders. Intergenerational tension flared along several fronts.

Generally, the first area of disagreement between a teenager and her family would be over her personal appearance. During the 1920s, a woman's decision "to bob or not bob" her hair assumed classic proportions in Mexican families.

After considerable pleading, Belen Martínez Mason was permitted to cut her hair, though she soon regretted her decision. "Oh, I cried for a month."[41] Differing opinions over fashions often caused ill feelings. One Mexican American woman recalled that when she was a young girl, her mother dressed her "like a nun" and she could wear "no makeup, no cream, no nothing" on her face. Swimsuits, bloomers, and short skirts also became sources of controversy. Some teenagers left home in one outfit and changed into another at school. Once María Fierro arrived home in her bloomers. Her father inquired, " 'Where have you been dressed like that, like a clown?' " "I told him the truth," Fierro explained. "He whipped me anyway. . . . So from then on whenever I went to the track meet, I used to change my bloomers so that he wouldn't see that I had gone again."[42] The impact of flapper styles on the Mexican community was clearly expressed in the following verse, taken from a *corrido* appropriately entitled "Las Pelonas" (The Bobbed-Haired Girls):

> Red Bandannas
> I detest,
> And now the flappers
> Use them for their dress.
> The girls of San Antonio
> Are lazy at the *metate.*
> They want to walk out bobbed-haired,
> With straw hats on.
> The harvesting is finished,
> So is the cotton;
> The flappers stroll out now
> For a good time.[43]

With similar sarcasm, another popular ballad chastised Mexican women for applying makeup so heavily as to resemble a piñata.[44]

Once again, bearing the banner of glamour and consumption, *La Opinión* featured sketches of the latest flapper fashions as well as cosmetic ads from both Latino and Anglo manufacturers. The most elaborate layouts were those of Max Factor. Using celebrity testimonials, one advertisement encouraged women to "FOLLOW THE STARS" and purchase "Max Factor's Society Make-up." Factor, through an exclusive arrangement with *La Opinión,* went even further in courting the Mexican market by answering beauty questions from readers in a special column—"Secretos de Belleza" (Beauty Secrets).[45]

The use of cosmetics, however, cannot be blamed entirely on Madison Avenue ad campaigns. The innumerable barrio beauty pageants—sponsored by *mutualistas,* patriotic societies, churches, the Mexican Chamber of Commerce, newspapers, and even progressive labor unions—encouraged young women to accentuate their physical attributes. Carefully chaperoned, many teenagers did participate in community contests from La Reina de Cinco de Mayo to Orange Queen. They modeled evening gowns, rode on parade floats, and sold raffle tickets.[46] Carmen Bernal Escobar remembered one incident where, as a contestant, she had to sell raffle tickets. Every ticket she sold counted as a vote for her in the pageant. Naturally, the winner would be the woman who had accumulated the most votes. When her brother offered to buy twenty-five dollars' worth of votes (her mother would not think of letting her peddle the tickets at work or in the neighborhood), Escobar, on a pragmatic note, asked him to give her the money so that she could buy a coat she had spotted while window-shopping.[47]

The commercialization of personal grooming made additional inroads into the Mexican community with the appearance of barrio beauty parlors. Working as a beautician conferred a certain degree of status, "a nice, clean job," in comparison to factory or domestic work. As one woman related: "I always wanted to be a beauty operator. I loved makeup; I loved to dress up and fix up. I used to set my sisters' hair. So I had that in the back of my mind for a long time, and my mom pushed the fact that she wanted me to have a profession—seeing that I wasn't thinking of getting married."[48] Although further research is needed, one can speculate that neighborhood beauty shops reinforced women's networks and became places where they could relax, exchange *chisme* (gossip), and enjoy the company of other women.

Conforming to popular fashions and fads cannot be construed as a lack of ethnic or political consciousness. In 1937, Carey McWilliams spoke before an assembly of 1,500 walnut workers in Los Angeles and was "profoundly stirred" by this display of grass-roots labor militancy on the part of Eastern European and Mexican women. In describing the meeting, he wrote, "And such extraordinary faces—particularly the old women. Some of the girls had been too frequently to the beauty shop, and were too gotten up—rather amusingly dressy."[49] I would argue that dressing up for a union meeting could be interpreted as an affirmation of individual integrity. Although they worked under horrendous conditions (actually cracking walnuts with their fists), their collective action and personal appearance give evidence that they did not surrender their self-esteem.

The most serious point of contention between an adolescent daughter and her parents, however, regarded her behavior toward young men. In both cities and rural towns, girls had to be closely chaperoned by a family member every time they attended a movie, a dance, or even church-related events. Recalling the supervisory role played by her "old maid" aunt, María Fierro laughingly explained, "She'd check on us all the time. I used to get so mad at her." Ruby Estrada recalled that in a small southern Arizona community, "all the mothers" escorted their daughters to the local dances. Even talking to male peers in broad daylight could be grounds for discipline.[50] Adele Hernández Milligan, a resident of Los Angeles for over fifty years, elaborated: "I remember the first time that I walked home with a boy from school. Anyway, my mother saw me and she was mad. I must have been sixteen or seventeen. She slapped my face because I was walking home with a boy."[51] Describing this familial protectiveness, one social scientist aptly remarked that the "supervision of the Mexican parent is so strict as to be obnoxious."[52]

Faced with this type of situation, young women had three options: they could accept the rules set down for them; they could rebel; or they could find ways to compromise or circumvent traditional standards. "I was *never* allowed to go out by myself in the evening; it just was not done." In rural communities, where restrictions were perhaps even more stringent, "nice" teenagers could not even swim with their male peers. "We were ladies and wouldn't go swimming out there with a bunch of boys." Yet many seemed to accept these limits with equanimity. "It wasn't devastating at all," reflected Ruby Estrada. "We took it in stride. We never thought of it as cruel or mean. . . . It was taken for granted that that's the way it was."[53] In Sonora, Arizona, as in other small towns, relatives and neighbors kept close watch over adolescent women and quickly reported any suspected indiscretions. "They were always spying on you," Estrada remarked. Women in cities had a distinct advantage over their rural peers in that they could venture miles from their neighborhood into the anonymity of dance halls, amusement parks, and other forms of commercialized leisure. With carnival rides and the Cinderella Ballroom, the Nu-Pike amusement park of Long Beach proved a popular hangout for Mexican youth in Los Angeles.[54] It was more difficult to abide by traditional norms when excitement loomed just on the other side of the streetcar line.

Some women openly rebelled. They moved out of their family homes and into apartments. Considering themselves free-wheeling single women, they could go out with men unsupervised, as was the practice among their Anglo peers. "This terrible freedom in the United States," one Mexicana lamented. "I do not have to worry because I have no daughters, but the poor *señoras* with many girls, they worry."[55] Those Mexican American adolescents who did not wish to defy their parents openly would "sneak out" of the house in order to meet their dates or to attend dances with female friends. A more subtle form of rebellion was early marriage. By marrying at fifteen or sixteen, these women sought to escape parental supervision; yet it could be argued that many of these child brides exchanged one form of supervision for another, in addition to taking on the responsibilities of child rearing.[56]

The third option sometimes involved quite a bit of creativity on the part of young women as they sought to circumvent traditional chaperonage. Alicia Mendeola Shelit recalled that one of her older brothers would always accompany her to dances, ostensibly as a chaperone. "But then my oldest brother would always have a blind date for me." Carmen Bernal Escobar was permitted to entertain her boyfriends at home, but only under the supervision of her brother or mother. The practice of "going out with the girls," though not accepted until the 1940s, was fairly common. Several Mexican American women, often related, would escort one another to an event (such as a dance), socialize with the men in attendance, and then walk home together. In the sample of thirteen interviews, daughters negotiated their activities with their parents. Older siblings and extended kin appeared in the background as either chaperones or accomplices. Although unwed teenage mothers were not unknown in the Los Angeles barrios, families expected adolescent women to conform to strict standards of behavior.[57] As can be expected, many teenage women knew little about sex other than what they picked up from friends, romance magazines, and the local theater. As Mary Luna remembered, "I thought that if somebody kissed you you could get pregnant." In *Singing for My Echo,* New Mexico native Gregorita Rodriguez confided that on her wedding night she knelt down and said her rosary until her husband gently asked, " 'Gregorita, *mi esposa,* are you afraid of me?' " At times this naivete persisted beyond the wedding. "It took four days for my husband to touch me," one woman revealed. "I slept with dress and all. We were both greenhorns, I guess."[58]

Of course, some young women did lead more adventurous lives. A male interviewer employed by Mexican anthropologist Manuel Gamio recalled his "relations" with a woman he met in a Los Angeles dance hall. Though born in Hermosillo, Elisa "Elsie" Morales considered herself Spanish. She helped support her family by dancing with strangers. Although she lived at home and her mother and brother attempted to monitor her actions, she managed to meet the interviewer at a "hot pillow" hotel. To prevent pregnancy, she relied on contraceptive douches provided by "an American doctor." Although Morales realized her mother would not approve of her behavior, she noted that "she [her mother] is from Mexico. . . . I am from there also but I was brought up in the United States, we think about things differently." Just as Morales rationalized her actions as "American," the interviewer also regarded her as "American," though in a distinctly less favorable sense of the word. "She seemed very coarse to me. That is she dealt with one in the American way."[59] In his field notes, Paul Taylor recorded an incident in which a young woman had moved in with her Anglo boyfriend after he had convinced her that such living arrangements were common among Americans. Popular *corridos,* such as "El Enganchado" and "Las Pelonas," also touched on the theme of the corrupting influence of U.S. ways on Mexican women.[60]

It is interesting to note that Anglo and Mexican communities held almost identical preconceptions of each other's young female population. While Mexicanos viewed Anglo women as morally loose, Latina actresses in Hollywood found themselves typecast as hot-blooded women of low repute. For example, Lupe Velez starred in such films as *Hot Pepper, Strictly Dynamite,* and *The Mexican Spitfire.*[61]

The image of loose sexual mores as distinctly American probably reinforced parents' fears as they watched their daughters apply cosmetics and adopt the apparel advertised in fashion magazines. In other words, "If she dresses like a flapper, will she then act like one?" Seeds of suspicion reaffirmed the penchant for traditional supervision.

Tension between parents and daughters, however, did not always revolve around adolescent behavior. At times, teenagers questioned the life-styles of their parents. "I used to tell my mother she was a regular maid," Alicia Shelit recalled. "They [the women] never had a voice. They had to have the house clean, the food ready for the men . . . and everything just so."[62] As anthropologist Tuck observed: "Romantic literature, still more romantic movies, and the attitudes of American teachers and social workers have confirmed the Perez children in a belief that their parents do not 'love' each other; that, in particular, Lola Perez is a drudge and a slave for her husband."[63]

However, I would argue that the impact of Americanization was most keenly felt at the level of personal aspiration. "We felt if we worked hard, proved ourselves, we could become professional people," asserted Rose Escheverria Mulligan.[64] Braced with such idealism, Mexican Americans faced prejudice, segregation, and economic segmentation. Though they considered themselves Americans, others perceived them as less than desirable foreigners. During the late 1920s, the *Saturday Evening Post,* exemplifying the nativist spirit of the times, featured inflammatory characterizations of Mexicans in the United States. For instance, one article portrayed Mexicano immigrants as an "illiterate, diseased, pauperized" people who bear children "with the reckless prodigality of rabbits."[65] Racism was not limited to rhetoric; between 1931 and 1934, an estimated one-third of the Mexican population in the United States (over 500,000 people) were either deported or repatriated to Mexico, even though many were native U.S. citizens. Mexicans were the only immigrants targeted for removal. Proximity to the Mexican border, the physical distinctiveness of *mestizos,* and easily identifiable barrios influenced immigration and social welfare officials to focus their efforts solely on the Mexican people, people whom they viewed as foreign usurpers of American jobs and as unworthy burdens on relief rolls. From Los Angeles, California, to Gary, Indiana, Mexicans were either summarily deported by immigration agencies or persuaded to depart voluntarily by duplicitous social workers who greatly exaggerated the opportunities awaiting them south of the border.[66] According to historian George Sanchez: "As many as seventy-five thousand Mexicans from southern California returned to Mexico by 1932. . . . The enormity of these figures, given the fact that California's Mexican population was in 1930 slightly over three hundred and sixty thousand . . . , indicates that almost every Mexican family in southern California confronted in one way or another the decision of returning or staying."[67]

By 1935, the deportation and repatriation campaigns had diminished, but prejudice and segregation remained. Historian Albert Camarillo has demonstrated that in Los Angeles restrictive real estate covenants and segregated schools increased dramatically between 1920 and 1950. The proportion of Los Angeles–area municipalities with covenants prohibiting Mexicans and other minorities from purchasing residences in certain neighborhoods climbed from 20 percent in 1920 to 80 percent in 1946. Many restaurants, theaters, and public swimming pools discriminated against their Spanish-surnamed clientele. In southern California, for example, Mexicans could swim at the public plunges only one day out of the week (just before they drained the pool).[68] Small-town merchants frequently refused to admit Spanish-speaking people into their places of business. "White Trade Only" signs served as bitter reminders of their second-class citizenship.[69]

In 1933, a University of California study noted that Mexicans in southern California were among the most impoverished groups in the United States. Regardless of nativity, they were often dismissed as cheap, temporary labor and were paid "from 20 to 50 percent less per day for . . . performing the same jobs as other workers."[70] This economic segmentation did not diminish by generation. Writing about San Bernardino, California, in the 1940s, Ruth Tuck offered the following illustration:

> There is a street . . . on which three families live side by side. The head of one family is a naturalized citizen, who arrived here eighteen years ago; the head of the second is an alien who came . . . in 1905; the head of the third is the descendant of people who came . . . in 1843. All of them, with their families, live in poor housing; earn approximately $150 a month as unskilled laborers; send their children to "Mexican" schools; and encounter the same sort of discriminatory practices.[71]

Until World War II, Mexicans experienced restricted occupational mobility as few rose above the ranks of blue-collar labor. Scholars Mario García and Gilbert González have convincingly argued that the curricula in Mexican schools helped perpetuate this trend. Emphasis on vocational education served to funnel Mexican youth into the factories and building trades.[72] In the abstract, education raised people's expectations, but in practice, particularly for men, it trained them for low-status, low-paying jobs. Employment choices were even more limited in rural areas. As miners or farmworkers, Mexicans usually resided in company settlements, where almost every aspect of their lives—from work schedules to wage rates to credit with local merchants—was regulated. In 1925, a newspaper editor in Greeley, Colorado, bluntly advocated "a caste system," even though, he alleged, such a system "will be worse upon us, the aristocracy, than upon the Mexicans in their serfdom."[73] Both in urban and rural areas, ethnicity became not only a matter of personal choice and heritage but also an ascribed status imposed by external sources.[74]

Considering these circumstances, it is no surprise that many teenagers developed a shining idealism as a type of psychological ballast. Some adolescents, such as the members of the Mexican American Movement, believed that education was the key to mobility, while others placed their faith in the application of Max Factor's bleaching cream.[75] Whether they struggled to further their education or tried to lighten their skin color, Mexican Americans sought to protect themselves from the damaging effects of prejudice.

Despite economic and social stratification, many Mexicanas believed that life in the United States offered hope and opportunity. "Here woman has come to have place like a human being," reflected Señora ——.[76] More common perhaps was the impact of material assimilation, the purchase of an automobile, a sewing machine, and other accouterments of U.S. consumer society. The accumulation of these goods signaled the realization of (or the potential for realizing) the American dream. As Margaret Clark has eloquently commented: "In Sal si Puedes [a San Jose barrio] where so many people are struggling to escape poverty and want, a 'luxury item' like a shiny new refrigerator may be the source of hope and encouragement—it may symbolize the first step toward the achievement of a better way of life."[77] One of Clark's informants made the point more directly: "Nobody likes to be poor."[78]

The World War II era ushered in a set of new options for Mexican women. In southern California, some joined unions in food-processing plants and negotiated higher wages and benefits. Still others obtained more lucrative employment in defense plants. As "Rosie the Riveters," they gained self-confidence and the requisite earning power to improve their standard of living. A single parent, Alicia Mendeola Shelit purchased her first home as the result of her employment with Douglas Aircraft.[79] The expansion of clerical jobs also provided Mexican American women with additional opportunities. By 1950, 23.9 percent of Mexican women workers in the Southwest held lower white-collar positions as secretaries or sales clerks.[80] They could finally apply the office skills they had acquired in high school or at storefront business colleges. Although beyond the scope of this study, intermarriage with Anglos may have been perceived as a potential avenue for mobility.[81]

Most of the thirteen interviewees continued in the labor force, combining wagework with household responsibilities. Only the oldest (Ruby Estrada of Arizona) and the youngest (Rosa Guerrero of Texas) achieved a solid, middle-class standard of living. While one cannot make facile correlations, both women are the only informants who attained a college education. Six of the eleven California women took their places at the shop floor in the aerospace, electronics, apparel, and food-processing industries. Two became secretaries and one a sales clerk at K-Mart. The remaining two were full-time homemakers. Seven of these eleven informants married Anglo or Jewish men; yet their economic status did not differ substantially from those who chose Mexican spouses.[82] With varying degrees of financial security, the California women are now working-class retirees. Their lives do not exemplify rags-to-riches mobility but, rather, upward movement within the working class. Though painfully aware of prejudice and discrimination, people of their generation placed faith in themselves and in the system. In 1959, Margaret Clark asserted that the second-generation residents of Sal si Puedes "dream and work toward the day when Mexican Americans will become fully integrated into American society at large."[83] The desire to prove oneself appears as a running theme in twentieth-century Mexican American history. I should hasten to add that, in the process, most people refused to shed their cultural heritage. "Fusion is what we want—the best of both ways."[84]

In this essay, I have attempted to reconstruct the world of adolescent women, taking into account the broader cultural, political, and economic environment. I have given a sense of the contradictions in their lives—the lure of Hollywood and the threat of deportation. The discussion gives rise to an intriguing question. Can one equate the desire for material goods with the abandonment of Mexican values? I believe that the ideological impact of material acculturation has been overrated. For example, a young Mexican woman may have looked like a flapper as she boarded a streetcar on her way to work at a cannery; yet she went to work (at least in part) to help support her family, as part of her obligation as a daughter. The adoption of new cultural forms certainly frightened parents, but it did not of itself undermine Mexican identity. The experiences of Mexican American women coming of age between 1920 and 1950 reveal the blending of the old and the new, fashioning new expectations, making choices, and learning to live with those choices.[85]

NOTES

1. Oscar Handlin, *The Uprooted* (New York: Grosset and Dunlap, 1951); Alfred Kazin, *A Walker in the City* (New York: Harcourt Brace, 1951).

2. Examples of this rich literature include John Bodnar, *The Transplanted* (Bloomington: University of Indiana Press, 1985); Kathy Peiss, *Cheap Amusements: Working Women and Leisure in Turn-of-the-Century New York* (Philadelphia: Temple University Press, 1986); Paula S. Fass, *The Damned and the Beautiful: American Youth in the 1920's* (New York: Oxford University Press, 1977); and Estelle B. Freedman and John D'Emilio, *Intimate Matters* (New York: Harper and Row, 1988).

3. The word *Mexicano(a)* designates someone of Mexican birth residing in the United States (either temporarily or permanently), while *Mexican American* denotes a person born in the United States with at least second-generation status. *Mexican* is an umbrella term for both groups. I use the term *Chicano(a)* only for the contemporary period, since most of the older women whose oral interviews contributed to this study did not identify themselves as Chicanas. *Latino(a)* denotes someone of Latin American birth or heritage.

4. Albert Camarillo, *Chicanos in a Changing Society: From Mexican Pueblos to American Barrios in Santa Barbara and Southern California, 1848–1930* (Cambridge, Mass.: Harvard University Press, 1979), pp. 200–201; Ricardo Romo, *East Los Angeles: History of a Barrio* (Austin: University of Texas Press, 1983), p. 61; T. Wilson Longmore and Homer L. Hitt, "A Demographic Analysis of First and Second Generation Mexican Population of the United States: 1930," *Southwestern Social Science Quarterly* 24 (September 1943): 140.

5. Manuel Gamio, *Mexican Immigration to the United States: A Study of Human Migration and Adjustment* (Chicago: University of Chicago Press, 1930; rpt. New York: Arno Press, 1969); Paul S. Taylor, *Mexican Labor in the United States,* 2 vols. (Berkeley: University of California Press, 1928, 1932); Emory S. Bogardus, *The Mexican in the United States* (Los Angeles: University of Southern California Press, 1934). *Pachucos* were young men who adopted the zoot suit, a badge of adolescent rebellion in Mexican and African American communities during World War II. Because of their dress and demeanor, they were subject to verbal and physical abuse by law enforcement officials and servicemen. Mauricio Mazón's *The Zoot Suit Riots: The Psychology of Symbolic Annihilation* (Austin: University of Texas Press, 1984)

and the Luis Valdez play and feature film *Zoot Suit* provide examples of the literature on *pachucos*.

6. Works that focus on Mexican women during this period include Rosalinda M. González, "Chicanas and Mexican Immigrant Families, 1920–1940: Women's Subordination and Family Exploitation," in *Decades of Discontent: The Women's Movement, 1920–1940,* ed. Lois Scharf and Joan Jensen (Westport, Conn.: Greenwood Press, 1983), pp. 59–83; and Vicki L. Ruiz, *Cannery Women, Cannery Lives: Mexican Women, Unionization, and the California Food Processing Industry, 1930–1950* (Albuquerque: University of New Mexico Press, 1987).

7. Ruth Zambrana, "A Walk in Two Worlds," *Social Welfare* 1 (Spring 1986): 12.

8. The age breakdown for the thirteen interviewees are as follows: two women were born between 1910 and 1912; six between 1913 and 1919; four between 1920 and 1929; and one after 1930.

9. Adelina Otero, "My People," *The Survey* 63 (May 31, 1931), rpt. in *Aspects of the Mexican American Experience,* ed. Carlos Cortés (New York: Arno Press, 1976), p. 150; Ruth Tuck, *Not with the Fist* (New York: Harcourt, Brace, 1946; rpt. New York: Arno Press, 1974), pp. 185–188; Vicki L. Ruiz, "Oral History and La Mujer: The Rosa Guerrero Story," in *Women on the United States–Mexico Border: Responses to Change,* ed. Vicki L. Ruiz and Susan Tiano (Boston: Allen and Unwin, 1987), pp. 226–227; interview with Belen Martínez Mason, in *Rosie the Riveter Revisited: Women and the World War II Work Experience,* ed. Sherna Berger Gluck (Long Beach, Calif.: CSULB Foundation, 1983), 23:24–25.

10. Interview with Ruby Estrada, August 4, 1981, conducted by María Hernández, "The Lives of Arizona Women" Oral History Project (On File, Special Collections, Hayden Library, Arizona State University, Tempe), p. 6.

11. Interview with Mary Luna, in *Rosie the Riveter,* 20:10. During the 1940s, bilingual education appeared as an exciting experiment in curriculum reform. See George I. Sanchez, ed., *First Regional Conference on the Education of Spanish-Speaking People in the Southwest* (Austin: University of Texas Press, 1946), pp. 1–22; rpt. in *Aspects of the Mexican American Experience.*

12. Margarita B. Melville, "Selective Acculturation of Female Mexican Migrants," in *Twice a Minority: Mexican American Women,* ed. Margarita B. Melville (St. Louis: Mosby, 1980), p. 161; Ruiz, "Oral History and La Mujer," p. 222.

13. Interview with Rose Escheverria Mulligan, in *Rosie the Riveter,* 27:16–17, 24; Ruiz, "Oral History and La Mujer," pp. 227–228; Taylor, *Mexican Labor,* 1:79, 205–206. Text quotation is from Taylor, 1:79.

14. Tuck, *Not with the Fist,* pp. 162–163, 190–191; Paul S. Taylor, "Women in Industry," field notes for his book *Mexican Labor in the United States, 1927–1930,* Bancroft Library, University of California, 1 box; Estrada interview, pp. 10–15; Escheverria Mulligan interview. Text quotation is from Taylor, *Mexican Labor,* 1:205. See also Paul S. Taylor, "Mexican Women in Los Angeles Industry in 1928," *Aztlan* 11 (Spring 1980): 99–131.

15. Lois Rita Helmbold, "The Work of Chicanas in the United States: Wage Labor and Work in the Home, 1930 to the Present," seminar paper, Stanford University, 1977, p. 53; Taylor field notes; Tuck, *Not with the Fist,* pp. 190–191; interview with Julia Luna Mount, November 17, 1983, conducted by the author.

16. John Bodnar, "Immigration, Kinship and the Rise of Working-Class Realism in Industrial America," *Journal of Social History* 14 (Fall 1980): 53–55; Tamara K. Hareven,

"Family Time and Industrial Time: Family and Work in a Planned Corporation Town, 1900–1924," in *Family and Kin in Urban Communities,* ed. Tamara K. Hareven (New York: New Viewpoints, 1977), p. 202; Taylor field notes; U.S. Department of Labor, Bureau of Labor Statistics, "Labor and Social Conditions of Mexicans in California," *Monthly Labor Review* 32 (January–June 1931): 89.

17. Mario Barrera, *Race and Class in the Southwest* (Notre Dame, Ind.: University of Notre Dame Press, 1979), p. 131; Taylor field notes. The percentage of Mexican women workers employed in industry was comparable to that of European immigrant women in the Eastern states, where one-third of ethnic women who worked outside the home labored in blue collar employment. See Alice Kessler-Harris, *Out to Work: A History of Wage Earning Women in the United States* (New York: Oxford University Press, 1982), p. 127.

18. Heller Committee for Research in Social Economics of the University of California and Constantine Panuzio, *How Mexicans Earn and Live,* University of California Publications in Economics 13, no. 1, Cost of Living Studies 5 (Berkeley: University of California, 1933), pp. 11, 14–17; Taylor field notes; Luna Mount interview; interview with Alicia Shelit, in *Rosie the Riveter,* 37:9. For further delineation of the family wage and the consumer wage economy, see Louise A. Tilly and Joan W. Scott, *Women, Work and Family* (New York: Holt, Rinehart, and Winston, 1978).

19. Taylor field notes; Helmbold, "The Work of Chicanos," pp. 15, 30–31, 36; Douglas Monroy, "An Essay on Understanding the Work Experience of Mexicans in Southern California, 1900–1939," *Aztlan* 12 (Spring 1981): 70; González, "Chicanas and Mexican Immigrant Families," p. 72.

20. Discussing popular magazines and movies helped build important cross-cultural bridges—bridges that would facilitate union organizing drives among southern California food-processing workers during the late 1930s and early 1940s. See Ruiz, *Cannery Women, Cannery Lives.*

21. Roland Marchand, *Advertising the American Dream: Making Way for Modernity, 1920–1940* (Berkeley: University of California Press, 1985), pp. 197–199, 219. Freedman and D'Emilio, *Intimate Matters,* p. 278.

22. Taylor field notes; Richard G. Thurston, "Urbanization and Sociocultural Change in a Mexican-American Enclave," Ph.D. diss., University of California, Los Angeles, 1957 (rpt. San Francisco: R and E Research Associates, 1974), p. 128; Helmbold, "The Work of Chicanos," pp. 42–44; interview with Carmen Bernal Escobar, June 15, 1986, conducted by the author.

23. Elizabeth Fuller, *The Mexican Housing Problem in Los Angeles,* Studies in Sociology 5, Sociological Monograph no. 17 (Los Angeles: Southern California Sociological Society, 1920; rpt. New York: Arno Press, 1974), pp. 4–5.

24. Ruiz, "Oral History and La Mujer," p. 226.

25. Shelit interview, p. 4; interview with Adele Hernández Milligan, in *Rosie the Riveter,* 26:14; Martínez Mason interview, pp. 59–60; Luna interview, pp. 18, 26; Clint C. Wilson II and Felix Gutiérrez, *Minorities and Media* (Beverly Hills, Calif.: Sage, 1985), pp. 85–86.

26. For examples, see *La Opinión,* September 16 and 18, 1926; May 13 and 15, 1927; June 3 and 4, 1927.

27. Ibid., September 23, 24, 27, and 30, 1926.

28. Ibid., March 2, 1927.

29. Taylor field notes. Referring to Los Angeles, two historians have argued that

"Mexicans experienced segregation in housing in nearly every section of the city and its outlying areas" (Antonio Ríos-Bustamante and Pedro Castillo, *An Illustrated History of Mexican Los Angeles, 1781–1985* [Los Angeles: Chicano Studies Research Center, University of California, 1986], p. 135). Ruth Tuck (in *Not with the Fist,* pp. 142–143) noted that Anglo-Americans also employed the term *Spanish* in order to distinguish individuals "of superior background or achievement."

30. Shelit interview, p. 32; Escheverria Mulligan interview, p. 14; Melville, "Selective Acculturation," pp. 155, 162.

31. Tuck, *Not with the Fist,* p. 133.

32. Gamio, *Mexican Immigration,* pp. 172–173; Bogardus, *The Mexican in the United States,* p. 75; Romo, *East Los Angeles,* p. 142; Ruiz, "Oral History and La Mujer," p. 224. "Some adolescents are stimulated to play the dual roles of being good Mexicans at home and good 'Americans' at school" (Bogardus, p. 75).

33. Ruiz, "Oral History and La Mujer," pp. 221, 224–225; Margaret Clark, *Health in the Mexican American Culture* (Berkeley: University of California Press, 1959), p. 21.

34. Clark, *Health in the Mexican American Culture,* p. 21.

35. Tuck, *Not with the Fist,* p. 108. The term "Los Conejos" refers to a village in Mexico.

36. Ríos-Bustamante and Castillo, *An Illustrated History,* p. 139; George Sanchez, "The Rise of the Second Generation: The Mexican American Movement," unpublished paper (courtesy of the author), 1986, pp. 26–27; interview with Luisa Moreno, August 12–13, 1977, conducted by Albert Camarillo.

37. Sociologist Norma Williams contends that contemporary Mexican Americans view the Catholic church almost solely in terms of social, life-cycle functions, such as baptisms and funerals (see *The Mexican American Family: Tradition and Change* (Boston: G. K. Hall, 1990).

38. Vicki L. Ruiz, "Dead Ends or Gold Mines? Using Missionary Records in Mexican American History," *Frontiers* 12 (1991): 33–56. Escheverria Mulligan interview, p. 24. For an interesting collection of Protestant missionary reports during this period, see Carlos Cortés, ed., *Church Views of the Mexican American* (New York: Arno Press, 1974).

39. Luna interview, p. 9.

40. George Sanchez, " 'Go After the Women': Americanization and the Mexican Immigrant Woman, 1915–1929," in *Unequal Sisters: A Multicultural Reader in U.S. Women's History,* ed. Ellen Carol DuBois and Vicki L. Ruiz (New York: Routledge, 1990), pp. 250–263.

41. Bogardus, *The Mexican in the United States,* p. 74; Martínez Mason interview, p. 44. During the 1920s, Mexican parents were not atypical in voicing their concerns over the attitudes and appearance of their "flapper adolescents." A general atmosphere of tension between youth and their elders existed—a generation gap that cut across class, race, ethnicity, and region. See Fass, *The Damned and the Beautiful.*

42. Shelit interview, p. 18; Taylor, *Mexican Labor,* 2:199–200; interview with María Fierro, *Rosie the Riveter,* 12:10.

43. Gamio, *Mexican Immigration,* p. 89. The verse taken from "Las Pelonas" in the original Spanish follows:

Los paños colorados
  Los tengo aborrecidos
Ya hora las pelonas
  Los usan de vestidos.

Las muchachas de S. Antonio
Son flojas pa'l metate
Quieren andar pelonas
Con sombreros de petate.
Se acabaron las pizcas,
Se acabó el algodón
Ya andan las pelonas
De puro vacilón.

44. Taylor, *Mexican Labor*, 2:vi–vii.

45. *La Opinión*, September 18, 1926; May 9, 1927; June 5, 1927. Using endorsements from famous people was a common advertising technique (see Marchand, *Advertising the American Dream*, pp. 96–102).

46. Rodolfo F. Acuña, *A Community under Siege: A Chronicle of Chicanos East of the Los Angeles River, 1945–1975* (Los Angeles: Chicano Studies Research Center, University of California, 1984), pp. 278, 407–408, 413–414, 418, 422; *FTA News*, May 1, 1945; Escobar interview. For an example of the promotion of a beauty pageant, see issues of *La Opinión*, June–July 1927.

47. Escobar interview.

48. Sherna B. Gluck, *Rosie the Riveter Revisited: Women, the War and Social Change* (Boston: Twayne, 1987), pp. 81, 85.

49. Letter from Carey McWilliams dated October 3, 1937, to Louis Adamic, *Adamic File*, Carton 1, Carey McWilliams Collection, Special Collections, University of California, Los Angeles.

50. Martínez Mason interview, pp. 29–30; Escobar interview; Fierro interview, p. 15; Estrada interview, pp. 11–12. Chaperonage was also common in Italian immigrant communities. Indeed, many of the same conflicts between parents and daughters had surfaced a generation earlier among Italian families on the East Coast (Peiss, *Cheap Amusements*, pp. 69–70, 152).

51. Hernández Milligan interview, p. 17.

52. Evangeline Hymer, "A Study of the Social Attitudes of Adult Mexican Immigrants in Los Angeles and Vicinity: 1923," M.A. thesis, University of Southern California, 1924 (rpt. San Francisco: R and E Research Associates, 1971), pp. 24–25.

53. Escobar interview; Estrada interview, pp. 11, 13.

54. Estrada interview, p. 12; also Shelit interview, p. 9; Ríos-Bustamante and Castillo, *An Illustrated History*, p. 153.

55. Taylor field notes; Thurston, "Urbanization," p. 118; Bogardus, *The Mexican in the United States*, pp. 28–29, 57–58.

56. Martínez Mason interview, p. 30; interview with Beatrice Morales Clifton, in *Rosie the Riveter*, 8:14–15.

57. Shelit interview, pp. 9, 24, 30; Escobar interview; Martínez Mason interview, p. 30; Hernández Milligan interview, pp. 27–28; Taylor field notes.

58. Luna Mount interview; Fierro interview, p. 18; Luna interview, p. 29; Gregorita Rodriguez, *Singing for My Echo* (Santa Fe: Cota Editions, 1987), p. 52; Martínez Mason interview, p. 62.

59. "Elisa Morales," Manuel Gamio field notes, Bancroft Library, University of California, Berkeley, 1 box.

60. Taylor field notes; Taylor, *Mexican Labor*, 2:vi–vii; Gamio, *Mexican Immigration*, p. 89.

The *corrido* "El Enganchado" (in *Mexican Labor,* vol. 2) offers an intriguing glimpse into attitudes toward women and Americanization.

61. Wilson and Gutiérrez, *Minorities and Media,* p. 86.

62. Tuck, *Not with the Fist,* p. 115; Shelit interview, p. 26.

63. Tuck, *Not with the Fist,* p. 115.

64. Taylor, *Mexican Labor,* 1:205–206; Ruiz, "Oral History and La Mujer," pp. 227–228; Sanchez, "The Rise of the Second Generation," pp. 7–10, 12; Escheverria Mulligan interview, p. 17.

65. Kenneth L. Roberts, "The Docile Mexican," *Saturday Evening Post,* March 10, 1928, as quoted in Sanchez, " 'Go After the Women,' " p. 8.

66. Rodolfo Acuña, *Occupied America: A History of Chicanos,* 2nd ed. (New York: Harper and Row, 1980), pp. 138, 140–141; Albert Camarillo, *Chicanos in California* (San Francisco: Boyd and Fraser, 1984), pp. 48–49; Abraham Hoffman, *Unwanted Mexican Americans in the Great Depression* (Tucson: University of Arizona Press, 1974), pp. 43–66; Francisco E. Balderrama, *In Defense of La Raza: The Los Angeles Mexican Consulate and the Mexican Community, 1929–1936* (Tucson: University of Arizona Press, 1982), pp. 16–20; Neil Betten and Raymond A. Mohl, "From Discrimination to Repatriation: Mexican Life in Gary, Indiana, during the Great Depression," in *The Chicano,* ed. Norris Hundley (Santa Barbara, Calif.: ABC-Clio Press, 1975), pp. 132, 138–139.

67. Sanchez, "The Rise of the Second Generation," p. 10.

68. Albert Camarillo, "Mexican American Urban History in Comparative Ethnic Perspective," Distinguished Speakers Series, University of California, Davis, January 26, 1987; Acuña, *Occupied America,* pp. 310, 318, 323, 330–331; Romo, *East Los Angeles,* p. 139; Tuck, *Not with the Fist,* pp. 51, 53; Shelit interview, p. 15.

69. Taylor, *Mexican Labor,* 1:221–224; interview with María Arredondo, March 19, 1986, conducted by Carolyn Arredondo.

70. Heller Committee, *How Mexicans Earn and Live,* pp. 68–69, 72. Text quotation is from Camarillo, *Chicanos in a Changing Society,* p. 215.

71. Tuck, *Not with the Fist,* pp. 209–210.

72. Barrera, *Race and Class in the Southwest,* pp. 82–91; Mario T. García, *Desert Immigrants: The Mexicans of El Paso, 1880–1920* (New Haven, Conn.: Yale University Press, 1981), pp. 110–126; Gilbert González, "Racism, Education, and the Mexican Community in Los Angeles, 1920–30," *Societas* 4 (Autumn 1974): 287–300.

73. González, "Chicanas and Mexican Immigrant Families," pp. 63–66; Taylor, *Mexican Labor,* 1:162–166, 176–179, 190–191, 217, 220, 227–228 (quote from p. 220).

74. Melville, "Selective Acculturation," pp. 159–160; John García, "Ethnicity and Chicanos," *Hispanic Journal of Behavioral Sciences* 4 (1982): 310–311.

75. Sanchez, "The Rise of the Second Generation," pp. 7–9; Guadalupe San Miguel, Jr., "Culture and Education in the American Southwest: Towards an Explanation of Chicano School Attendance," *Journal of American Ethnic History* 7 (Spring 1988): 15, 17; *La Opinión,* June 5, 1927.

76. "Sra. ——," Manuel Gamio field notes.

77. Clark, *Health in the Mexican American Culture,* p. 92.

78. Ibid.

79. Ruiz, *Cannery Women, Cannery Lives;* Shelit interview, pp. 52–55; Sherna Berger Gluck, "Interlude or Change: Women and the World War II Work Experience," pp. 14,

32–34 (rev. version of paper originally published in *International Journal of Oral History* 3 [1982]; courtesy of author); see also Gluck, *Rosie the Riveter Revisited.*

80. William H. Chafe, *The American Woman: Her Changing Social, Economic, and Political Roles, 1920–1970* (New York: Oxford University Press, 1972), pp. 137–143, 146; Barrera, *Race and Class in the Southwest,* pp. 131, 140–145.

81. Shelit interview, p. 32; Escheverria Mulligan interview, p. 14; Richard Griswold del Castillo, *La Familia: Chicano Families in the Urban Southwest, 1848 to the Present* (Notre Dame, Ind.: University of Notre Dame Press, 1984), pp. 120–122.

82. Many of the husbands were skilled workers in the aerospace industry. The highest occupation for a spouse was firefighter.

83. Clark, *Health in the Mexican American Culture,* p. 20.

84. Tuck, *Not with the Fist,* p. 134. According to historian Richard Griswold del Castillo (in *La Familia,* p. 126), "present-day Chicano families are a bridge between the social and cultural heritages of Anglo and Latin America."

85. I gratefully acknowledge the research assistance of Amagda Pérez and Christine Marin. I appreciate the generosity and longstanding support of Sherna Gluck, who has given me permission to quote from eight volumes of the *Rosie the Riveter Revisited* oral history collection housed at California State University, Long Beach. I also wish to thank the American Council of Learned Societies and the Committee on Research, University of California, Davis, for financial support of this project. Roland Marchand, Ramón Gutiérrez, and Howard Shorr provided incisive comments on earlier drafts, and I appreciate their interest in my work.

EIGHT

The Mother Motif in *La Bamba* and *Boulevard Nights*

Rosa Linda Fregoso

Filmmaking was one of the new cultural practices to emerge out of the Chicano and Chicana Cultural Renaissance of the 1960s. Besides encoding a vision of social reality, filmmakers sought to challenge the authority of the dominant culture—an authority that rested on stereotyped characterizations, omissions, and distortions about the population of Mexican origin in this country. The Chicano and Chicana themes in these films contested the dominant group's historic license to define and delimit the Chicano and Chicana social experience. The filmmakers' cinematic practices, albeit didactic, nevertheless offered an alternative historical account of our social conditions. Most of the early films were financed by public means, such as grants from the Corporation for Public Broadcasting, the National Endowment for the Arts, and other grant agencies. The ascent of Reaganomics marked a turning point for alternative filmmaking. As public funds for alternative cinema were curtailed by the Reagan regime, filmmakers sought to secure other means, from "private" sources, in order to finance their cultural products. These means included but were not limited to the Hollywood studio apparatus.

Former Teatro Campesino director Luis Valdez, for instance, obtained a modest (by Hollywood standards) budget of $2.5 million from Universal Studios to film the stage production of *Zoot Suit*. The filmed play was released in 1981 throughout the country. Part of a corporate strategy to reach Chicano audiences (or, as Universal's executive Ned Tanen would say, "to break into the 'Hispanic' market"), *Zoot Suit* failed to provide the projected market returns.[1]

In the late 1970s, the Coors Corporation designated the 1980s the Decade of the Hispanic. However, not until the commercial success of *La Bamba* (1987) and *Born in East L.A.* (1987) was the Hollywood film industry once again convinced of the market viability of Chicano cinema.[2] The international success of both films exemplifies a broader trend, by no way limited to Chicano cinema, of capitalizing on minority groups and the market potential for their "marginal" subject matter. For Chicanos and Chicanas, this "crossover phenomenon" exemplifies a new phase in filmmaking, since it marks the interest by a wider audience in our cultural themes. However, the "crossover phenomenon" also marks a major shift not only in the reception but also in the production of Chicano cinema. That is, in this new phase, the audience for Chicano cinema has expanded beyond the "restricted" small circle of viewers in universities, public broadcasting stations, schools, and cultural (film) festivals and into the broader sphere of popular culture. At the same time, production within the dominant film "apparatus" may compromise certain crucial aspects of the symbolic struggle against the hegemonic forms of the dominant culture.[3] The adoption of the Hollywood model by Chicano cultural producers signals the transformation of Chicano cinema from an alternative form into a genre within dominant cinema.

This essay is peripherally concerned with contesting the celebratory posture of access by Chicano filmmakers to the commercial mainstream. My analysis, however, specifically deals with the reproduction of the dominant model for imaging Chicanas.[4] Through an analysis of the mother motif, I will illustrate the extent to which a Chicano-directed film, *La Bamba,* reproduces the dominant discourse on woman. A comparative reading of two films will demonstrate that this dominant mode of representing motherhood is also encapsulated in another non-Chicano-directed film with significant Chicano thematic content, *Boulevard Nights* (1978).

Feminist analysis of the images of woman has shifted from an initial phase of enumerating "positive" and "negative" stereotypes to an examination of the way that women operate or function as characters in the narrative. This textual focus has resulted from studies of the ways in which subjectivity is constructed in the film-viewing process. In other words, feminist film analysis focuses on ways to understand the viewers' productive relation to the film text by reaffirming the text's ability to "map" a social vision for the viewing subject. Through semiotics and linguistically based psychoanalysis, used as tools for decoding dominant discourse, conjoined with the feminist critique of male-centered principles inherent in Lacanian and Freudian models,[5] analysts have deciphered the major strategy for imaging woman in the dominant cinema: in films, woman is represented as spectacle, as object, as fetish, and as the embodiment of male desire. As Teresa de Lauretis sums it up: "The dominant cinema specifies woman in a particular social and natural order, sets her up in certain positions of meaning, fixes her in certain identifications."[6]

My analysis departs from the concern with "positive" or "negative" stereotypes of Chicanos and Chicanas in cinema.[7] I am concerned primarily with discourse as a means of expression in film. Therefore, instead of focusing on the image as a reflection of "real women," I will consider woman as a structure within the organization of the narrative. In contrast to the "tendency to collapse the opposition between sign (the image) and the 'real,' " which informs studies of stereotypes, discourse analysis seeks to unveil how the woman character is situated in a specific position within the text."[8] A formal approach that concerns "how" meaning is produced, or the process of meaning production, within the film text helps us understand the degree to which the woman image operates as signifier. Since characters are vehicles for narrative action, discourse analysis explains the way in which the woman is arranged deliberately and functions as a sign, a signifier, and the embodiment of male desire in the narrative. I will consequently be concerned with how mother is positioned as the "bearer" rather than the "maker" of narrative meaning—that is to say, how she is thus "representation." Of the various images of woman portrayed in the dominant cinema, I will center my study on that of the mother, which, as Williams and Rich concede, "has been one of the most censored and distorted images produced by patriarchy."[9]

THE MOTHER MOTIF IN DOMINANT DISCOURSE

Central concerns for feminism are the female body—and, by extension, control over the site of human reproduction, the womb—as well as the question of motherhood, the capacity to reproduce the human species. In recent times, motherhood has surfaced as a crucial site of contestation in feminist analysis, filmmaking, and women's writings. Julia Kristeva's analysis of the Renaissance artists Giovanni Bellini and Leonardo da Vinci, for example, addresses the male rendition of motherhood in their paintings. The Mother, as the agent and possessor of a "tangible space of production in the womb,"[10] not only is absent as a speaking subject from the dominant discourse of Western thought but her voice has been appropriated by that discourse. "This becoming-a-mother, this gestation, can possibly be accounted for by means of only two discourses. There is *science;* but as an objective discourse, science is not concerned with the subject, the mother as site of her own proceedings. There is *Christian theology* (especially canonical theology); but the theology defines maternity only as an impossible elsewhere, a sacred beyond, a vessel of divinity, a spiritual tie with the ineffable godhead, and transcendence's ultimate support—necessarily virginal and committed to assumption."[11]

The appropriation takes a perverse form in the science of the subject, psychoanalysis, which, as it has been applied to women, follows the trajectory of other objective sciences. The inability to specify the moment-of-becoming that is necessarily maternity, the impossibility of grounding the contradictory subject in the mother's position, however, is central to the symbolic distortions and absences that Kristeva deconstructs: "As long as there is language-symbolism-paternity, there will never be any other way to represent, to objectify, to explain this unsettling of the symbolic stratum, this nature culture threshold, this instilling the subjectless biological program into the very body of a symbolizing subject, this event called motherhood."[12] The moment and the act have, as Kristeva's essay discloses, nonetheless been described and represented in the various cultural forms produced by the dominant discourse.

Moreover, two modalities inhabit these dominant depictions of motherhood from outside the mother-subject. First, there is idealization, or the "cult of the mother—tenderness, love and the seat of social conservation";[13] second, one finds the "patriarchal illusion of an all powerful and whole phallic mother."[14] Both forms are inscribed in dominant ideology's views of the mother. Chodorow and Contratto, for instance, trace this inscription of motherhood to the ideology of the nineteenth century and locate it in recent post-Freudian psychology. The authors propose that, as a result of these dual beliefs, one can both "blame mothers for any failings in their children" and at the same time "idealize possible mother perfection."[15] The contradiction in dominant ideology is, in turn, reinforced by "the contradiction of woman's experience in patriarchal culture," which, according to Kegan Gardiner, "defines the 'mind' as male and mother as mindless mat(t)er whose responsibility is total and whose authority is denied."[16] More important, however, dominant ideology is scaffolded by the "modern" predicament of the mothering practice. In other words, it is an ideology that, as Chodorow and Contratto explain, "gains meaning from and is partly produced by infantile fantasies that are themselves the outcome of being mothered exclusively by one woman."[17]

From a child-centered perspective, the mother is both feared and idealized. As a mother, the woman envelops the totality of the child's universe. She is the *giver* and, by a strange logic, the potential *taker* of the child's life: "For the infant, the mother is not someone with her own life, wants, needs, history and social relationships, work. She is known only in her capacity as mother."[18] And if the center of this universe, the child, develops pathology, blame is directed at the mother. As Spiegel aptly states: "To whatever extent we have believed that mothers do something special for their children, we have always been more willing to believe that failures in mothering do something devastating to children."[19]

In this scenario, the child assumes the bench of bequeathing both judgment and perpetual distortions about motherhood. The child maneuvers from a site that Kristeva calls the "point of view of social cohesion, which is the place where legislators, grammarians and even psychoanalysts have their seats; which is where everyone is made homologous to the male speaking body."[20] In contemporary thought, the dominant specification of the mother in a particular order, however, is incomplete without a mention of its framing by Freudian accounts of sexuality. For the site from which the child passes judgment feeds on male fantasies and male-derived accounts, which posit woman as the castrating mother. In psychoanalysis, according to Kristeva: "The dominant discourse of analysis proves that the desire for motherhood is without fail a *desire* to bear the child of the father (a child of her own father) who, as a result, is often assimilated to the baby itself and thus returned to its place as a *devalorized man*, summoned to accomplish his function, which is to originate and justify reproductive desire."[21]

This narrative on sexuality and on the female predicament that Freud would refer to as "penis envy" reveals a child speaking as a male, speaking as a psychoanalyst. All three male subjects thus form a trinity that abrogates the mother as the speaking subject in the same Oedipal stroke that they uphold the "myth of maternal omnipotence."

THE MOTHER MOTIF IN CINEMA

The Oedipal narrative on maternity, as well as on female sexuality and the position of women in the social order, finds an appropriate form in dominant cinema. In recent years, feminist film theory has shown the extent to which mainstream films rearticulate various Freudian themes.[22] Because of its capacity for symbolizing reality, cinema contributes to the reproduction of reality; yet this process is in no way innocent or without social consequences, for as de Lauretis reminds us: "What is called reproduction—as women well know—is never simply natural or simply technical, never spontaneous, automatic, without labor, without pain, without desire, without engagement of subjectivity."[23] Therefore, in a complicity with authoritative discourse, mainstream films have encoded hegemonic forms of motherhood. Through a device that Williams and Rich identify as devaluation and sanctification, even the Hollywood genre of *women's films,* a genre that assumes the female point of view, presents distorted forms of the mother: "Pretending to sanctify the institution of motherhood, they more often exalt its ideal while punishing and humiliating the individual women who participate in it."[24]

THE MOTHER MOTIF IN CHICANO CINEMA

Boulevard Nights, directed by Michael Pressman, was released in 1978. The film reconstructs the Chicano barrio experience in East Los Angeles from a dominant perspective. In other words, drawing from the hegemonic forms of the dominant media, *Boulevard Nights* encodes Chicanos as social problems. It was the forcefulness of the tropes on Chicanos—namely, the reproduction of the dominant media's images about Chicano violence, gangs, and drug use—that prompted boycotts and pickets in the Los Angeles area.[25]

La Bamba, directed by Luis Valdez, concerns the rise to fame of rock star Ritchie Valens (or Ricardo Valenzuela), a California Chicano. The story's plot is propelled by means of a dream sequence and the triangular relation between two brothers, Ritchie and Bob, and their mother, Connie. *La Bamba* begins with a dream sequence of a plane crash and ends in the fulfillment of the dream: the tragic death of Ritchie Valens along with two other rock stars, Buddy Holly and the Big Bopper. The film registers a circular view of history in prefiguring its own ending through the dream sequence. Moreover, director Luis Valdez renders the story of Ritchie Valens from the point of view of Bob, the "bad" brother. The relationship of these brothers-as-subjects to the mother-character-object moves the narrative action.

As depicted by *Boulevard Nights,* the story of Chicano barrio life is rendered in terms of a character contrast between two brothers: the elder, Ramon, and the younger brother, who is referred to only as "Chuco." As in *La Bamba,* the brothers in *Boulevard Nights* embody the dichotomy of "good" Chicano / "bad" Chicano. Ramon, for instance, works for a living, has a "decent" girlfriend, and exhibits a protective attitude toward his mother. Chuco, on the other hand, leans to the gang life-style. Despite his brother's efforts to provide guidance, Chucho is destined to reproduce the vicious cycle of gang behavior. The younger brother's death at the end of the film befits the life framed by the dominant culture's perspective on the Chicano/a social experience.

La Bamba begins in 1957 in a farmworkers' camp in northern California. Ritchie, three siblings, and the mother are working on the orange harvest. As the credits begin, Bob enters the film, riding on a motorcycle at high speed and sporting a leather jacket and dark sunglasses. Coded this way to embody the "dark" side of pleasure, the good-looking Bob seductively low-rides down the highway to the background music, "Who do you love" by Bo Diddley, and into the migrant camp where his family is living. The film establishes the structural contrast between the "good"/"bad" brothers in the initial sequences. We learn that Bob has served "time" in the penitentiary while Ritchie displays a passion for music and a dedication to his *familia.* Bob comes to visit his family in order to take them out of the poverty of farmwork, an effort that of course requires money. When Bob gives his mother a roll of dollars, the mother casts doubt on their origin: "I mean honest money," she says. Bob assures her that he has been working. Yet while he does provide the means for his family to leave the misery of migrant work, the following scene denies Bob the ability to assume the "good" son-provider role.

Casting further doubt on Bob, an early scene shows him in sexual intercourse with Ritchie's "virgin" girlfriend while Ritchie is at the campside entertaining the farmworkers with his guitar and songs. This tendency to image Bob as the "bad" brother gains momentum as the film progresses. During the first quarter of the film, in alternating sequences between separate cinematic spaces of Bob and Ritchie, Bob sells marijuana while Ritchie makes his first attempts to join a rock band. Other contrasts maintained in this alternating sequence include the unhealthy relationship between Bob and Rosie (Ritchie's farmworker girlfriend) and Bob's "bad" behavior; he rarely comes home at night, drinks, smokes marijuana, and forces sex on Rosie when he does come home. Ritchie, on the other hand, hangs around with "clean-cut" musicians, attends high school, and experiences his first adolescent love, for an impeccable white girl, Donna. Additionally, this polarity between the two brothers gains added meaning by the absence of a literal father—an absence that artistically reflects the contemporary historical circumstances of Chicanas as single heads of household. The role of the father substitute necessarily falls to the eldest male; however, Bob's depiction as the "bad" son precludes that role for him. Ritchie thus becomes the proper stand-in for the absent father at the same time that he assumes the role of the family's main provider. And, while the mother has her own interests in work outside the home, she is narratively rendered, to the detriment of Bob, as obsessed with the "good" son's own career as a rock musician.

Similarly, the story of *Boulevard Nights* depends on the absence of a father character as well as on the absence of the mother as speaking subject within the narrative. The "good" brother thus functions as the father-husband substitute in relation to both the mother and the "bad" brother. Although the mother character in *La Bamba* occupies more screen time, what is striking about *Boulevard Nights* is the centrality of the mother character to the plot's development. The mother character in this film serves a dual narrative function. In the first place, contrary to the interactions of mother and "good" brother, the film never shows any genuine closeness between Chuco and the mother. Second, her murder during Ramon and Shady's wedding by the rival 11th Street Gang sparks Chuco's act of revenge, which ultimately brings about his own death. In order to deconstruct the mechanism that positions mother as a narrative function and as an object in the process of narrativization, we must first examine in greater detail how the male characters are constructed as subjects in both films.

The "Good" Brother as Father-Husband

Ritchie's character incarnates the Chicano desire for a piece of the American pie. The "good" brother is, after all, the Chicano version of the all-American, clean-cut type. The minor reference to racism in the 1950s is made by Donna's father, who comments that Ritchie looks Italian—an ethnic designation which, for an Anglo Californian, distanced from the East Coast Anglo-Italian conflicts, certainly signifies "better Italian than Mexican." The fact that Ritchie makes it as a rock musician, on the dominant culture's terms, reinforces the hegemonic belief in individualism. This illusory ideology corresponds to the film's romanticization of the life-style and social experience of rock musicians.[26]

A poor working-class boy rising to the stars and winning the love of a proper middle-class girl symbolizes Chicano social mobility. Ritchie, moreover, represents everything a Chicano mother could dream of. After Ritchie's refusal to record his first song without the rest of the members of his band, the promoter poses the following choice for Ritchie: "What's more important, your friends or your music?" Like an exemplary Chicano, Ritchie responds: "My family." Consequently, the mother, as her comments illustrate, looks on Ritchie as an ideal son: "Oh, Ritchie, you're the best." "Look at my Ritchie, shining like a star." "Ritchie is wonderful." In her excess of love for the "good" son, Connie becomes a perverse subject. In his all-enveloping goodness, the film represents Ritchie as an illusory, unified, noncontradictory, and "essentially" Chicano subject.

In the narrative of *Boulevard Nights,* Ramon occupies the space of the "good" brother with both "normal" and "healthy" relationships and occupations. He lifts weights, has a steady job at the Body Shop, and has maintained a stable relationship with a woman who comes from a "normal" Chicano family. While he exhibits a fascination with cars (evident in the kind of job he holds, in the care he takes of his own car, and in his enjoyment of cruising down the boulevard on weekend nights), Ramon abandons this adolescent fetish at the insistence of a girlfriend who wants to get married. The film also draws attention to the fact that, as a barrio boy, Ramon had been previously involved in gang activity. While this reference to Ramon's earlier history is outside the narrative setting, it nonetheless functions to solidify the mature role that the "good" brother character is destined to occupy within the process of narrativization.

The first part of the film sets the parameters for Ramon's place as the father substitute. In the first sequence, as the 11th Street Gang member defaces graffiti on VGV turf, Chuco and the home boys gang up on the *bato* from 11th Street. Ramon arrives to end the gang-style beating and thus establishes his role as the regulator of Chuco's behavior. In the next sequence, Ramon, lifting weights, assumes the parental function of waking up the child by yelling, "Chuco, get your ass up, man, and get dressed." Ramon maintains this fatherlike stance throughout the film; however, it is a role that in this sequence is reinforced by the mother character's remarks to Ramon: "Chuco's gonna be late. At least make sure he looks good." The next sequence reveals that they are worried about Chuco's appearance because Ramon is taking him to the Body Shop to get him a job. During this job interview with Gil, we learn why Chuco is a high school dropout: "There was a fight in the cafeteria. . . . I wasn't in it but I took out my *filero* just in case . . . and the principal busted me for it."

The "Bad" Brother as Victim-Child

Chuco's account of the cafeteria incident recapitulates a dominant textual strategy contained in the film: the victimization of the "bad" brother. Things, indeed, happen to Chuco. In the opening sequence, a member of the 11th Street Gang penetrates VGV turf and thereby pays for this violation. The beating by the VGV then propels the plot's development. In retribution for this initial beating, the 11th Street Gang retaliates against VGV on the boulevard. Here Chuco accidentally stabs an 11th Street Gang member. Later a VGV member is beaten as is Ramon, and the VGV takes revenge by decimating an 11th Street member's car. In an endless cycle of action and reaction, the point to highlight is the progressive incarceration of the "bad" brother within a unidirectional narrative space. This narrativization, however, underscores that circumstances beyond Chuco's control and against his will provoke his transgressions. In a painful exchange with Ramon, Chuco explains: "I wanted to be at your wedding, man. I just get real mad and I wanna do something . . . but I don't know what to do . . . I just get real mad and fuck up and I do something wrong."

Chuco's efforts to maintain a stable job fail, and the VGV home boys pull him further into the cycle of drugs and violence. However, Chuco is not imaged with the same "deviant" and "violent" codes as are his home-boy friends. In addition to the narrative focus that absolves Chuco, the film encodes the "bad" brother in childlike features. This quality evokes viewer sympathy for Chuco and offers instances whereby we may interpret Chuco's behavior as that of an adolescent who needs attention. The film's coding of Chuco in facial features that are almost pathetic, innocent, and childlike draws viewers to identify with the character's plight and to feel sorry for the evil he encounters. Ramon's words to Shady reiterate Chuco's victimization: "I knew when to get out. I don't know about Chuco. The shit's coming down and he's gonna be right in the middle of it all."

The dominant character attributes associated with Chuco are those of a victim-child in need of guidance and attention. And two scenes where the "bad" brother interacts with a caged bird reinforce this sympathetic reading. In a sequence at the beginning of the film, Chuco asks the bird: "Hey, Negrito, are you my friend? Are you my friend?" If Ramon and the caged bird circumscribe Chuco's affective universe, the progressive involvement of Ramon with his girlfriend permits the VGV home boys to draw Chuco further into their domain. Consequently, as Ramon spends more time planning his wedding, Chuco's involvement with the VGV in acts of crime, drugs, and violence intensifies. He sniffs paint, is late for work, and spends his nights on the streets with the VGV. Finally, in a fight scene at the Body Shop, Chuco accidentally strikes the boss and is fired. The furious Ramon yells at Chuco: "I gotta watch over you all the time or you fuck up. You think you're bad but you're dumb." With a painful but defiant face, Chuco responds: "I ain't dumb." That comment—as well as the fact that, living in East Los Angeles, Chuco has "never been to the beach before"—elicits sympathy for the younger brother-victim.

Contrary to the illusion of a unified subject that the "good" Chicano Ritchie represents, one finds a complexity in Bob's characterization. The "bad" brother is the contradictory subject of the film. At one level, the film encodes Bob with negative attributes; for instance, he is physically and emotionally abusive to his live-in girlfriend, Rosie. After he forces intercourse on Rosie, she reveals: "I'm pregnant. Aren't you gonna say anything." For a brief moment, it seems as though Bob will change his behavior toward Rosie. However, subverting the conventional expectations of both viewers and Rosie, Bob responds: "What's there to say? It's not my first, or my last."

To Ritchie, Bob often exhibits jealousy and scorn. At the same time, the film emphasizes Bob's love for his younger brother. For example, scenes where Bob manifests jealousy or scorn are followed by scenes in which Bob is helpful and supportive toward Ritchie. This contradiction is best illustrated by the discrepant representation of Bob in two sequences filmed back to back. In a kitchen scene, Bob is ridiculed by Ritchie, the mother, and Rosie for his lack of talent. Bob storms out of the house in a fury. Yet in the scene following this incident, and even after the mother has referred to Bob as a "flunky," a series of alternating sequences depict Bob staying up late in Ritchie's room and designing the posters announcing Ritchie's performance. Moreover, Bob, along with his drug-abusing biker friends, joins the family in distributing posters for Ritchie's debut.

This discrepancy in the process of narrativizing the "bad" brother figures as a cinematic strategy for infusing Bob with the character attributes of victim. A deeper reading of the characterization reveals that, even though the "bad" brother's actions may often seem distasteful, the negative codes demand reading in their relation to the other side of Bob's psyche. As we learn, Bob is not the "natural" son of Steve, Ritchie's father. During the scene where he sleeps in Ritchie's room, Bob notices Steve's picture on Ritchie's night stand. After learning that the mother had given Ritchie this picture, the "bad" brother shares his regret for missing Steve's funeral but adds: "He was your dad anyway and not mine." Closer to the end of the film, as Ritchie's success becomes more prominent, Bob's jealousy intensifies. During a welcoming party in Ritchie's honor, Bob leaves the party for the guest house. Ritchie enters the scene to find Bob looking at the picture of Steve. The following emotional dialogue culminates in the only violent exchange between the brothers:

Ritchie: What's your problem, man.
Bob: Ol' Steve, boy, he always said you were gonna be somebody and I bought it too. That's the way Steve wanted it and that's the way it was gonna be. Even after he told me he wasn't my dad. Then when I knew he was full of school, I understood, man. I realized why he always treated you a little bit better. That's how much I loved him, like a god-damned dog!
Ritchie: Hey Bob. We don't have to talk about this right now.
Bob: No, shit no. I wanna talk about it and you're gonna listen to me.
Ritchie: This is a crock of shit.
Bob: No. He set you up to conquer the world and he didn't leave me shit.
Ritchie: Nobody told you to throw your life away, man. I'm only sorry I didn't say something about you being drunk half the time. You did it to yourself.

Since his love for his stepfather is signified by his holding the picture, the film encodes the "bad" brother as fatherless victim. Ritchie's response during this encounter carries minimal semantic weight in light of other prevalent attributes assigned to Bob in the textualizing process.

For instance, Bob often appears childlike, as is evident in the scene during his rounds as a garbage collector. As Bob finds a stack of drawings in a trash can, he says to his partner: "Hey, look at this, it's Woody Woodpecker. . . . They make cartoons out of this." This discovery prompts Bob to enter a drawing contest, where he succeeds in winning the grand prize of $500 in art supplies. Rosie's attitude of minimizing his prize provokes Bob's angry response: "You don't respect anything I do." Later Ritchie comes in and finds Bob appearing depressed as he is playing with a pet rabbit. The importance of this depiction rests on its place within the narrative, for the sequences that feature Bob's involvement with cartoon drawing are interlaced with sequences showing Ritchie's involvement in the more socially prominent world of recording. Thus, in comparison to Ritchie's success in the real (adult) world, Bob's accomplishment cannot be taken seriously. Bob's cartoon drawings and the prize he obtains signify an adult succeeding in a childish world. For Chicano/a viewers, Bob's "little" success evokes a favorite cultural commentary of *pobrecito* (poor little one). With this understanding of how the brothers are imaged, we can begin to deconstruct the narrative function of the mother as object within the text.

The Phallic Mother

Inscribed in the polarities of "good/bad" brothers, we find the mother displaced from any subject position within the narrative. In both films, her relationship with one brother stands in opposition to her relationship with the other brother. The narrative's development centers on this contrast between the mother's interaction with each of the brother characters. In the first place, we find a positive interaction with the "good" brother. For example, the second sequence of the film establishes the "healthy" exchange between Ramon and the mother. As both discuss Chuco, the mother makes reference to her strained back, which Ramon then proceeds to massage. Throughout the film, whenever the "good" brother and the mother characters interact, their mutual physical and emotional closeness is visually reinforced. This spatial proximity is further accentuated with dialogue, such as the mother's words "Ay, que guapo mijo. Porque me parezco a ti." The fact that Ramon regulates Chuco's behavior, coupled with the absence of a literal father and the mother's recurring references to Chuco's misbehavior, serves to position Ramon as the stand-in for the absent father. Moreover, the positive mother–"good" son relation functions as a mechanism whereby viewers can levy judgment against the mother–"bad" brother interaction.

In contrast to her intimacy with Ramon, the mother character is fabricated as distant from Chuco. This lack of closeness between Chuco and the mother helps to legitimate the "bad" brother's pathology. The prevalent imaging of Chuco in childlike qualities emphasizes his need for maternal warmth. His apparent innocence begs for nurturing. He warrants an understanding touch and a sympathetic look from the mother, which he does not receive. Moreover, in her concern for Chuco, questions such as "How's he doing?" or "Does Gil like him?" are directed at Ramon. In fact, throughout the film, the mother appears only three times in the same visual space as Chuco. Each time, moreover, their mutual exchange is problematic. In their first interaction, the mother simply says: "It's late, Chuco." Her look appears critical and distant, and she is thereby faulted for Chuco's negativity.

Thus, the central ideological imperative of the film reinforces the dominant culture's tendency to blame the mother for the child's pathology. Her spatial distance from Chuco positions viewers as the mother's critics. Since we are shown her positive interaction with Ramon, the film is mapping a judgment against the mother character, who is ultimately made responsible for Chuco's destiny.

Besides blaming the mother, *Boulevard Nights* also inscribes her as a castrating mother. For example, in the scene that follows the fight on the boulevard, Chuco's subsequent arrest, and his release, the mother waits in the car parked outside the jail. She sits silently in the front seat as Ramon and Chuco enter. Chuco sits in the back seat, and, as Ramon drives off, Chuco approaches the mother: "Ma, I just wanna say . . ." The mother interrupts: "No, quiero oir nada." The next sequence visualizes Chuco outside, looking sadly at the bird Negrito. The mother's attitude toward Chuco thus devalorizes the "bad" brother. Faced with a castrating mother, Chuco projects his desire for maternal love and warmth onto Negrito. Since she fails in her socially assigned function of comforting, protecting, and nurturing, she is thus imaged as a bad mother to Chuco.

After he is fired from his job, Chuco disappears for over a week. He fails to show up for the wedding but does come to the party. In his conversation with Ramon, Chuco appears to repent and to indicate that he will change his old ways. It is thus fitting that the only positive exchange between Chuco and the mother takes place in this scene. When Chuco enters the house with Ramon, the mother asks Chuco to dance with her. He reluctantly accepts. However, the scene turns to melodrama, for—as Chuco is happily learning how to dance—a gunshot meant for Chuco strikes the mother. She tragically falls from Chuco's arms. Her death, nonetheless, functions as a vehicle for narrative action. The mother's murder is a signifier for the "bad" brother's need to avenge the action. In other words, the mother's death serves as a mechanism that propels the brother character once again into gang violence. Ultimately, the "bad" brother kills the responsible 11th Street Gang member, yet Chuco will pay with his own death as well.

In *La Bamba,* the maternal figure is excessively absorbed in the "good" son. The mother overinvests in the details of Ritchie's career. She organizes his first debut, she watches his performance, she wants to be his manager, etc. Her endless obsession with Ritchie is contrasted with the cinematic distance she maintains from Bob. Ritchie lives up to her expectations. In fact, toward the end of the film, Ritchie buys Connie the "home of her dreams." By this time, viewers may well have forgotten that Bob provided the money for them to leave the migrant camp in the first place. More pronounced than in *Boulevard Nights,* the major strategy of *La Bamba* is to blame the mother for Bob's misfortunes. As such, the film degrades the mother figure by blaming her both for Bob's misfortunes and for his behavior. She embodies the maternal phallus: possessive with Ritchie, hostile to Bob. The mother's narrative function is to serve as textual (visual and narrative) reinforcement for Bob's negativity.

Bob's negative actions are visually and narratively linked to the mother's presence within the film. For instance, in the early scene where Bob is having intercourse with Ritchie's farmworker girlfriend, the mother is visually implicated in the act. The scene alternates between Ritchie playing his guitar to a group of farmworkers around the campfire and Bob and Rosie making love in the woods. Each cut from the campsite to the woods is preceded by a camera focus on the mother, who is shown looking off-screen left. The shot signifies her suspicion and distrust of Bob, but it also serves to interlink the mother with Bob's offense. While the visual rendition here suggests "mother in concern," as the plot develops and as viewers progressively identify with Bob, the mother becomes the narrative's causal factor for Bob's misbehavior.

The scene after Ritchie and Bob's performance in the country bar provides a textual glimpse of Connie's ridiculing attitude toward Bob: "You can be my flunkie"—a reference to the mother's wish to be Ritchie's manager. In this case, the mother and Ritchie are united in a mocking attitude toward Bob. However, Ritchie's debut, which his mother has organized at the VFW Hall, clearly accentuates the narrative distance between Bob and the mother. While Ritchie is performing, Bob enters the dance hall visibly drunk. His lewdness precipitates a full-fledged fight that ends Ritchie's performance. The following exchange between the mother and Bob illustrates Bob's internal turmoil:

Mother: How could you do this to Ritchie?
Bob: To Ritchie? I did this to me. You don't understand a god-damn thing.

For spectators, this exchange images Bob's deeper psychological trauma. As the story evolves, spectators are drawn to link Bob's trauma, his negativity and deviance, to a singular causal factor: the mother. The final element for piecing together the central locus of Bob's pathology surfaces in a scene toward the end of the film. Again in a drunken state, Bob wants to enter the house to see his daughter. Both Connie and Rosie are by the door, urging him to go away. "I just want to see my daughter," Bob yells. To that, the mother says: "Go downstairs and sober up. I have enough to worry about with Ritchie." Overwhelmed with indignation, Bob turns violent and yells back: "You always worry more about Ritchie. What about me? I know you don't give a damn about me. You had me turned in. You had me locked up. You think I could ever forgive you for that?" Neither will the viewers, for, through her son's own words, the mother character is ultimately to blame. As the speaking subject of the film, the "bad" brother imputes blame onto the mother, thereby excusing his actions and justifying his behavior.

This analysis of the Oedipal themes reproduced in both films would be incomplete without a mention of two other significant elements: eroticization and retribution. Both films, for instance, dramatize post-Freudian psychological accounts of the mother-son relation. The Freudian and Lacanian formulations about relations between the sexes are reinforced by the lack of the "real" father and the absence of the mother's involvement in other sexual relations in both films. And, while the split between the mothers and the "bad" brothers is thematically and concretely accentuated, the "good" brothers' girlfriends mediate "actual" incest between the mothers and the "good" sons. Both films eroticize the "good" son–mother relation through intimate touching and emotional-visual proximity. Connie's obsession with Ritchie clearly positions the mother as seductress. However, the girlfriends, as Mary Ann Doane explains about other similar films, "effectively block . . . the eroticization of the mother/son relation."[27] Structurally, since the mother character sublimates her desire for the "good" son in the girlfriend, in both films the mother character commits symbolic as opposed to "actual" incest.[28]

Particularly pertinent to the psychological orientation of both *La Bamba* and *Boulevard Nights* is the element of retribution. Both films end by punishing the mother for her own transgression. In *Boulevard Nights*, the mother's failure in her socially assigned functions of providing comforting and nurturing results in punishment through her own death. The fact that *La Bamba* is based on a "true" story does not minimize the element of retribution against the mother, particularly if we examine in detail how the film renders this historical fact.

Narrative closure takes place with the radio bulletin announcing the death of Ritchie Valens. Having heard this news bulletin, Bob goes to his mother's house. They face each other, and then the mother takes several steps away from Bob. As she is walking back, she begins to cry out, "No, no, not Ritchie. Never Ritchie, Bob. Not my Ritchie, not Ritchie. Not Ritchie, Bob." The final embrace between Bob and the mother articulates poetic irony. Certainly, since the words spoken by the mother begin as she is looking at Bob and culminate with their emotional embrace, viewers are moved to interpret her words as meaning something else as well. The narrative thrust forces us to interpolate that she must be thinking or perhaps wanted to say: "It should have been you, Bob. Why not you, Bob." Since the film's dominant tendency is to refuse the mother a subject role within the narrative at the same time that it disallows her any other interests or desires apart from Ritchie, the Ritchie Valens story advances an image of a sacrificial mother whose only object of desire is the "good" son. The film's portrayal of the mother in this manner necessitates her "just" reward. Thus, the death of Ritchie, her sole object of desire, signifies her punishment. More clearly than *Boulevard Nights, La Bamba* contains a buried "misogynist" subtext in this critique and punishment of the mother. As this final scene makes evident, the mother is left with a son-object whom she least desires. Consequently, in *La Bamba,* retribution is stronger, since the mother is punished twice: on the one hand, for her obsessive love for Ritchie, she is denied this object; on the other hand, for her devalorization of the "bad" brother, she is left, in the end, with Bob.

CONCLUSION

Both *La Bamba* and *Boulevard Nights* reproduce patriarchal-informed accounts of motherhood. In their representation of the mother character, both films deny the mother a subject position, and they blame the mother for "deviance" associated with the negative son, consequently providing a problematic and perverse rendition of the "good" son–mother relation. In their critique of the mother, both films are exceedingly informed by an infant's perspective on motherhood. Both films thereby exemplify the dominant culture's tendency to blame and idealize the mother. In *La Bamba* and in *Boulevard Nights,* she is idealized by the "good" son and blamed by the "bad" son. In this manner, the mother character in both films embodies what Doane has termed "the logic of the excluded middle," or the fact that in one subject we cannot locate a "happy medium." While it may appear that the mother character represents a contradictory or a nonunified essence, the films' textualizing process instead renders her as a polarized or a schizophrenic mother. To the good brother, she represents singular goodness; to the bad brother, badness. She thus embodies the maternal phallus, a polarized subject that serves to sublimate those fears associated with the maternal. As Doane indicates, the polarization of the mother "is a strategy for defusing, minimizing the effects of another diametrically opposed understanding of the maternal as the site of the collapse of all opposition and the confusion of identities."[29] The Oedipal construction of motherhood, rearticulated by both films, reaffirms as well what Julia Kristeva has shown: the impossibility of the mother-as-speaking-subject within male discourse. The cleavage of the maternal image advanced by both *La Bamba* and *Boulevard Nights* reflects the symbolic and social threat posed by women's sexuality. The male-derived fear of women's power to produce and reproduce the human species ultimately drives Gayatri Spivak to propose that the Freudian term for the construction of sexual difference and the marker for the subject's entry into the symbolic order, "penis envy," be replaced with a more appropriate designation: "womb envy."[30]

NOTES

1. Pat Aufderheide, "*Zoot Suit,*" *Film Quarterly* 36 (Winter 1983): 44–47.

2. Released in August of 1987, *La Bamba* grossed $51.5 million during its sixteen-week run in English and $15 million through its Spanish-language run of seventeen weeks ("Movie Studios Habla Español," *Hispanic Business,* July 1988, pp. 8–13).

3. "Ideological" consequences, for instance, have been noted by Jason Johansen, who warned that Chicano filmmakers needed to examine the effects of producing through Hollywood channels, which do not promote "questioning or reflection" ("Notas sobre el cine Chicano," *La Opinión,* November 16, 1980).

4. I am using *imaging* as Teresa de Lauretis defines the term: "the articulation of meaning to image, language and sound, and the viewer's subjective engagement in that process." Cinema's imaging, according to de Lauretis, plays a "role in the production of social reality" (*Alice Doesn't* [Bloomington: Indiana University Press, 1984], pp. 46–47).

5. See de Lauretis, *Alice Doesn't,* pp. 12–36; and Julia Kristeva, *Desire and Language: A Semiotic Approach to Literature and Art,* trans. Thomas Gora, Alice Jardine, and Leon Roudiez (New York: Columbia University Press, 1980).

6. De Lauretis, *Alice Doesn't,* p. 15.

7. The limitations of this concept are addressed by E. Ann Kaplan, who writes that the sociological approach to cinema "tends to blur the distinction between the realms of lived

experience (the social formation) and that of representation (images of film)" (*Women and Film: Both Sides of the Camera* [New York: Methuen, 1983], p. 15). According to Annette Kuhn, this method moreover assumes that images can be viewed individually and as unified essences rather than as elements in relation to other elements within the narrative whole (*Women's Pictures: Feminism and Cinema* [London: Routledge, Melbourne and Henley, 1982], p. 76).

8. Mary Ann Doane, *The Desire to Desire* (Bloomington: Indiana University Press, 1987), p. 7.

9. Linda Williams and B. Ruby Rich, "The Right of Re:Vision: Michelle Citron's Daughter Rite," *Film Quarterly* 35, no. 1 (Fall 1981): 360.

10. Gayatri Chakravorty Spivak, *In Other Worlds: Essays in Cultural Politics* (New York: Methuen, 1987), p. 79.

11. Kristeva, *Desire and Language,* p. 237.

12. Ibid., p. 242.

13. Ibid., p. 237.

14. Linda Williams, "Something Else Besides a Mother: Stella Dallas and the Maternal Melodrama," *Cinema Journal* 24, no. 1 (Fall 1984): 11.

15. Nancy Chodorow and Susan Contratto, "The Fantasy of the Perfect Mother," in *Rethinking the Family: Some Feminist Questions,* ed. Barrie Thorne and Marilyn Yalom (New York: Longman, 1982), pp. 64–65.

16. Judith Kegan Gardiner, "Mind Mother: Psychoanalysis and Feminism," in *Making a Difference,* ed. Gayle Green and Coppelia Kahn (London: Methuen, 1985), p. 114.

17. Chodorow and Contratto, "The Fantasy of the Perfect Mother," p. 65.

18. Ibid.

19. David Spiegel, "Mothering, Fathering and Mental Illness," in *Rethinking the Family,* p. 95.

20. Kristeva, *Desire and Language,* p. 242.

21. Ibid., p. 239.

22. These themes include Freudian views of the family, marriage, and sexuality, as well as attempts to reinsert women within the symbolic or Law of the Father.

23. de Lauretis, *Alice Doesn't,* p. 58.

24. Williams and Rich, "The Right of Re:Vision, p. 360.

25. "CCC Releases Statement on 'Boulevard Nights,' " *Chicano Cinema Coalition Newsletter,* June 1979. For accounts of the boycotts and pickets of the film by Chicano and Chicana college students in the Los Angeles area, see Daniel G. Solorzano, "Teaching and Social Change: Reflections on a Freirean Approach in a College Classroom," *Teaching Sociology* 17 (April 1989): 218–225.

26. The film downplays racism against minority musicians just as it omits the actual exploitation of many minority musicians by greedy white promoters. *La Bamba* fails to address the fact that the Ritchie Valens story does not end with his funeral. In fact, in "real" life the mother was left poverty-stricken, precisely by his promoter.

27. Doane, *The Desire to Desire,* p. 88.

28. Ibid., pp. 88–92.

29. Ibid., p. 82.

30. This essay was written for the Chicano Culture: Text and Context conference at the University of California, Davis, in 1988. I would like to thank Angie Chabram Dernersesian for inviting me to participate and for encouraging me to study Chicano and Chicana cinema.

PART THREE

Contested Domains: Economy and Family

NINE

Gender, Class, and Households

Migration Patterns in Aguascalientes, Mexico

María de los Angeles Crummett

Much of the recent research on migration in Mexico and elsewhere in Latin America has been preoccupied with determining the unit of analysis most appropriate to an understanding of the migratory process. The choice of analytical unit has become especially important because migration studies are no longer concerned merely with descriptive statistics such as the volume and direction of migration or the socioeconomic characteristics of migrants (sex, age, education, income, occupation, place of origin, and destination). At present, the focus is on the impact of rapid demographic change on family life and composition (Brambila Paz, 1985); the relationship between population growth, income levels, the organization of production, land tenure, and migration (Dinerman, 1982; López Castro, 1986; Roberts, 1981); and migration as a strategy of economic reproduction and survival in rural communities (Mines, 1981), to cite a few examples.

Feminist scholars in particular have been at the forefront of research examining the role of women in migration. Research efforts in this direction have considered, for example, the specificity of female migration; the effects of gender and age-specific migration on the division of labor, agricultural production, and family structure; and the impact of the migration of men on women's status in the household and in the community (see, for example, Arizpe, 1985; Casillas, 1986; Dottin, 1987; Chaney, 1983; Crummett, 1987b; Margolis, 1979; Pessar, 1982; Young, 1978).

These studies view migration as a complex and varied phenomenon in which the autonomous actions of individuals are conditioned by larger socioeconomic processes. To a great extent, contemporary research has sought to capture the dynamic character of migration by linking two different levels of analysis, micro and macro, to form a single conceptual framework. Significantly, the family or household unit has emerged as the "critical unit of analysis" in migration studies

(Caces et al., 1985). In this context, the household is conceptualized as an intermediate variable capable of bridging the gap between individual and social levels of analysis (Schmink, 1984:87).

The present study is based on a sample survey of over two hundred rural households in Aguascalientes, Mexico. By focusing on the household, scholars shed light on the division of labor by gender and show how this factor in turn shapes and reinforces specific migration patterns. However, this study maintains that the household approach is deficient unless it is accompanied by an analysis of class structure that locates the domestic unit within a broader context of social relations of production.

The first section, "Households and Migration," examines the contribution of the household unit to migration theory. The second section, on "Class, Household Structure, and Gender Selectivity in Migration," emphasizes the importance of viewing the household within the context of regional class structures and reviews several studies that have taken such an approach. The third section presents an analysis of the relationship among classes, households, and migration in Aguascalientes.

HOUSEHOLDS AND MIGRATION

The focus on the household unit emerged in reaction to what were perceived to be significant conceptual and methodological shortcomings on the part of two dominant and competing theories of migration: the neoclassical model and the historical-structural approach. (See Wood, 1982, and Crummett, 1987c, for extended critiques of these two paradigms.)

In the neoclassical or micro model, the individual's economic behavior constitutes the primary level of investigation. The motives of individual migrants were explored through the forces of supply and demand operating in regional labor markets or through the existence of rural-urban wage differences (Todaro, 1969). Typically, individuals seek to maximize benefits or minimize losses; therefore, they migrate to areas of greater labor demand and greater economic reward (Verdera, 1986:20). Critics of this model argue that it is seriously limited in its capacity to place individual motivations and preferences within a larger context. This model assumes that individual considerations based on economic opportunities and constraints motivate migration, yet it fails to specify the various contexts in which these decisions are taken or to address the decisive role of the family in migration (Stark, 1985). Moreover, little consideration is given to identifying basic macroeconomic processes of change and conflict that may also affect the decision to migrate.

In sharp contrast to the microeconomic model, the historical-structural approach considers migration a result of macroeconomic forces in the wider economy. According to this model, structural factors—primarily the structure of the agrarian sector—are responsible for the rural exodus. The unequal distribution of income, the decreasing viability of peasant agriculture, the concentration of agricultural resources, particularly land, among a small number of producers—all these factors contribute to high rates of rural out-migration. Above all, the structural perspective regards migration as a historically determined social process that cannot be studied in isolation from demographic, social, and economic factors. It consequently assumes that the unit of analysis is not the individual but the group or social class (Singer, 1974).

This analytical perspective, although comprehensive in its consideration of the historical and structural dimensions of migration, remains exclusively at the level of macro processes. If the neoclassical model emphasizes to an unrealistic degree the role of individual choices, the historical structure approach is overdeterministic in that it underplays the role of individual preferences. The emphasis on social class clearly adds a vital dimension to this paradigm by broadening the analysis beyond the consideration of static rural factors, such as land concentration and rural stagnation. Nonetheless, as Dinerman (1982:6) notes: "The use of the term 'class' as an inclusive category blurs issues to why some members of the class choose to migrate and others do not, why men in some cases migrate in larger numbers than women, and what effect, if any, purely local circumstances have on migration patterns."

The limitations of the microeconomic and historical-structural frameworks have led migration scholars to search for more comprehensive theoretical perspectives that relate the autonomous actions of individuals to larger cultural, economic, and social processes. Several authors (Dinerman, 1982; Wood, 1982; Pessar, 1982) claim that the household unit successfully integrates the dynamics of micro and macro perspectives. Briefly, the argument proceeds as follows: With the unit of analysis shifted to the household, migration can be viewed, on the one hand, as a group decision-making process on the part of individuals and, on the other, as a process conditioned by overall factors—insofar as households are linked to one another through larger communal and regional ties (Dinerman, 1982). The migration process itself is conceived as an adaptive strategy responsive to changing internal characteristics of households as well as to external structural conditions (Dinerman, 1982; Wood, 1981).

Almost from the outset, the household perspective also illuminated a critical issue overshadowed in traditional frameworks—that is, the gender-specific character of migration. In the structural framework, the model's aggregate perspective renders women (and men for that matter) largely invisible (Long, 1983). And the micro model, in highlighting the experiences of individual migrants, makes the implicit assumption that the determinants and consequences of female migration mirror those of male migration (Thadani and Todar, 1979). In short, both models fail to consider that micro and macro forces may affect men and women differently.

By contrast, in the household approach, the internal dynamics of the family and the household provide the basis for understanding potential differences in the characteristics of male and female migration. For example, women's roles as wage laborers and unpaid family workers in the household division of labor are highlighted as key components shaping and defining migration patterns.

It seems clear that an inquiry into the household more thoroughly captures the actions of individuals and locates these actions in the context of variable macro processes. Its attention to gender in migration also represents an important advance over both atomistic micro models and abstract structural perspectives. Nonetheless, in a number of important respects, the household model falls short of its goal of bridging the theoretical gulf separating behavioral and structural approaches and, consequently, of capturing the essence of the migration process. In particular, by focusing on the common budget in its analysis of the household's economic functioning, this model reduces the domestic unit to an undifferentiated group of individuals working toward the collective well-being. Wood, for example, defines the household as a core group of individuals whose decision making and labor are directed toward maintaining and reproducing the unit by generating and allocating a "collective income fund" (1981:338). As the model stands, household structure is merely the sum of individual motivations and calculations; the household itself appears as an autonomous unit unconnected to other social and economic structures.

Such conceptualizations of the household as a static, harmonious unit, where individuals contribute to the common good, fail to grasp the different and often unequal roles played by household members in the domestic unit. For example, although the household may operate on a common budget, it is critical to ask who controls the outcome of production and how it is distributed among the various members of the household. By failing to consider the domestic unit's internal organization, or the contributions of individuals to the unit's sustenance, the model does not provide a cogent explanation of why some members migrate and others do not.

It is only within the context of an analysis of class relations that the household becomes a useful analytical tool to investigate the unequal impact of migration on the sexes. Class is to be seen by no means as external to the household unit but, rather, as an integral part of it. Sen (1978:55) provides a concise example of the kind of household framework we are attempting to specify. She highlights three critical themes. First, a sound basis is provided for considering the household, and not the individual, as the proper unit of analysis. Second, the household emerges as substantially more than a group of persons sharing a common residence and a common budget (Wood, 1981; Dinerman, 1982). The existence of authority relations suggests that conflict and tension between different household members can also be expected (Schmink, 1984). Third, there is the implicit assumption that the evolution and functioning of the household are affected by external structures, relations, and functions.

CLASS, HOUSEHOLD STRUCTURE, AND GENDER SELECTIVITY IN MIGRATION: AN OVERVIEW

In the Mexican context, the type of analysis discussed in the preceding section has illustrated the social, economic, and historical processes that generate a migratory labor force; it has also attempted to show how such processes vary over time, affecting some classes, households, and individuals and not others. The present section reviews texts of Lourdes Arizpe (1985), Kate Young (1978), and Ina Dinerman (1982). (The studies by Arizpe and Dinerman are analyzed in greater detail in Crummett, 1987b.) These studies provide valuable insights into the dynamic interaction among social classes, households, and migration in Mexico as well as setting the stage for an analysis of the Aguascalientes data.

Arizpe's research in the Mazahua region of the state of Mexico offers a detailed view of the changes in the rural sector that have contributed to high rates of out-migration among the poorest stratum of the rural population. These changes—the integration of the local economy into the national market, demographic pressures on the land, land fragmentation, and the growth of Mexico City as a major industrial center—have transformed rural households' access to means of production. Arizpe maintains that migration represents a basic survival strategy among households most severely affected by declining access to productive resources. She found that household members undertake *migración por relevos* (relay migration). First, the adult male migrates on a temporary basis to Mexico City. Later he is "relieved" by his older sons and daughters, who move to the capital to work. This type of temporary, rotational migration enables households to retain their legal rights to the land and ensures the continuation of agricultural production.

Relay migration among the Mazahua tends to occur in larger households, which are capable of sponsoring greater numbers of circular migrants. According to Arizpe, this type of strategy to obtain basic needs explains why smallholding agriculturalists continue to have large families, even though they do not have resources to distribute among so many dependents and despite limited opportunities for employment locally.

In spite of its positive contribution to the long-term survival of the household, relay migration is altering the traditional division of labor, adversely affecting the type and extent of women's work. On the one hand, the migration of husbands, sons, and daughters has led mothers to participate to a greater extent in unpaid domestic activities and subsistence production. On the other hand, given the link between the household's economic situation and family size and fertility, women are shouldering the physical cost of bearing and rearing large numbers of children. In short, the women who remain behind are increasingly responsible for the economic, social, and biological reproduction of the household.

Young (1978) postulates that the transformation of agrarian structures has led to class stratification, which in turn has resulted in a new division of labor by gender. Although this restructuring of women's roles permeates all classes of the peasantry, the most severely affected are poor and landless women. These women work longer and harder days as they struggle to meet basic subsistence requirements. They also work as wage laborers for better-off peasant families.

As suggested above, one of the consequences of agricultural transformation has been an increase in family size among the poor peasantry. With the disappearance of reciprocal labor exchange, these households have to depend to a greater extent on their own labor resources, thus placing greater emphasis on women's reproductive capacities. For households dependent on wage labor for survival, a large family will increase the number of potential income earners, thus benefiting the household as a whole. However, as Arizpe has demonstrated, this situation, by accentuating their work load in both wage work and domestic work, has deleterious effects on the women of the poor peasantry.

The need for money income among the poor peasantry of Oaxaca has led to the expulsion of working-age children. In this case, however, young single girls overwhelmingly comprise the rural-urban migrant stream. According to Young, the expulsion of daughters rather than sons occurred for two main reasons. First, the division of labor within the household placed the burden of agricultural production on men. Second and more important, many of the economic activities carried out by mothers and their daughters—the making of food and clothing and the preparation of products for sale on the local market—were being undercut by more efficiently produced manufactured goods.

Young also stresses the impact of migration on the gender and age division of labor. For example, the expulsion of daughters from smallholder households places increased demands on many mothers' unpaid domestic chores. The care of young children, traditionally a responsibility of older daughters, is added to the mother's already heavy work load. A number of tasks entrusted to children, such as animal care and wood collecting, also become the mother's charge.

Dinerman's comparative study of two rural communities (Huecorio and Ihuatzio) in Michoacán examines several of the themes considered by Arizpe and Young: the role of women in the peasant economy, the impact of migration on the division of labor, and the relationship between family structure and migration. Here again, the household's changing position in the rural class structure provides important insights into the causes and consequences of migration.

In the period 1960–1980, Huecorio and Ihuatzio experienced dramatic changes in the structure of production. Dinerman argues that government policies favoring the cultivation of commercial and export crops led to a decrease in the production of basic food crops, primarily corn and beans, and an increase in the production of alfalfa, a commercial crop used for livestock fattening. The number of landless peasants also increased markedly as many households, unable to compete effectively on the market, abandoned agricultural production altogether. At the same time, employment opportunities in the cities, after having been fueled by rapid industrial growth in the 1940s and 1950s, dwindled in the following decades. In addition to the changes in agriculture and off-farm employment, the expansion of the tourist industry signaled a shift from goods manufactured for the local population to artisan production for national and international markets.

In response to these changes in the local and regional economy, migratory wage labor, both to the United States and internally to Mexico City, has become an integral part of many poor peasant and landless households. Yet the volume and direction of migration, its importance to household maintenance, and its effects on the household division of labor vary between the two communities.

In Huecorio, for example, the increased cultivation of alfalfa at the expense of corn brought changes in the division of labor. Alfalfa production requires relatively little labor and consequently allows the family labor force to engage in other productive activities. The women raise small animals for sale on the market, while the men migrate on a temporary basis to the United States. Women's commercial activities are indispensable to migrant households. The income received from this work not only supports the household during periods of male migration but also finances a major portion of the expenses incurred in international migration. In turn, remittances are invested in women's economic activities.

Because of the large numbers of landless households and the shortage of employment opportunities outside the agricultural sector, Ihuatzio has concentrated its energies in handicraft production for the tourist market. For households that are poor in resources, artisan production represents an efficient and relatively risk-free use of the family labor force. Handicrafts do not entail a strict division of labor by gender or age, and the entire household can participate in all stages of production throughout the year. For these reasons, migration occurs less frequently than in Huecorio; those individuals who do migrate tend to be male heads of households involved in temporary moves to Mexico City.

One other variable is responsible for the different migratory patterns witnessed in the two communities: household organization. In Huecorio, the extended family predominates. Dinerman argues that in this type of family structure, composed of two generations of adult workers, a greater number of persons contribute to household income. At the same time, it is easier to replace the work and income of a migrant. In Ihuatzio, by contrast, the dependence on craft production, along with income pressures, has contributed to sustaining a nuclear family structure. In this community, the low recompense for artisan work implies that the domestic unit has difficulty supporting persons that do not contribute economically to its maintenance. Moreover, because nuclear households in general have a smaller pool of labor than extended units, migration reduces more drastically the labor force available to each unit.

To summarize, these three case studies show that economic pressures provoke multiple strategies of survival and reproduction among different rural groups. These strategies—among them, the decision to migrate—affect not only particular households but also particular individuals within households. Clearly, then, an analysis of the relationship between the household's specific role in the productive structure (i.e., class position) and the internal characteristics of households deepens our understanding of the determinants and effects of migration.

CLASS, HOUSEHOLD STRUCTURE, AND MIGRATION: THE CASE OF AGUASCALIENTES

The Aguascalientes survey is a stratified random sample of rural communities in three distinct agricultural zones. It covers a total of 21 communities and 211 households. All data pertain to the period May 1981 to June 1982. (See Crummett, 1984, for an extended discussion of the region and the survey methodology.) Using the Aguascalientes survey data, I will attempt to show how different migration rates by class affect and are affected by the internal structure and composition of the household and by its division of labor by gender. This analysis goes beyond other studies of migration by providing an empirical construct of class and utilizing it to explain rural out-migration.

Agrarian Economic Development and Migration

Aguascalientes, like much of the rest of Mexico, witnessed a major transformation of land tenure relationships in the rural sector after the 1910 revolution. Government-sponsored agrarian reform measures, which promoted the *ejido* system while simultaneously supporting the development of large-scale, irrigated commercial agriculture, laid the foundations for a highly differentiated agrarian structure (Exter, 1976). (An *ejido* is a landholding unit in which ownership and administration are legally vested in a community responsible for allocating cropland to individual members. By law, *ejido* land cannot be sold or rented.)

Aguascalientes was one of the first states in Mexico to experience this dual strategy of agricultural development. In 1924, at the beginning of the agrarian reform movement in the state, rain-fed *ejido* lands were created in order to satisfy the peasantry's demand for land redistribution. Three years later, the first major irrigation system in the country's history was under construction for the purpose of fostering commercial agriculture for export (Rojas Nieto, 1981).

This growing irrigation infrastructure brought with it a number of qualitative changes in the structure of the state's rural production. Most important, between 1925 and 1959 traditional crops, such as corn and beans, were gradually displaced by fruit and vegetable production (and later by grains for animal feed), both in area cultivated and in the value of production. The state's two most important commercial crops, grapes (primarily for wine production) and guava, were introduced during this period. By 1974, the state's agrarian structure was almost completely transformed from rain-fed production of staple crops to irrigated production of high-value fruit crops.

The development of large-scale commercial agriculture profoundly altered the composition of the agrarian population. From 1925 to the present, the percentage of the labor force engaged in agriculture has decreased from 51 percent to 36 percent. The proletarianization of the peasantry has been particularly acute in the last couple of decades. In 1960, 26 percent of the labor force was classified as agricultural wageworkers, in contrast to 55 percent in 1975. Additionally, the landholdings in the *ejido* sector have been increasingly fractionalized.

The commercialization of agriculture seriously eroded the economic viability of rain-fed agricultural smallholdings; as a result, the number of landless agricultural wageworkers increased, and so did the migration of rural inhabitants. Between 1940 and 1960, the migrant stream was composed largely of young single women from poor peasant and landless laborer households. In the following decades, however, young men—displaced by the increasing mechanization in irrigated areas of the state—constituted a far greater percentage of the migrant population (Crummett, 1987c:251).

The erosion of women's productive activities in the rural area and the demand for female labor in the cities partially explain the early tendency for women to dominate the migrant stream. The sharp decrease in female migration after 1960 appears to be a result of increasing opportunities for women in both rural and urban areas in the state. Women's participation in agricultural wagework increased in those phases of production calling for temporary, seasonal labor. Grape cultivation, for example, employs women during the harvest, the most labor-intensive period of production. Additionally, the growth of the textile and garment industries in Aguascalientes City in the 1960s caused an increase in the demand for a permanent female labor force. These industries also flourished in numerous rural communities, employing a predominantly young and female work force. The textile and garment industries in turn promoted the growth of *maquila doméstica* (piecework in the home)—an activity exclusively employing women (Crummett, 1987c:251).

Class Position and Household Structure

The research by Arizpe, Young, and Dinerman and my own work in Aguascalientes have highlighted key variables that help to explain the nature of socioeconomic class in rural areas: the degree of access to land and other productive resources, the extent of participation in agricultural production, and the importance to household subsistence of wage labor. Class, however, has not been defined in narrow terms. As discussed, both the overall economic status and the internal structure of the rural household—the gender and age division of labor, household size and organization, and the family life cycle—are taken into account.

To test the proposed relationship between class and household, a set of variables sensitive to these characteristics was generated, and a factor analytic test was applied to the Aguascalientes data to determine class divisions among rural groups.[1] For example, it is postulated that the upper stratum of rural households will dominate the region's agrarian structure (the access to land, mechanized instruments of production, production for the market, and the use of hired labor in production). It is also expected that in the upper strata of the peasantry, women and children will not contribute significantly to household subsistence through either wage work or other income-generating work; a rigid gender division of labor may confine women to domestic chores and men to farm responsibilities.

By contrast, rural households that are struggling to meet subsistence requirements in the face of inadequate or nonexistent means of production should have high participation rates of women and children in productive work—both in wage labor and in farm activities. Greater household size and an extended family structure should also be strongly associated with households at the lower end of the class scale.

The statistical results (presented in detail in Crummett, 1987a) confirm that internal household demographic features, on the one hand, and external structural factors of households, on the other, are interrelated and that they provide, when taken together, a solid foundation for differentiating rural groups.[2] Table 9.1 shows the three main class types—commercial, subsistence, and landless—that characterize the agrarian structure in Aguascalientes. These three groups emerging from the factor analytic test are composite indices in which traditional indicators of socioeconomic status correlate strongly and positively with a particular household type.

The "commercial" units of production, which account for the smallest percentage of households in the sample survey, 12.3 percent, pertain to the upper stratum of the landholding sector in Aguascalientes. These households produce the most profitable crops in the state, grapes and guava, and make use of wage labor accompanied by a high degree of agricultural inputs (chemical fertilizers, herbicides, insecticides, etc.) and mechanization. In commercial units, agricul-

TABLE 9.1 Classification of Rural Households

Class Type	*Number of Households*[a]
Commercial	26 (12.3)
Subsistence	99 (46.9)
Landless	86 (40.8)
Total	211 (100.0)

[a] Numbers in parentheses indicate percentage of total households sampled.

tural production constitutes the primary source of income. (Nearly 88 percent of their income is derived from the sale of agricultural goods.)

"Subsistence" producers comprise the largest percentage of rural households in the sample survey (47 percent). These households cultivate basic food crops, corn and beans, for their own consumption and, to a lesser degree, for sale on the market. They lack sufficient land and other productive resources to survive through agricultural production alone. Rather, wage labor constitutes their principal income source. The "landless," 40.8 percent of the total number of households in the Aguascalientes sample, depend almost entirely on wagework for material reproduction.

The data presented in Tables 9.2 and 9.3 allow us to examine the relationship between demographic and economic features in the three main rural groups. Although households are large in all strata, the subsistence sector has on average significantly larger families than either commercial or landless units. As expected, the extended family structure is most pronounced in the subsistence sector. The data also indicate that women form an important part of the wage labor force in the two lower strata but not in commercial households. The landless stand out from the landholding classes in that they are relatively "young" households, as

TABLE 9.2 Family Structure Characteristics of Rural Households by Class (averages)

Class	*Age of Female Head*	*Household Size*	*Household Type (%)*[a]			*No. of Wageworkers*	
			N	E	O	Male	Female
Commercial	41.5	7.5	80	20	—	0.4	0.2
Subsistence	43.7	8.8	55	42	3	2.0	1.0
Landless	35.5	7.1	72	22	6	1.7	0.8

[a] N = Nuclear, E = Extended, O = Other. ("Other" refers to individuals living alone and to households headed by females.)

TABLE 9.3 Average Household Income and Agricultural Output by Class, 1981–1982 (pesos per year)

Class	*Average Household (Money) Income*	*Wagework as % of Income*	*Value of Agricultural Output*[a]
Commercial	319,748	2.6	341,280
Subsistence	140,464	78.3	33,104
Landless	143,975	94.3	—

[a] Refers to the value of marketed and nonmarketed agricultural products.

shown by the age of the female head of household (35.5 years) and smaller household size (7.1).

These two tables highlight the extremely precarious economic situation of the smallholding or "subsistence" sector of the peasantry. First, because commercial agriculture is profitable, the upper stratum of the peasantry has on average a total income over two times greater than that of subsistence agriculture units; the difference in value of agricultural output is almost tenfold between the two classes: 341,280 as opposed to 33,104 pesos.[3] Furthermore, the fact that subsistence households derive the greater part of their income from wagework (78 percent) points to a profound process of pauperization, in which the need for money income is vital for this sector of the peasantry.

Second, subsistence households are larger and more involved in wage labor than the completely proletarianized sector (the landless), as evidenced by family size and the average number of wageworkers per household, respectively. And although subsistence households have more wage earners per household than the landless, they earn less. Significantly, women are somewhat more involved in paid work in the subsistence sector than in the landless. On average, subsistence households contain one female wage laborer per household, whereas landless households have fewer than one per household (see Table 9.2).

Class, Gender, and Migration: Survey Results

Table 9.4 presents data on rural out-migration by class status for the period 1981–1982.[4] A salient trend emerging from the data is that commercial units of production account for the lowest percentage of households with migration, 8.8 percent. Subsistence agriculture units account for the greatest percentage, 54.4 percent, followed by landless households with approximately 37 percent.

Table 9.5 depicts the gender composition of the migrant pool by class. Male selectivity in migration is clearly evident across all class types. The volume and

TABLE 9.4 Households with Migration, 1981–1982

Class	*Households*[a]	*Households with Migration*[a]
Commercial	26	10
	(12.4)	(8.8)
Subsistence	99	62
	(47.4)	(54.4)
Landless	84[b]	42
	(40.2)	(36.8)
Total	209	114
	(100.0)	(100.0)

[a] Numbers in parentheses indicate percentage of total households sampled.
[b] Two missing cases.

TABLE 9.5 Gender Composition of Migrant Pool by Class, 1981–1982

	Individual Migrants[a]	
Class	Men	Women
Commercial	11 (7.6)	5 (8.9)
Subsistence	84 (58.3)	35 (62.5)
Landless	49 (34.1)	16 (28.6)
Total	144 (100.0)	56 (100.0)

[a] Numbers in parentheses indicate percentage of individuals in total migrant pool.

intensity of male migration, however, differ markedly by class. Commercial households contribute the fewest individuals to the male migrant pool, while subsistence households account for the greatest number of migrants. The landless also contribute strongly to the male migrant pool.

Although women do not constitute a substantial portion of the migrant pool, the data do indicate that the rate and intensity of female migration also relate to class structure, with the bulk of migrants concentrated among the lower strata of the rural sector and particularly among subsistence households. Although women of all three groups in the Aguascalientes survey migrated almost exclusively within Mexico, the type of migration varied by class status. Female migration from the upper class largely consisted of single daughters migrating to Mexico City or Guadalajara to study or pursue careers in secretarial work and nursing. The vast majority of female migrants from subsistence and landless households sought employment in domestic service and, to a lesser degree, factory work in nearby urban centers, primarily Aguascalientes City.

These differing patterns of migration by class and gender relate in large part to households' economic standing within the agrarian structure and their internal structure and organization. For example, financial stability in the economically dominant class appears to be a factor in reducing out-migration from this stratum. Among the commercial households that do sponsor migrants, international migration is the primary destination. While migration remittances did not constitute a significant proportion of total income (7.4 percent), such income was directed toward the purchase of means of production and not basic needs. In 81 percent of migrating commercial households, farm equipment and livestock were the two principal purchases.

The particularly high rates of migration found among subsistence units of production is in great part a response to their inability to meet consumption needs from the land. For these households, access to land does not mean that agricultural production contributes significantly toward household maintenance and reproduction. In fact, in over 40 percent of subsistence households, agricultural output was either nonexistent or so low that farm production did not contribute at all to household welfare.

In these households, migratory wage labor represents an important strategy to meet basic consumption needs. Through the permanent and temporary migration of some household members, subsistence units acquire resources that contribute to household survival. In contrast to commercial units, 79 percent of migrating subsistence households used remittances to purchase such basic necessities as food and clothing rather than to invest in agricultural equipment. The precarious economic base of these peasants, however, greatly restricts international migration. Despite the attraction of higher wages in the United States, this sector does not have the economic wherewithal to send a migrant across the border; migration patterns are decidedly regional and national in character.

In this class, sons and daughters dominate the migrant pool. The high tendency for sons to migrate relates to increasing demographic pressure on the land in the face of fixed and decreasing resources. In *ejidatario* households, for example, only one son, usually the oldest, will eventually inherit his father's plot. (With the exception of widows, women do not generally inherit land.) Sons from subsistence households therefore opt for employment opportunities elsewhere rather than investing in farming, an enterprise that at best provides only a small portion of reproduction requirements. Daughters are drawn away from the rural sector by wage opportunities in the cities, especially in domestic service and in textile and garment factories.

Household size and composition also account for the volume and intensity of migration in this stratum. As evidenced in Table 9.2, subsistence units contain larger households than either the commercial stratum or the landless. On average, the subsistence sector contains 8.8 members, in contrast to 7.5 members in commercial units and 7.1 members among the landless stratum. Furthermore, it is the class with the largest proportion of extended households.

The subsistence sector, because of its large household size and extended family units, has sponsored more than 70 percent of total migrants. If land rights depend on annual cultivation of the soil, as in the *ejido,* a large household can sponsor a migrant, usually a son, while other family members remain to do the agricultural work.

Two other factors also suggest that migration rates in the subsistence sector are especially responsive to household structure characteristics. This class has a higher percentage of its household members between the ages of fifteen and fifty-nine (the age group most likely to be engaged in migration) than either the commercial or the landless classes. Indeed, the age composition of the household may be a more powerful predictor of migration than absolute household size. Among subsistence households in Aguascalientes—and other studies of migration have confirmed this finding (see Wiest, 1973; Casillas, 1986)—migration occurs most frequently in households containing several members old enough (over age fifteen) to support the family economically during the absence of the laborer. Not surprisingly, subsistence households are at a later stage in the domestic cycle, as shown by the average age of the female head of household (forty-four years), than either commercial or landless units (see Table 9.2).

In subsistence households, the greater tendency to expel male household members and retain women has increased women's involvement in agricultural work on the family holding and in paid labor. In addition to such tasks as weeding and spreading fertilizers, women of subsistence households are increasingly involved in tasks traditionally assumed by men—plowing, sowing, and cultivation. In the interim before remittances are sent, women also increase household income, either through agricultural wagework or through a variety of casual jobs such as selling food products to neighbors or taking in laundry or ironing.

In sum, the dominance of the subsistence sector in migration arises from its weak economic standing. This factor, coupled with these households' distinctive domestic structure, appears to promote and support a migratory labor force.

Among the landless, temporary cyclical migration to the United States constitutes a dominant pattern, and international migrants are overwhelmingly male heads of households. The temporary character of the migrant stream and male selectivity in migration are particularly evident in one region of the study area, Calvillo. In this region, male migration relates strongly to the existing gender and age division of labor within the region and in the household. Two key factors operate here: widespread male underemployment and women's roles in productive and reproductive activities.

The vast majority of landless households depend on wagework in order to meet consumption needs. In Calvillo, wage income is obtained primarily from work in the guava fields or through *maquila*. Overall, more than 75 percent of households depend on either guava or *maquila* for employment. Guava employs adult men and male children, whereas *maquila* exclusively employs women; almost all female children from the age of seven or eight are involved in *maquila* as unpaid family laborers.

The limited range of salaried work available to male household members shapes the pattern and intensity of migration. Employment in guava is seasonal, the harvest period extending from late September through early February. Few jobs are available in guava during the off-season, and other employment opportunities are sporadic. During the off-season, the adult male work force, primarily heads of households, migrates across the northern border in search of agricultural or service-sector work.

Women's activities also shape the composition of the migrant labor force. *Maquila* provides the household with a dependable source of income throughout the year. The availability of year-round, albeit poorly remunerated, work means that basic needs are being met in the interim before remittances arrive. Moreover, the nature of *maquila*—paid work in the home—enables child care and other household tasks to be performed alongside wagework. Women's activities thus represent a critical means to maintain the household's economic and social viability during periods of male migration (Crummett, 1987c:254). The availability of homework also appears to reduce out-migration among young females.

Unlike migrating subsistence units, migration to the United States allows landless households to secure basic needs substantially above a bare subsistence level. Migration remittances were used to purchase durable consumer goods (television sets, automobiles, household appliances, and the like). Health and educational expenses were also met through remittances.

Another factor relating to households' internal structure further distinguishes these international migrants from the internal migrants of the subsistence group. Both sectors are dominated by male migration; yet male heads of households largely comprise the international migrant labor force among the landless, while sons account for the majority of internal migrants among the subsistence sector. The tendency for male heads of households to migrate in the landless group relates in part to our discussion of regional labor demand and the division of labor. The prevalence of relatively "young" nuclear family units also suggests that households contain a large number of dependent children—a factor limiting migration to the male head of household.

In conclusion, this study has shown that the factors shaping migration must be analyzed within a framework that includes larger macroeconomic processes and both class and household characteristics. The particularly strong covariance evidenced among class, household organization, and migration in Aguascalientes underscores the importance of differentiating social groups in the rural sector on the basis of their place in the agrarian productive structure *and* also of internal demographic features of households.

For the three classes identified in the survey region—commercial, subsistence, and landless—decisions to migrate are uniquely grounded in the household's productive base. The study also demonstrated how the internal structure of different rural households affects and is affected by migration. The division of labor by gender and household size and composition vary across classes and have a decisive effect on the migration patterns of households.

Among landless and subsistence households in particular, male migration has important consequences for the division of labor. Women increase their participation in agricultural production and wagework and also have continued responsibility for traditional domestic and unpaid tasks. This kind of insight into intrahousehold dynamics sharpens the analysis of class structure by revealing how and which household members are affected by migration. By considering both class and household characteristics, this study not only helps to explain why migration occurs but also discerns the uneven effects of migration on rural households.

NOTES

1. The objective of factor analysis is to group a series of variables into smaller sets of hypothetical variables, or "factors." Factor analysis explores the data for new concepts and detects underlying dimensions that might indicate data-reduction possibilities. In this study, factor analysis determines whether the survey data can be subdivided into categories that would differentiate among rural groups. The factor methods and procedures for this study are presented in Crummett (1987a).

2. Eighteen variables were employed in the factor analysis to test the interaction between class and household characteristics. These included eleven variables addressing households' status within the rural productive structure (i.e., type of land in use—rain fed or irrigated; use of wage labor in production; off-farm employment; total household income; agricultural output; the value of capital stock; etc.) and seven household structure variables (i.e., type of household—extended or nuclear; involvement of women and children in agricultural production and wagework; family life cycle; age and sex of household members; etc.). The three main groups emerging from the factor test are composite indices of these eighteen variables. Descriptions of the variables are presented in Crummett (1987a).

3. Before the devaluation of the peso in February 1982, one U.S. dollar was equivalent to approximately 26 Mexican pesos. Between February and August 1982, one U.S. dollar was equivalent to 49 pesos.

4. The tables on migration refer to both temporary and permanent migrants. A temporary migrant is someone who left the community for at least one month for work purposes and returned within the study period. A permanent migrant is someone who was living and had lived more than half a year out of the community when the survey was taken.

REFERENCES

Arizpe, L.
1985. *Campesinado y migración.* México: Secretaría de Educación Pública.

Bach, R., and L. A. Schraml.
1982. "Migration, Crisis and Theoretical Conflict." *International Migration Review* 16, no. 2:320–341.

Brambila Paz, C.
1985. *Migración y formación familiar en México.* México: El Colegio de México.

Caces, A., et al.
1985. "Shadow Households and Competing Auspices: Migration Behavior in the Philippines." *Journal of Development Economics* 17, no. 1–2:5–25.

Casillas, A.
1986. *La mujer en dos comunidades de emigrantes (Chihuahua).* México: Secretaría de Educación Pública.

Chaney, E.
1983. "Scenarios of Hunger in the Caribbean: Migration, Decline of Smallholder Agriculture and the Feminization of Farming." Working Paper Series on

Women in International Development, no. 18. East Lansing: Office of Women in International Development, Michigan State University.

Crummett, M.

1984. "Agrarian Class Structure and Migration: A Comparative Regional Analysis from Aguascalientes, Mexico." Ph.D. diss., New School for Social Research.

1987a. "Class, Household Structure and the Peasantry: An Empirical Approach." *Journal of Peasant Studies* 14, no. 3:363–379.

1987b. "Migración rural femenina en América Latina y el Caribe y su efecto en las pequeñas unidades campesinas." In *Mujeres campesinas en América Latina.* Santiago, Chile: Food and Agriculture Organization, United Nations.

1987c. "Rural Women and Migration in Latin America." In *Rural Women and State Policy: Feminist Perspectives on Latin American Agricultural Development,* ed. C. D. Deere and M. Leon. Boulder, Colo.: Westview Press.

Dinerman, I.

1982. *Migrants and Stay-at-Homes: A Comparative Study of Rural Migration from Michoacán, Mexico.* Monograph Series no. 5. La Jolla: Center for U.S.-Mexican Studies, University of California, San Diego.

Dottin, M.

1987. *Indicadores sobre mujer y familia rurales en República Dominicana: Encuesta Nacional de Mujeres Rurales, 1985.* Santo Domingo: El Centro de Investigación para la Acción Femenina.

Exter, T.

1976. "Rural Community Structure and Migration: A Comparative Analysis of Acatic and Acatlan de Juárez in Jalisco, Mexico." Ph.D. diss., Cornell University.

Long, J.

1983. "Economic Outcomes for Women Migrants to Mexico City." Paper presented at the Conference on Women and Industrialization, Bellagio, Italy.

López Castro, G.

1986. "Migración temporal a Estados Unidos en una comunidad rural mexicana." In *Se fue a volver.* Seminario sobre migraciones temporales en América Latina. México: El Centro de Estudios de Población, El Colegio de México.

Margolis, J.

1979. "El papel de la mujer en la agricultura del Bajío." *Iztapalapa* (México) 1, no. 1:158–159.

Mines, R.

1981. *Developing a Community Tradition of Migration: A Field Study in Rural Zacatecas, Mexico, and California Settlement Areas.* Monograph Series no. 3. La Jolla: Center for U.S.-Mexican Studies, University of California, San Diego.

Pessar, P.

1982. "The Role of Households in International Migration and the Case of U.S.-Bound Migration from the Dominican Republic." *International Migration Review* 16, no. 2:352–365.

Roberts, K.

1981. "Agrarian Structure and Labor Migration in Rural Mexico." Working Papers in U.S.-Mexican Studies, no. 30. La Jolla: Center for U.S.-Mexican Studies, University of California, San Diego.

Rojas Nieto, B.
1981. *La destrucción de la hacienda en Aguascalientes.* México: El Colegio de Michoacán.

Schmink, M.
1984. "Household Economic Strategies: Review and Research Agenda." *Latin American Research Review* 19, no. 3:87–101.

Sen, G.
1978. "Rural Women and the Social Organization of Production: Some Conceptual Issues." Unpublished manuscript.

Singer, P.
1974. "Migraciones internas, consideraciones teóricas sobre su estudio." In *Las migraciones internas en América Latina,* ed. H. Muñoz et al. Buenos Aires: Nueva Vision.

Stark, O.
1985. "Introduction." *Journal of Development Economics* 17, no. 1–2:1–3.

Thadani, V., and M. Todaro.
1979. *Female Migration in Developing Countries: A Framework for Analysis.* New York: Center for Policy Studies, Population Council.

Todaro, M.
1969. "A Model of Labor Migration and Urban Unemployment in Less Developed Countries." *American Economic Review* 59, no. 1:138–148.

Verdera, F.
1986. *La migración a Lima entre 1972 y 1981: Anotaciones desde una perspectiva económica.* Monograph no. 14. Lima: Instituto de Estudios Peruanos.

Wiest, R.
1973. "Wage-Labor Migration and the Household in a Mexican Town." *Journal of Anthropological Research* 29, no. 3:180–209.

Wood, C.
1981. "Structural Change and Household Strategies: A Conceptual Framework for the Study of Rural Migration." *Human Organization* 40, no. 4:338–344.
1982. "Equilibrium and Historical Structural Perspectives on Migration." *International Migration Review* 16, no. 2:298–319.

Young, K.
1978. "Economía campesina, unidad doméstica y migración." *América Indígena* (México) 38, no. 2:279–302.

TEN

Hard Choices and Changing Roles among Mexican Migrant *Campesinas*

Adela de la Torre

Women's roles in agricultural economic development have been the subject of many studies during the last decade. Research in this area, by scholars such as Ester Boserup (1970) and Carmen Diane Deere and Magdelena Leon (1982), has challenged the myth of male production dominance in the agricultural sector. For example, Boserup illustrates the complementarity between the sexes in Third World peasant production, highlighting the economic significance of women's work within the agricultural sector, even though much of it is unpaid labor. Furthermore, this body of literature illuminates the contradictory impact of agricultural capitalist development on women: capitalist development within peasant society often results in an erosion of women's economic, social, and health status. According to Sen and Grown (1987:30–31):

> The patriarchal ideology of the colonists was only partly responsible for the worsening of women's economic position. The inherent inequality and poverty-creating character of economic and political processes was an equally important factor. While large numbers of both women and men were impoverished by these processes, women tended to suffer more. When private property in land was introduced, for example, women more often than men lost traditional land-use rights. It was women's labour that tended to be unpaid and ill specified under systems of tenancy and debt peonage. When traditional manufactures decayed it was often female employment and incomes that were affected most, as for example food processing. Women were often left with meager resources to feed and care for children, the aged, and the infirm when men migrated or were conscripted into forced labour by the colonists.

The central thesis of this chapter is critically linked to these scholars' analyses, which provide an important basis for examining the gender-specific impact of capitalist development on Mexican migrant women's roles in the United States. When capitalism enters into less developed rural communities, these women also experience a mixed return from their seasonal migrant employment. Moreover, the net economic gain of female labor force participation is offset by a double workday—that is, a workday that includes time spent on domestic chores and child rearing, as well as on paid seasonal employment. Unfortunately, women's household work produces commodities that have use value for the family but limited exchange value; therefore, from a market point of view, the wage value of their time is very low—thus further undermining their perceived contribution to the household (Chaney, 1987). Furthermore, the devaluation of "women's work" and their added paid-labor responsibilities can result in direct negative health consequences for the family.

Four general sections comprise this chapter. The first section provides a brief review of the salient points developed by researchers who have examined Third World countries and assessed the division of labor by gender. The second section discusses the labor needs of California agriculture and describes the sample used for this study. The third section analyzes the impact on maternal and infant death, gender perceptions, and levels of household control for these Mexican migrant women. General conclusions are provided in the final section.

LITERATURE REVIEW

Ester Boserup, in her seminal work *Women's Role in Economic Development* (1970), was the first scholar to identify male and female farming systems. Her research demonstrated the important link between levels of rural proletarianization and/or plough cultivation and the shift away from female to male farming systems, the former generally reflecting a more egalitarian system in tribal peasant communities. Her findings, based primarily on the African experience, illustrate the way changes in technology, such as capital intensity levels and irrigation, lead to alterations in agricultural gender relations.

Boserup's identification of gender divisions in farming systems was further developed by Deere and Leon in *Women in Andean Agriculture* (1982). They pointed out that a farming system based on the criterion of who provides the largest labor input "serves to obscure the fact that so-called male agricultural systems still depend on the active participation of women" (Deere and Leon, 1982:4). They proposed additional criteria in gender classification of farming systems: not only labor input but also access to the means of production, participation in decision making, and control over the outcome of the productive process. The criteria of access and control allowed them to differentiate between patriarchal and egalitarian farming systems—the egalitarian system clearly linked to levels of female access and control. They also linked farming systems to the process of capitalist development in agriculture and social differentiation of the peasantry. At different stages of capitalist development in several Third World countries, women were rarely the beneficiaries of this development process in agriculture. Even during periods of progressive agrarian reforms, women rarely benefited from these programs (Lago, 1987; Deere and Leon, 1987).

In general, much of the research on rural women in the Third World has examined the negative effects of capitalist development on female control, both in household and in market production; the unequal impact of modernization on rural women of different classes; and the negative consequences for the material well-being of these women and their children (Young, 1978).

Several of these studies supported the conclusion that agricultural economic development does not lead automatically to greater equality for women. For example, depending on their class position, proletarianization could have differential impacts, either positive or negative, on the household and women. Indeed, patriarchal relationships often prevailed with economic development. Perceptions of male-female roles in the household helped to maintain patriarchal relationships that would often conflict directly with the economic realities of these individuals. Young's study in Oaxaca, Mexico, concludes that "the women's very active participation in the economic life of the village, which involves their increased social visibility, is not rewarded. . . . The cultural prescription that a woman's place is in the home ensures that those who have to work outside it to maintain it in existence derive no social benefit from their work" (Young, 1978:151).

To assess any program's effects on domestic relations, one must establish points of reference and methods to measure levels of inequality within households. Measuring inequality among peasant households, particularly among women within the varying peasant strata, is problematic. However, many researchers have attempted to isolate critical variables that determine the increased burdens placed on peasant women—variables such as the employment status of these women, their conditions of employment, and the resulting household nutritional status after a modernization strategy. However, maternal employment and nutritional status are subject to intervening variables, such as the mother's earnings, proportion spent on food, cost of substitute for mother's milk, and maternal and nonmaternal child-care costs (Carloni, 1984).

With their insights into gender-related economic issues in less developed countries, these studies present empirical evidence of women's roles in the agricultural production process and suggest a framework to analyze women's roles in agriculture. They also challenge traditional beliefs that women's economic participation in the wage labor market will necessarily alter patriarchal relationships in the home and in production. Furthermore, this literature calls into question the assumption that the introduction of new production systems results in net social and health benefits.

The results of these studies can be generalized and applied to the experience of Mexican migrant workers in the United States. Rural migration of women to the United States does not reflect an individual's decision to seek higher wages in the U.S. labor market; rather, it reflects the uneven impact of capitalist development on the Mexican household, where women disproportionately bear the burden of adverse impacts. However, as suggested by Crummett (1987:253), "Women are not always 'victims' of migration; they often take active parts in the migration process even when they do not go themselves." On the one hand, I would argue, Mexican women who migrate to the United States actively participate in making critical household decisions and also provide needed income for the family. On the other hand, the capitalist development process, which pushes migrant workers to the United States to increase their household income, undermines these women's control over household decision making and constrains the health-care choices available to them and their children. In other words, with their entry into the U.S. agricultural labor market, the benefits from their paid labor increase, but at the same time the demands on their unpaid labor also increase. The net results are a loss of control in household decision making and a severe reduction in the quality of care available to their children.

ROLE OF MIGRATORY WORKERS IN CALIFORNIA AGRICULTURAL PRODUCTION

Labor Needs

California agriculture primarily relies on Mexican-origin seasonal workers to cultivate and harvest its labor-intensive specialty crops. Historically, most of these immigrant nonwhite laborers have been single males. However, within the last twenty years, a new group—Mexican-origin women—has appeared in the California fields. These women have become important contributors to the economic survival of the Mexican migrant household. A report by the California Commission on the Status of Women (Halfon et al., 1978) indicates that many of these women are employed in low-status and low-paying tasks of weeding, thinning, hoeing, and harvesting. In addition, female employment is greater in particular speciality crops, such as tomatoes, lettuce, grapes, and field crops. When these crops become mechanized, there is a concentration of women in the lowest tier of the harvest hierarchy. For example, few women are employed as harvester supervisors or in processing; generally, these women are employed in sorting and cleaning on the harvesting machine. Thus, although they are found in increasing numbers in California agriculture, they are employed in the lowest tiers of the agricultural labor market hierarchy.

A significant number of female migrant workers are from rural communities in Mexico and share many of the characteristics of the women left behind. Just as many nonmigrating Mexican women face disruptive forces because of uneven Mexican agricultural development, Mexican migrant women must adjust their lives to the uneven forces of employment in California agriculture. In the preceding chapter, María de los Angeles Crummett has shown that both household division of labor and class position are critical factors in the migration decision of households in Aguascalientes. These forces, combined with the impact of their legal status, compound the problems faced by many Mexican *campesinas.*

Description of the Sample

For this study, 137 women in seasonal farm labor households in three major California agricultural counties—San Joaquin, Stanislaus, and Tulare—were interviewed. Although a convenience sample was used, all interviewed women lived in farm labor households where harvest employment was the major source of income for the family, and all were of Mexican origin—that is, they were born in Mexico or were of Mexican descent. Approximately sixty specific and open-ended questions were asked concerning basic socioeconomic information, prenatal nutrition, pregnancy, perinatal outcomes, child care, and infant-feeding practices. Interviews were administered in labor camps and in rural health clinics by trained bilingual interviewers. Several of the clinics were located in or near the labor camps and were selected because of their accessibility to the migrant community. (For a further detailed discussion of the data, see de la Torre and Rush, 1987.)

As in many studies of migrant workers, no control group was developed to compare nonworking migrant women with working migrant women. The major objective of this convenience sample was to provide an overview of employment decisions, health behaviors and choices, and gender relations of migrant women and not to rely a priori on one explanatory variable, such as employment or nativity, as the major factor influencing these women's choices. Therefore, a case-control approach would be far too narrow in scope and would not contribute to greater methodological rigor.

The mean age of the sample was 28.2 years, 95 percent were married, and 70 percent were employed as seasonal harvest laborers during the time of the interview. The mean education was 6.6 years, slightly more than the equivalent of *primaria* in Mexico, and over 80 percent of the sample were born in Mexico. Sixty-four percent of the respondents identified themselves as migrants; in general, migrants were slightly older than permanent seasonal agricultural workers.

The vast majority of the women surveyed were from rural areas of Mexico. Although a specific question concerning their Mexican class status was not asked, other migration studies suggest that, in general, migrants who enter the United States are not from the lowest strata of the Mexican peasantry. Rather, given the high economic cost of migration for these families, their class background would reflect the more mobile semiproletarian and/or small-landholding strata of the peasantry (Taylor, 1987). Nevertheless, even though these women do not necessarily reflect the lowest strata of the Mexican peasantry, similar cultural norms concerning women's roles transcend these differences. That is, even though the level of paid labor force participation may vary across peasant strata, the actual perception of women's social and economic contribution remains constant. Thus, for many of the women working outside the home, their paid economic contribution to the household will be undervalued with respect to its significance in maintaining the household income, so as to project the more important housewife and mother image.

MIGRANT EMPLOYMENT AND MATERNAL AND INFANT HEALTH

This study illustrates the contradictory nature of migrant agricultural female employment and family well-being: on the one hand, migration to and employment in an advanced capitalist economy may provide a higher pecuniary return to the family; at the same time, it may jeopardize the healthy reproduction of these families in the long run.[1] Specifically, the dual workday, the illegal status, and the limited kinship networks available may severely restrict traditional infant- and child-care practices used by these women in Mexico.[2] Studies of the impact of employment on infant-feeding practices—specifically, breast versus formula feeding of infants—illustrate this point.

Within the last fifteen years, a general consensus has developed among the medical community concerning the superiority of breast over bottle feeding for infant and maternal health. With respect to infant health, human milk is superior to its substitutes because of its nutritional quality, protective effects against infection such as *Escherichia coli* diarrhea, antiallergic effects, and influence on maternal-neonate bonding (Jeliffe and Jeliffe, 1977). In addition, prolongation of the period of postpartum amenorrhea and suppression of the mother's ovulatory cycle assist in preventing unwanted pregnancies and promote child spacing (Akin et al., 1981). Both birth spacing and contraception in underdeveloped countries have been associated with decreasing maternal morbidity and mortality (Lillig and Lackey, 1982).

A major study of the Hispanic population along border counties suggests that Mexican-origin women are relatively less likely to breast-feed than the majority population (Smith et al., 1982). Another study focusing on Mexican-origin agricultural migrants observed low rates of breast feeding (Mines and Kearney, 1982), and the women in this sample had similar low rates. Of the sample, 24 percent breast-fed their infants for six months, 45 percent fed their infants commercial formula, and 27 percent breast-fed initially and also used formula. Comparable results were found in the study by Mines and Kearney in Tulare County (see Table 10.1).

Given past studies, the observation of lower breast-feeding rates among mi-

TABLE 10.1 Breast versus Bottle Feeding during the Last Pregnancy

	% Sample[a]	*% Tulare Survey*[b]
Breast	23.6	22.9
Bottle	45	55.1
Both	27.4	22.0
Other	4	—

[a] *N* = 137.
[b] From Mines and Kearney, 1982. *N* = 118.

grant women may not be surprising. But what motivated the women to make this choice? Are these women's infant-feeding practices constrained or influenced by their surrounding environment? Do their choices reflect actual shifts in preferences or tastes? Or are economic reasons motivating and constraining their preferences?

From the survey, a summary of rationales for infant-feeding practice was developed (see Table 10.2). Many women who preferred to formula-feed their infants indicated that work was the primary motive for their decision, 32 percent. The next most common response was that they did not like to breast-feed, indicating a choice linked to individual preference. The third most common response was that the mother lacked breast milk. When the "lack of breast milk" response is included with the "work" response, the percentage of work-related reasons increases to 45.5 percent. The current medical literature in this area

TABLE 10.2 Infant-Feeding Practices of Working Mothers and Explanations Cited for Choice of Method[a] (% of sample)

A. Choice of breast milk (*N* = 31)	
Best method	71
Easier	13
Medical advice	6
Other	10
B. Choice of formula only (*N* = 59)	
Work	32
Dislike nursing	14
Lack of breast milk	13.5
Baby refused to nurse	10
Peer/family pressure	5
Illness	5
Coraje[b]	3
Other	7.5
C. Choice of both (*N* = 11)	
Work	42
Dislike nursing	2.7
Lack of breast milk	33
Medical advice	11
Coraje	2.7
Other	8.6

[a] The numbers in the three categories do not add up to 137 (the total sample) because the remainder of the respondents gave inadequate information.

[b] Anger—in the sense of a severe emotional upset.

HUMBOLDT CREW WANTS YOU!

WHAT IS CREW?

A great sport!
New FUN Friends.
Crew is having no previous sport experience.
Having the desire to live an active lifestyle.
It is getting into the best shape of your life.
It is learning to row on the open waters of Humboldt Bay.
It is traveling to Washington, Oregon and So-California
to compete against other Universities.

For more information please call

Women's Team
Deanna 822-7347
Dawn 826-9493
Women's Coach-Robin 822-9227

Men's Team
Elke 822-6601

We will be recruiting in the quad on September 5-8, look for us!

We will have slide shows on September 8, at noon and again at 4:30p.m. in the Kate Buchanan Room in Nelson Hall.

The women's team invites you to informal land work-outs on the track from 4-5:30p.m. starting August 30th, come join the fun!

TUESDAY SEPTEMBER 24 3PM

Ladysmith Black Mambazo

Second show added
by popular demand!!
Van Duzer Theatre

$22 General
$16 Students & Seniors

MORE INFORMATION

Call the ticket office at 826-3928

suggests that there are few if any biological constraints to breast feeding (Richardson, 1986). However, successful lactation does require sustained infant sucking. Therefore, "lack of breast milk" as a response is most likely a result of the *campesina*'s interruption of a sustained sucking by the infant, as opposed to an actual biological condition. Those who combined breast feeding with formula feeding for their infants recognized that this practice would ease their dual role as mothers and workers. Not surprising, then, is the finding that, among those who chose to combine breast and formula feeding, 42 percent stated that their work required them to include formula feeding in their infant diet. An analysis of these data supports the hypothesis that the probability of breast feeding declines when these migrant women work outside the home (de la Torre and Rush, 1987). Such a finding has been supported in other studies where socioeconomic changes, such as employment, adversely affect the incidence and duration of breast feeding (World Health Organization, 1983).

Given these findings, one can conclude that migrant women are often forced to choose between the optimal source of infant nourishment and seasonal work that is necessary to supplement the household income. Their behavior does not merely express a shift in preferences resulting from their immigrant status in the United States, since many of these women attempt to maintain traditional infant and postpartum-care practices such as *la cuarentena*, use of *faja* on the umbilicus, and kinship networks.[3] (See Table 10.3.)

Cultural factors alone are a strong intervening variable in the decision-making practices of Mexican migrant women; however, they cannot completely shield these women from their new immigrant and employment status. Reproduction of specific Mexican practices of maternal and infant health care is one manifestation of the strong role of cultural tradition despite severe socioeconomic forces placed on migrants. These same cultural norms, which may provide useful strategies in health care, may also permeate other levels of household decision making. Cultural norms also affect gender roles, perceptions, and practices in migrant households.

TABLE 10.3 Use of Traditional Practices in Maternal and Infant Health Care (% of sample)

	La Cuarentena[a]			*Use of Faja*[b]		
	Yes	No	NA[c]	Yes	No	NA
Work in fields	.68	.30	.02	.29	.68	.03
Work at home	.68	.29	.03	.29	.62	.09

[a] Dietary and sexual restrictions on women's activities during the postpartum period.
[b] Binding of the newborn child's umbilicus.
[c] NA = no answer.

ECONOMIC CONTRIBUTION, GENDER PERCEPTION, AND CONTROL

Perceptions of women's roles affect women's economic contribution and influence the division of labor within the home. Both in less developed and more developed nations, capitalist economic growth has not diminished the traditional gender-specific division of labor in the home. Indeed, the euphemism of the "double day" is readily accepted in most advanced capitalist nations, even though the term is used to obscure the loss of control women experience in the sphere of production and in the home. With the emergence of market-dependent economies in many rural sectors of underdeveloped countries, changes in women's roles have resulted in a similar loss of control. Increasingly, women must provide greater paid remuneration for the household as well as maintain the same level of household production. Thus, the perceived benefits of increased female labor force participation may not be completely positive, and, indeed, could even be negative if there are no adequate support systems for household chores and child care.

Table 10.4 illustrates the contradictory relationship between actual migrant women's roles in paid seasonal employment and their perceived household contribution. First, both employed and currently nonemployed migrant women said that their husbands were the major providers of economic security for the family; only 6 percent of the sample stated that their income was the major source of household support, and only 30 percent of the women who worked outside the home considered that their employment was of equal significance for maintaining the family.

Table 10.5 assesses the impact of female employment on the household division of labor. The choice of food preparation (consisting of menu planning and meal preparation) and grocery purchases as proxies for household division of labor tasks is reasonable, since these tasks are more likely to attract male participation and are less sex typed. Also, with increased economic mobility, food preparation in particular may be perceived positively by male household members. Thus, initial changes in gender roles within the domestic sphere may be first apparent in food preparation (Pesquera, 1985).

TABLE 10.4 Perceived Gender Contribution to Total Household Income as Indicated by Mexican Migrant Respondents (% of sample)

	Man	*Woman*	*Both*	*No one*
Work in fields (*N* = 111)	.63	.06	.30	.01
Work at home (*N* = 24)	.91	.06	.03	.00

NA (no answer) = 2.

TABLE 10.5 Household Division of Labor
(% of sample)

	Work in Fields (N = 111)			*Work at Home (N = 24)*		
	Men	Women	Both	Men	Women	Both
Menu planning	0	.95	.05	0	.88	.12
Meal preparation	.01	.95	.01	0	.97	.03
Grocery purchase	.09	.60	.31	.18	.53	.20

NA (no answer) = 2.

The evidence from this survey indicates that among migrant Mexican households the traditional segregation of female household chores was not substantially altered with female employment. Nor were there significant differences among employed and nonemployed women with respect to grocery purchase. However, the highest level of male participation was found in the area of grocery purchase. Although no data are available on these practices in households in Mexico, one might conclude that there is some male participation in domestic chores, specifically grocery purchase. However, the net gain for women from male participation in grocery purchase is highly suspect. As one study in rural households of less developed countries has noted, "in market dependent households, women's influence on the menu and quantities per meal depends on *who* does the shopping" (Carloni, 1981:9). The fact that men purchase groceries, therefore, may not reflect greater egalitarianism within the home; rather, it may remove from women the little control they have over household income and family consumption patterns. Selective male participation in household tasks, particularly when linked to use of household income, may minimize women's decision-making power in the home.

CONCLUSION

Familial migration is often considered to result in net gains for the family. Clearly, the economic return with respect to female employment is higher in the United States than in Mexico. However, by emphasizing the financial advantages of migration, one may overlook the real cost in terms of family health and women's roles.

This study suggests that migration to a more advanced capitalist economy may not translate into greater social equality for migrant women. As has been demonstrated, the demands of agricultural employment may have negative consequences for infant and maternal health care. Breast-feeding decisions by migrant women were constrained by seasonal employment. At the same time, cultural norms, which would promote more traditional health practices with respect to postpartum and infant care, were widely observed by the survey respondents. This finding suggests that the choice to formula-feed does not merely reflect shifts in the preference structure due to migration.

A second important finding from this study suggests that traditional gender roles in the household are not radically altered with female seasonal employment. Even though increased labor-force participation of migrant women may increase the gross income of a migrant household, for many migrant women the overall work burden increases as the household responsibilities continue to stay within the woman's domain.

NOTES

1. "Healthy reproduction of the family" is a health-status measure rather than an economic-status measure. It refers to the ability of the family unit to meet its basic physical and psychological needs.

2. With the passage of the Immigration Reform and Control Act (1986), many of these women may have enrolled in the program offered under the law's amnesty provisions for special agricultural workers. Thus far, little is known about the effects of this legislation on workers, because many of the final regulations have only recently appeared and no published surveys have been made available. It would be reasonable to assume, given the current paucity of data, that many of the constraints placed on migrant women will not change radically with the amnesty provisions of the new law.

3. *La cuarentena* and use of the *faja* reflect culturally specific practices of traditional rural Mexican women. The former practice consists of both dietary and sexual restrictions that limit women's activities during the postpartum period. The latter requires the mother, relative, or friend to bind the umbilicus of the newborn to prevent undesirable umbilical cord bulging and entry of *mal aire* (bad air) that would be harmful to the infant (Zepeda, 1982).

REFERENCES

Akin, J., et al.

1981. "The Determinants of Breast-Feeding in Sri Lanka." *Demography* 18, no. 3:287–307.

Boserup, E.

1970. *Women's Role in Economic Development.* New York: St. Martin's Press.

Carloni, A. S.

1981. "Sex Disparities in the Distribution of Food within Rural Households." *Food and Nutrition* 7, no. 1:3–12.

1984. *The Impact of Maternal Employment and Income on the Nutritional Status of Children in Rural Areas of Developing Countries: What Is Known, What Is Not Known, Where the Gaps Are.* New York: United Nations Administrative Committee on Coordination, Subcommittee on Nutrition.

Chaney, E. M.

1987. "Women's Components in Integrated Rural Development Projects." In *Rural*

Women and State Policy: Feminist Perspectives on Latin American Agricultural Development, ed. C. D. Deere and M. Leon. Boulder, Colo.: Westview Press.

Crummett, M. de los Angeles.
1987. "Rural Women and Migration in Latin America." In *Rural Women and State Policy,* ed. C. D. Deere and M. Leon. Boulder, Colo.: Westview Press.

de la Torre, A., and L. Rush.
1987. "The Determinants of Breastfeeding for Mexican Migrant Women." *International Migration Review* 21, no. 3:728–742.

Deere, C. D., and M. Leon.
1982. *Women in Andean Agriculture.* Geneva: International Labor Office.
1987. *Rural Women and State Policy.* Boulder, Colo.: Westview Press.

Halfon, S., et al.
1978. *Campesinas: Women Farmworkers in the California Agricultural Labor Force.* Sacramento: California Commission on the Status of Women.

Jeliffe, B., and E. F. Patrice Jeliffe.
1977. "Breast Is Best: Modern Meanings." *New England Journal of Medicine* 297, no. 17:912–915.

Lago, M. S.
1987. "Rural Women and the Neo-Liberal Model in Chile." In *Rural Women and State Policy,* ed. C. D. Deere and M. Leon. Boulder, Colo.: Westview Press.

Lillig, K. K., and C. J. Lackey.
1982. "Economic and Social Factors Influencing Women's Infant Feeding Decisions in a Rural Mexican Community." *Journal of Tropical Pediatrics* 28, no. 5:240–247.

Littlefield, C., and C. L. Stout.
1987. "A Survey of Colorado's Migrant Farmworkers: Access to Health Care." *International Migration Review* 21, no. 3:688–708.

Magnus, P. D.
1983. "Breastfeeding among Hispanics." *American Journal of Public Health* 73, no. 5:597.

Mines, R., and M. Kearney.
1982. *The Health of Tulare County Farmworkers: A Report of 1981 Survey and Ethnographic Research for the Tulare County Department of Health.* Sacramento, Calif.: Department of Health Services, Rural Health Division, Farmworkers Health Section.

Pesquera, B.
1985. "Work and Family: A Comparative Analysis of Professional, Clerical, and Blue Collar Chicana Workers." Ph.D. diss., University of California, Berkeley.

Richardson, B. D.
1986. "The Vicissitudes of Breastfeeding." *Journal of Tropical Pediatrics* 32, no. 3:102–103.

Sen, G., and C. Grown.
1987. *Development, Crisis, and Alternative Visions: Third World Women's Perspectives.* New York: Monthly Review Press.

Smith, J. C., et al.

1982. "Trends in the Incidence of Breastfeeding for Hispanics of Mexican Origin and Anglos on the U.S. Border." *American Journal of Public Health* 72, no. 1:54–61.

Taylor, J. E.
1987. "Undocumented Mexico-U.S. Migration and the Returns to Households in Rural Mexico." *American Journal of Agricultural Economics* 69, no. 3 (August): 626–638.

World Health Organization.
1983. "The Dynamics of Breast-Feeding." *WHO Chronicle* 37, no. 1:6–10.

Young, K.
1978. "Modes of Appropriation and the Sexual Division of Labor: A Case Study from Oaxaca, Mexico." In *Feminism and Materialism: Women and Modes of Production,* ed. A. Kuhn and A. M. Wolpe. London: Routledge and Kegan Paul.

Zepeda, M.
1982. "Selected Maternal Care Practices of Spanish-Speaking Women." *JOGN Nursing* 11, no. 6:371–374.

ELEVEN

"In the Beginning He Wouldn't Lift Even a Spoon"

The Division of Household Labor

Beatríz M. Pesquera

Research on the division of household labor demonstrates a persistent pattern: married women continue to perform all or most household tasks even when they are employed (Berk, 1985; Hartmann, 1981; Vanek, 1980). Similar patterns have been reported among Chicano families. However, these patterns are analyzed and reported in diverse ways. Some researchers stress the participatory role of husbands in the division of household labor to emphasize a trend toward egalitarianism (Ybarra, 1982), but even those who adhere to this line of thought acknowledge male reluctance. Ybarra and Arce (1981) found that husbands might participate in some household chores but that tasks such as cooking and laundry are resistant to "defeminization." Flores (1982) reported a traditional sex-role division, with women doing the majority of the housework; and other researchers support the tenacity of the traditional division of household labor (Mirandé and Enríquez, 1979, Segura, 1984).

Among Chicano couples, the most significant factor affecting the redistribution of household labor is women's employment. Ybarra (1982) and Baca-Zinn (1980) argue that there is a correlation between women's employment and increased male involvement in household labor. Zavella (1987), however, points out a key fact: although women's employment somewhat altered the distribution of labor, tasks remained sex-gender segregated. Data from my study of professional, clerical, and blue-collar Chicana workers collaborate these findings. Women's employment generally does bring about greater male involvement in household labor, but it does not lead to an egalitarian redistribution of tasks.

This essay analyzes the relationship between the ideology and practice of the division of household labor among a select group of Chicana workers. It also describes the process whereby that division of labor is altered or reproduced. I suggest that the distribution of household labor is shaped by the women's level of economic contribution to the household and their employment demands.

METHODOLOGY AND SAMPLE PROFILE

This study is based on information obtained through in-depth interviews with professional, clerical, and blue-collar married Chicana workers between the ages of twenty-five and forty. Each category included a selected sample of eight women; each informant met three criteria: (1) spouses must be of Mexican origin, (2) children must be present in the home, and (3) the women must have been employed full-time for at least five years. The employment criterion was essential, since the study analyzes the impact of work on family life. Because most of the women interviewed were in their childbearing years, I took maternity leaves into account.

To obtain a sample with these characteristics, I contacted professional associations, community groups and agencies, human service agencies, labor unions, and key persons who have contact with Chicana women. Informants were selected from names generated through the above referral system. Generalizability of the study is limited both by the relatively small sample size and by the method of sample selection.

The informants and their spouses came from lower- and working-class backgrounds. Although some of the women had early-childhood experiences in migrant workers' families, all have lived in urban settings the majority of their lives. At the time of the study, they resided in northern California.

Chicana professionals have at least a bachelor's degree, and five earned postgraduate degrees. Three husbands have the same level of education as their wives, two are more highly educated, and the remaining three have less education (with one a college student at the time the interview took place). Chicana professionals are all concentrated in the public sector; the majority are administrators, and two are teachers. Five of the husbands are either administrators or lawyers, one is self-employed, one is a student, and the other was at the time of the interview an unemployed teacher. Clerical workers are also employed primarily in the public sector. All but one of the clerical workers have from one to two years of community college or business school training. The majority of their husbands are blue-collar workers. Except in one case, where the husband has a bachelor's degree, the clerical workers have higher levels of education than their spouses. Among blue-collar workers, 75 percent also have some community college education. Their spouses tend to have lower levels of education; half did not complete high school, two have high school degrees, one has a bachelor's degree, and one has technical training. Except for one blue-collar worker who drives a delivery truck, all the women in this category work in factories. Their spouses are mainly employed as factory workers or in the skilled trades; one is a human service professional.

Data on the division of labor were generated through the use of various techniques. On a scaled written questionnaire, the women indicated the level at which each family member participated in household tasks and their own level of satisfaction with these arrangements. In addition, in a series of personal interviews, I asked the informants to describe in detail an average workday and an average weekend; open-ended questions were used to explore women's beliefs, expectations, and strategies. Disagreements or conflicts arising from the division of household labor were explored. Significant discrepancy existed between women's answers to the scaled questionnaire and their detailed descriptions of household routines. Overall, informants tended to report a higher level of male participation in household chores and a higher level of satisfaction with existing arrangements on the questionnaire than they expressed in their interviews. These differences between written and verbal descriptions of daily life require closer examination. They should give us an insight into the dynamics of household labor.

The analysis presented here emerged from the contradictions in the data and provides a glimpse into the mundane interactions of Chicana workers in this sample. These interactions represent an important area for the study of gender politics. The division of household labor is a critical factor, since it is an arena where gender relations are negotiated, altered, and reproduced.

IDEOLOGY AND PRACTICE

The following sections discuss the relationships between the ideology and the practice of professional, clerical, and blue-collar Chicana workers. The discussion will focus primarily on "gender strategies"—that is, peculiarities in types of strategies used by wives and husbands in the struggle over "who will do what." These strategies—such as "stalling" (used by men) and "coaching" (used by women)—articulate the ideological underpinnings in the "political struggle" over household labor. By *ideology,* we mean the belief system that incorporates what women "think" husbands ought to do and what they concretely "expect" them to do. The *practice* of household labor refers to "behavior," including strategies used in the struggle over household chores. The term *political struggle* is borrowed from Hartmann (1981), who proposes using housework to illustrate the conceptualization of family as a "locus of political struggle" over the fruits of labor.

The overwhelming majority of women in this study "think" that their husbands should participate equally in household labor. Expectations of actual performance, however, differ considerably. Thus, at the level of "thought," the responses are uniform. At the level of "expectations," however, this ideological convergence is altered. In particular, clerical workers did not "expect" their husbands actually to perform household labor on an equal basis.

Differences in the level of "expectation" reflect what takes place in practice within these families. Professional and blue-collar Chicana workers have greater expectations and observe greater male participation in household tasks. The different levels of male involvement reflect not only different expectations but also the women's willingness to engage in conflict and struggle with their husbands in order to increase their share of household work. That is, professional and blue-collar Chicana workers not only expect more but are willing to demand more from their husbands. Therefore, their husbands do considerably more than the husbands of clerical workers. The high level of "expectation" did not, however, translate into an equal division within these households. Although these women were firm in expressing their expectations, half of them admitted that these expectations were not actually fulfilled. As one women stated, "It doesn't mean it's going to happen."

To understand the complex dynamic between ideology and behavior, we must examine the gender strategies of these households by occupation. As pointed out, at the level of ideology, there was a divergence by occupation; differences also exist at the behavioral level. These findings are discussed in the following sections, which are organized by occupational categories.

Professional Workers

Households of Chicana professionals are the least sex-role segregated of this sample (Table 11.1). Nonetheless, these women perform more of the household labor than their husbands do. Although professional women's expectations are not being translated into equitable household division of labor, half of these women reported a high degree of satisfaction with existing arrangements. The reported level of satisfaction was called into question, however, as Chicana professionals articulated their frustrations, conflicts, and struggles during the interview. Furthermore, the reported level of male involvement in the division of household labor on the scaled questionnaire often did not coincide with the women's descriptions of daily activities in the home.

The struggle over the division of household labor among professional couples tends to generate various levels of conflict. For some, it was minimal; for others, it was open warfare. Perhaps Linda was most adamant in expressing this conflict:

TABLE 11.1 Division of Household Labor: Professional (% of sample, in round numbers; $N = 8$)

	Respondent[a]	*Both*[b]	*Spouse*[a]
Plans/prepares meals	37	50	12
Cleans up after meals	50	37	12
Cleans house	62	37	—
Buys groceries/household needs	50	37	12
Does laundry	50	50	—
	High	*Low*	*Neutral*
Level of satisfaction	50	37	12

[a] Performs these chores all or most of the time.
[b] Perform these chores about equally.

> Well, he says that I need to do more around the house. I'm sure that whatever he says, it is because he is feeling that I'm not putting in my part. But frankly, I don't give a shit. I mean, I do, but I'm thinking I'm doing a lot, too. I tell him I'm not superwoman. And if I start taking what he says really seriously, then I would probably have a nervous breakdown. I wouldn't be able to function.

Yolanda felt that she was doing more of the household work than she should. Her husband's lack of participation and his cultural expectations were constant sources of conflict. She complained that her husband consistently compared her to other women in order to discredit her expectations. She also has come to the conclusion that other women are willing to accept a minimal amount of male participation.

> What happens, what blows my mind, is I consider the fact that my husband does what to me is a minimal amount of work around the house, and my friends will come over and it will blow their minds at how much he does. Oh, Tony cooks, and washes dishes. Yeah, and it blows their mind, because their husbands do even less.

"Stalling" or not completing the task properly are strategies employed by men to avoid doing housework. Women sighed with resignation and said that often it was just easier to do the work themselves. Teresa Godinez explained:

> The balance between how much is done or expected to be done creates tension. I think at any point when something isn't done there is a "who will do it." In his mind the easiest answer is that no one does it and that's okay with him. In my mind if it doesn't get done, then I'm unhappy about it, so I end up doing it. It's not so much an argument of "who will do it," but just it has to be done. It probably goes back to the superwoman image. I want a good house. I don't want somebody to walk in and see this mess. It is not going to be Mike that they think didn't clean up the mess. It's going to be me.

Selia, who has difficulties with her husband's stalling strategies, rationalized his behavior as "casual, laid-back." She stated that her husband was extremely committed to his career and spent several hours every evening on his work. His zeal and commitment to his work call into question his "laid-back" attitude toward household labor. Rather, his casual attitude toward housework appears to be a strategy to avoid the work.

Overall, men married to professional Chicanas do more household work than other men in this sample. In a few families, their involvement is not a product of constant tension. For the most part, however, the only way women have altered the distribution of labor has been through conflict and confrontation.

Clerical Workers

In marked contrast, men married to clerical Chicanas do much less housework than all other husbands in the sample (Table 11.2). Although women were solely or primarily responsible for the household tasks, only three expressed dissatisfaction. The division of household labor in these households did not generate the

TABLE 11.2 Division of Household Labor: Clerical
(% of sample, in round numbers; N = 8)

	Respondent[a]	*Both*[b]	*Spouse*[a]
Plans/prepares meals	87	12	—
Cleans up after meals	87	12	—
Cleans house	75	25	—
Buys groceries/household needs	50	37	12
Does laundry	75	25	—
	High	*Low*	*Neutral*
Level of satisfaction	37	37	25

[a] Performs these chores all or most of the time.
[b] Perform these chores about equally.

same level of conflict as was found in households of Chicana professionals. Instead of open conflict, clerical workers thankfully accepted whatever their husbands were willing to give, or they attempted to "school" their husbands through gentle nonconfrontational tactics. Their behavior reflects a clear ideological division between what they "think" and "expect" regarding household labor. Some women said that they did not expect equal sharing because of their cultural upbringing. Gloria, for example, said:

> I think if I was raised differently and he had been raised differently I would, but I don't expect it. I'm not going to be the type that nags and says you do your share. I don't because it makes the house a little more comfortable, rather than have the constant nagging.

Laura, a swing-shift worker at the telephone company, whose husband is a full-time student, does not expect him to take equal responsibility and attempts to avoid conflict. Before she leaves for work in the afternoon, she usually prepares dinner for her husband and nine-year-old son. Although she arrives home after midnight, she gets up in the morning to take care of her son's needs and drives him to school.

> There are times when I wish I could come home and the sink was clean and there were no dishes from dinner. But I overlook it. They are going to get done, I'm going to do them, and I see no sense in making an upheaval about it. I never hold him accountable. So if it gets done fine; if it doesn't, well it will get done somehow. It's not something I harp on.

Norma, a secretary, talked about how men had to be "retrained." She also attempts to avoid conflict, nagging, or demanding tactics. Instead, she has taken the advice of older Mexican women, who have told her that "tienes que hacerlo por la buena" (you have to do it on good terms).

> I usually try to do it "a la buena." I kind of play little tricks, get him into a good mood or whatever. I just make sure that everything feels kind of neutral, like at night when no one is feeling grouchy or angry. And I will say, "Oh, help me with this, or bring me that, and can you do this for me. Oh, thank you, honey" or whatever and I kind of pat him on the back.

Norma's efforts have met with some success, in that her husband is beginning to become more involved in household labor. Juan is now working a four-day, ten-hour shift and is home Fridays. "On Fridays, when he is home, he fixes his own breakfast, and he will clean up a little bit, like he washes the dishes, vacuums, and fixes things up."

Norma also recently began to "school" him on how to do the laundry. While she feels responsible for laundering his work and personal clothing, she decided that he can take care of his athletic clothing. Juan belongs to a soccer team that plays every weekend and practices several times a week; so extra work is required for the upkeep of his gym clothes. Recently, after gentle prodding from her, he began to take responsibility for doing his own gym clothes.

The division of labor has also changed somewhat over the course of the marriage in Flor's household, but she is still responsible for the majority of the work, with help from her teenage daughter.

> It's changed. In the beginning he wouldn't lift even a spoon. As they say in Spanish: "No levanta ni una cuchara." That's true. He wouldn't babysit his own children; he wouldn't pick up his things, he wouldn't take his dish to the sink. Everything had to be done for him. It remained like that while I was at home. After I started working, things weren't getting done by me. After a long time he finally decided he could carry his dish to the sink by himself, and he could watch his own kids. Little by little he has just kind of gotten into doing things for himself. If there wasn't a pair of pants ironed, well, he just had to iron them himself. He has also learned to prepare his own breakfast and lunch for himself. So now he does for himself, and he doesn't really get into any household things for anybody else. If he does, then we hear about it.

Flor's husband, like Norma's, is involved in sports tournaments and practices several times a week. Like Norma, Flor also recently decided that she should not have to be responsible for his gym clothes.

Clerical workers also complained that their husbands utilize stalling techniques. Even though women recognize these tactics, they nevertheless fall prey to their husband's strategies. As Yvette explained:

> There were times when the garbage is there and I'll ask him, "Victor, will you please take out the garbage?" and he will say, "OK babe, I'll do it later." It's two hours later and I look and the garbage is still there and I will think, "I'll fix that." I'll get another bag and I'll start making another little garbage bag. And it's already in the evening and I'll ask him, "Aren't you going to take out the garbage," "Oh yeah, babe, I'll do it later." Then I'll think, "I'll fix this guy, I'll do it myself." I feel like

> I'm torturing him because I didn't give him the opportunity to take out the garbage, but all along I'm torturing myself, right?

While clerical workers do expect their husbands to "fill in their shoes" when necessary, they cling to traditional gender-role ideology. Although Yvette's situation has changed over the course of the marriage, with her husband taking on more responsibilities, a clear division of "his" and "her" realms persists, and both view his participation as a "help" to her.

> Things have changed. Now if he takes off his clothes and leaves them around, I just put them into a little pile. So a few days later, he will say, "Where are my slacks?" You see that pile over there? Well, what are they doing there? Look, I don't wear them, those are your clothes. If you know they are clean, you hang them up, and if they are dirty, then I will get to them.

Clerical workers in particular bring up gender-role socialization to explain contemporary gender behavior and realms of responsibility. As Yvette explained:

> In my house my father did nothing, my mother did everything. The house was the responsibility of my mother and the children. So in my mind, the father was to go to work and bring home the bread and butter, and it was the mother's responsibility to have the bread and butter on the table. That is why I say, my dishes, my laundry, because those are my responsibilities up front.

Chicana clerical workers differ from women in both professional and blue-collar jobs in their acceptance of traditional gender-role divisions. They uniformly stated that they did not expect their husbands to share equally in the division of household labor, they relied on gender-role ideology to explain their situation, and they utilized nonconfrontational strategies to attempt to change this division of labor.

Blue-Collar Workers

Chicana blue-collar and professional workers articulated similar expectations and willingness to engage in household struggle. Although husbands of blue-collar workers do less housework than husbands of Chicana professionals, the level of satisfaction with the division of household labor was similar for both groups. Half of the blue-collar women expressed a high level of satisfaction (Table 11.3).

One blue-collar worker stated that she expected her husband to do his equal share "right from the beginning," but most of the blue-collar workers adopted a militant stance on household labor later in their marriages. The overwhelming majority of blue-collar marriages started out highly sex-role segregated. During the course of the marriage, however, women began demanding—and receiving—more help from their husbands to accommodate their working schedules.

Christina, a delivery truck driver, who has the most egalitarian relationship in

TABLE 11.3 Division of Household Labor: Blue-Collar Workers (% of sample, in round numbers; $N = 8$)

	Respondent[a]	*Both*[b]	*Spouse*[a]
Plans/prepares meals	75	25	—
Cleans up after meals	50	37	—
Cleans house	50	50	12
Buys groceries/household needs	50	37	12
Does laundry	65	25	12
	High	*Low*	*Neutral*
Level of satisfaction	50	25	25

[a] Performs these chores all or most of the time.
[b] Perform these chores about equally.

this sample, was very clear about what she expected from her husband from the beginning of her marriage.

> Well, in the beginning we would have arguments, but I told him, I can't do everything. Right from the beginning we said what was expected. I wanted to work but I didn't want to come home to clean up the house. Like some of my girlfriends, their husbands work and they come home and that is it. They don't do anything. And on Friday nights they go out and have fun with their friends and the women have to stay home with the kids. I can't accept that. That is not right.

Christina reported joint division of labor on almost all items on the scaled questionnaire. However, when she talked about what occurred on a daily basis, it was clear that although her husband does a considerable amount of work, she does more. At the end of the interview, she became aware of this contradiction, looked up at me, and said: "I think I do more. But he doesn't just sit around the house. He puts his share in, but I do more."

Perhaps the most dramatic change has occurred in Maria's family as a result of her demands. Maria has a full-time job in a furniture factory, working the swing shift. She also works on-call at a motel during the week and works two eight-hour shifts on the weekends. Of all the women interviewed in this sample, she has had the most oppressive relationship. Prior to her newfound militancy, she did all the household labor.

> This just started recently, about two years ago. Before, I used to do everything. Now I put my cards on the table and he is doing his chores. In other words, we have made an agreement that he does so much and I do so much. I have worked hard for this, that is why it has changed.

When I asked her what brought on the change, she replied:

> I just got tired of it. *I'm nobody's slave.* Like I told him, I never used to take care of myself. Now I'm taking care of me. Before, I was too busy taking care of everything. I didn't have time, now I have time. Before, he demanded that I get up at 4:00 A.M. to prepare his breakfast and lunch, and now he does it himself. So now I get a full rest. I don't have to worry about washing clothes because he washes every week. If I prepare dinner, he will wash dishes. And when I don't feel like preparing dinner, he makes dinner and washes dishes too.

Like Chicana professionals, blue-collar women have had to fight an uphill battle that has gained them some tangible results. But even though men are doing more, most of the women are still responsible for the majority of household labor. Although men married to blue-collar women are sharing in the household labor, there is a great deal of resistance on their part. Women, however, continue to strive for greater male involvement. Victoria discusses resistance and change in gender relations in her marriage:

> It hasn't been easy. Richard was brought up *muy macho.* When I started working, I told him, "I'm tired. Why don't you help me do this?" At first he would say, "You can do it." It was getting to be too much. To this day Richard does not bathe the girls, Richard does not cook, he doesn't wash the toilet. I do that. But he washes clothes, mops the floor, and vacuums.

Richard's subversive techniques are similar to those employed by other husbands in this sample. Victoria, like other women, falls prey to these strategies, ultimately doing the job herself.

> For Richard to give the girls dinner, he will go to Wendy's and feed them. For him to be able to pay the PG&E bill, he will wait for two months to pay it. For Richard to make sure that the floor is clean, he will let it go. He will eventually do it but not when it needs to be done. I know he can do it, pero se hace tonto [but he plays dumb]. So I'll say, "Get out of here and let me do it."

Victoria has attempted a variety of techniques in her struggle. Outright confrontation and nagging have netted some results. Recently she has become increasingly impatient with her husband and has gone on strike.

> So I found another way of doing it. Which is I don't wash for him, I don't cook for him. I'm getting to the point in which I only make certain foods for the girls and I. Then he will come to, he gets the message.

Not only are blue-collar Chicanas willing to make demands on their husbands, but also at the ideological level they label their husbands' attitude as sexist. Victoria very adamantly told me: "One day I called Richard a male chauvinist pig. Boy, was he shocked."

Like other husbands, blue-collar men compare their wives to other women as a mechanism of social control in their attempts to maintain their privileges. Lisa related an incident that happened at her mother-in-law's house.

> He tries to pull these little numbers. Like "That is not the way my mother does it." Well, once we were at his mother's house and she had some beans on the stove, and he told his mother the way he wanted the beans cooked. And I thought to myself, if he had told me that, he would have been wearing the beans. I just thought, no way. I'm not going to put up with that, no way.

The data reveal that both men and women employ a variety of "gender strategies" to manipulate the situation to their advantage. Men use stalling tactics and perform tasks in a slipshod manner to avoid domestic work. They attempt to compare their wives to other women, as a means of social control and in order to discredit their wives' requests. Women also utilize a variety of strategies in their daily struggle: they retrain, coach, and praise husbands for a job well done. At times, they resort to slowdowns or work stoppages, so that eventually men are forced to contribute more to household labor.

Clerical workers are unique in their underground approach, which, for the most part, avoids verbal confrontations and open power struggles. Professional and blue-collar workers also utilize underground resistance in combination with confrontation techniques. This tactic has been successful for blue-collar and professional women; they have been able to alter the distribution of household labor on their behalf to a much greater degree than clerical workers. A strong relationship emerged between women's willingness to engage in "political struggle" and the level of male involvement in household labor.

The analysis of the household division of labor in this sample illustrates the complexity of the relationship between ideology (the belief system that incorporates what women "think" and what they "expect") and practice (as expressed in their behavior). At the ideological level, all the respondents believe that their husbands should have equal responsibility for household chores. However, clerical workers unanimously stated that they did not expect equal sharing, whereas blue-collar and professional workers expected equal sharing but did not believe it would actually happen. The category "expectations" operates at two levels: what women want, and what they think will happen realistically. At the level of practice, clerical workers behaved according to their nonexpectations. They did not demand or struggle for male involvement. They also articulated more sex-linked attitudes regarding male and female roles in the family. At the abstract level, they embrace an egalitarian stance on household labor. At the same time, they also expressed strong ideological and emotional ties to sex-typed roles. Perhaps this commitment to traditional roles accounts for their lack of expectations and their nondemanding attitudes. They can't expect their husbands to participate equally, since they themselves are not convinced that there *should* be equal participation. Professionals and, to a lesser degree, blue-collar workers were more successful in translating their beliefs and expectations into practice. Their willingness to struggle with their husbands also attests to the strength of their convictions and expectations.

ANALYSIS

I believe that women's earnings and work demands are contributing factors, at the ideological and behavioral levels, in the "political struggle" over the distribution of household labor. They are not the only factors, but they represent two plausible links between employment and the division of household labor that emerged from this sample.

Income

In *Becoming a Two Job Family,* Hood (1983) found that, in her sample of midwestern American couples, income ratio strongly influenced power relations in the family. Similarly, data from this study suggest a link between women's earnings and their ability to negotiate for greater male involvement in household labor. Most women viewed their economic contribution as a bargaining chip in the marriage power struggle. However, most of the women in this sample were unable to translate "income power" into marriage power, probably because they earned less than their spouses. This wage differential was most acute in the clerical category.

Clerical workers earned considerably less than their spouses, seven of whom are blue-collar workers and one a supervisor. Three clerical workers earned half or less than half as much as their spouses earned, and two earned $5,000 less. The other three women were primary supporters: one husband was a student on the GI bill, one collected disability insurance after an industrial accident, and the other husband received unemployment benefits.

While blue-collar Chicana women earned less than their blue-collar husbands, the gap was much less than for clerical women. In the blue-collar category, six Chicanas earned $5,000 to $10,000 less than their spouses, one earned the same salary, and one earned $2,000 more.

Among professional workers, two women were primary supporters, two earned $10,000 to $15,000 more than their spouses, two earned the same salary, and two earned $10,000 to $15,000 less than their husbands. Husbands of professional women were also professional workers, except in one case, where the husband was a student. For professional Chicanas, the economic gap was also much less than for the clerical workers.

Among the eight professional Chicanas in the sample, four of the husbands assumed considerable responsibility for household chores. In three of these four households, the women were providing most of the income to the household and had jobs with higher status than those of their husbands; one husband was a student, one was in a transitional job that he was going to quit in order to study for the bar, and one was attempting to build up a law practice. In one other household, the husband was unemployed and the wife was the sole supporter, but she was still responsible for most of the household tasks. This household exhibited a high level of conflict. In households where wives provided either similar or less income, or had similar or less prestigious employment status, women were responsible for more of the household labor.

Among blue-collar households, the relationship between women's earnings and the division of household labor was not readily apparent—probably because the earning gap between men and women was minimal. Although blue-collar men were assuming a share of the household labor, their involvement fell short of that of men married to professional women. Blue-collar households were similar to professional households in that there was a high level of struggle.

Clerical women were at an economic disadvantage vis-à-vis their husbands. This disadvantage was reflected in the lack of male participation in household work. Overall, clerical workers did most or all of the household work. In the two households where men were assuming more responsibility, the husbands were providing less household income. In one, the husband was a student receiving GI benefits; in the other, the husband was on disability. Since clerical Chicanas earn considerably less than their spouses, their economic power for bargaining strategies was practically nil. Furthermore, some of the men openly utilized their earning advantage in their efforts to circumvent their wives' attempts to involve them in household labor. These husbands used their higher salaries as leverage to maintain a measure of economic and social control and justify their resistance to doing "women's work."

Work Demands

The work demands for professional and blue-collar Chicanas are greater than for clerical workers; therefore, greater male involvement in household chores is required if these women are to handle both work and family concerns. Clerical workers have set limits to their labor, whereas the demands of professional and blue-collar jobs are not so easily contained. Clerical workers, for example, have set hours, and though they do bring home their work-related problems and frustrations, they are generally better able to separate work from family life. Though they generally complain about fatigue and stress from the job, they are not required to bring work home, and generally they are not required to work overtime or work a shift that conflicts with their familial duties.

For blue-collar workers, work schedules can vary. These workers complained that, although theoretically overtime is voluntary, they must work overtime if they are to stay in the good graces of the supervisor. A worker's willingness to put in overtime hours is taken into account when evaluations are made and promotions given. Work shifts can also vary; consequently, husbands often are forced to assume a greater share of household and child-care tasks, whether they want to or not.

Professional workers have to contend with fatigue and stress from juggling work and family and are unable to keep work from spilling into family life. Professional Chicanas have to take work home and often must attend evening meetings. Furthermore, the pressures from being a woman of color increase their level of tension, expectations, and stress. As Luisa stated,

> It's the double-triple role you have to uphold. Like I was telling my boss, I said, "You know, I have to succeed in this job. Because if I don't, I fail as a Chicana, as a female and as me," where if I was a white man, it would be different. It's that responsibility that we carry.

The work demands and the political nature of their jobs give Chicana professionals a degree of leverage for negotiating greater male involvement in household labor.

CONCLUSION

The degree of husbands' participation in household labor varied considerably in this sample. Professional men married to professional women did a greater share than most other men. The lack of a substantial earning gap, the energy and time demands of the women's careers, and their ability to pressure their husbands into doing their share had a positive effect on male involvement.

Blue-collar men married to clerical women did the least amount of household labor. In these families, a substantial earning gap, working schedules that allow women to continue to fulfill their familial responsibilities, and the women's ideological stance had a cumulative negative effect on male involvement in household labor.

The earning gap between blue-collar men and women was virtually nil. The lack of earning gap—in conjunction with women's demanding and often unpredictable working schedules and their willingness to press for greater male participation in household labor—had a positive result. Blue-collar men married to blue-collar women are more involved in household labor than blue-collar men married to clerical workers; but, except for a few cases, blue-collar men did less of the household labor than professional men.

Most of the women in this study have made some gains in moving their relationships with their partners toward less sex-role-segregated arrangements. In general, however, these marriages are not egalitarian in household chore allocation. The portrait that emerges from this study is a tendency toward a reproduction of the traditional household division of labor juxtaposed with a minimal degree of task reallocation. The study points to the important role that qualitative research plays in uncovering critical dynamics in the household division of labor.

The relationship between income, demands of work, and the ideological and behavioral dimensions of the struggle over the division of household labor needs to be tested with larger samples.

REFERENCES

Baca-Zinn, Maxine.
1980. "Employment and Education of Mexican American Women: The Interplay of Modernity and Ethnicity in Eight Families." *Harvard Educational Review* 50: 47–62.

Berk, Sarah Fenstermaker.
1985. *The Gender Factory*. New York: Plenum.

Flores, Yvette Gisele.
1982. "The Impact of Acculturation on the Chicano Family: An Analysis of Selected Variables." Ph.D. diss., University of California, Berkeley.

Hartmann, Heidi.
1981. "The Family as the Locus of Gender, Class and Political Struggle: The Example of Housework." *Signs* 6:336–394.

Hood, Jane C.
1983. *Becoming a Two Job Family*. New York: Praeger.

Mirandé, Alfredo, and Evangelina Enríquez.
1979. *La Chicana: The Mexican American Woman*. Chicago: University of Chicago Press.

Segura, Denise A.
1984. "Labor Market Stratification: The Chicana Experience." *Berkeley Journal of Sociology* 29:57–91.

Vanek, Joann.
1980. "Household Work, Wage Work, and Sexual Inequality." In *Women and Household Labor*, ed. Sarah F. Berk. Beverly Hills, Calif.: Sage.

Ybarra, Lea.
1982. "When Wives Work: The Impact on the Family." *Journal of Marriage and the Family* 2:169–177.

Ybarra, Lea, and Carlos H. Arce.
1981. "Entra Dicho y Hecho Hay Gran Trecho: The Division of Household Chores in the Chicano Family." Paper presented at the National Association for Chicano Studies conference, Riverside, Calif., April.

Zavella, Patricia.
1987. *Women, Work and the Chicano Family: Cannery Workers of the Santa Clara Valley*. Ithaca, N.Y.: Cornell University Press.

PART FOUR

Social Reproduction: Institutional and "Uninstitutional" Lives

TWELVE

Slipping through the Cracks

Dilemmas in Chicana Education

Denise A. Segura

At ——— High, I started "slipping." There wasn't any interest. You have to be interested in the classes to do well. And the teachers have to be interested in you. That just wasn't there.

CYNTHIA P., CLERICAL WORKER WITH A GED (HIGH SCHOOL EQUIVALENCY DIPLOMA)

I was raised to believe that the woman stays home and has the children and cares for the family. I was perfectly willing to stay home—I was even looking forward to it! [laughs] When I had to work, I was shocked out of my life!

VELIA M., TEACHER AIDE WITH A GED

Year after year, about half of all Chicanas slip through cracks in the educational system and do not obtain high school diplomas.[1] Without "good" academic skills or appropriate credentials, a majority (about 70 percent) of Chicanas like Cynthia and Velia work in unskilled or semiskilled jobs (Sokoloff, 1980; Segura, 1984). Research demonstrates that the occupational chances of Mexican Americans can improve with additional schooling (Snipp and Tienda, 1984). Yet surprisingly little research analyzes what impedes the educational attainment of "low-achieving" Chicanas who enter the secondary labor market. (On the other hand, both Vásquez, 1982, and Gandara, 1982, have examined barriers to education experienced by high-achieving and professional Chicanas.)

The purpose of this essay is to identify and analyze the barriers to education faced by a selected sample of Chicanas and Mexicanas who were not "successful" in school (e.g., "low achievers" and/or school dropouts). To provide a context for this analysis, I first examine research on impediments to the education of "disadvantaged" groups, including Chicanos. Second, I draw on experiential data to examine how social-class origin and gender-specific expectations within the family (such as those expressed by Velia) restrict educational attainment. Third, I analyze the manner whereby institutional practices, curriculum, and social dynamics in schools (alluded to by Cynthia) shape schooling. Inasmuch as the women in the present study eventually participated in an adult education/employment training program, I conclude by pointing to ways that the education and employability of other undereducated Chicanas can be improved.

EXPLANATIONS FOR LOW EDUCATIONAL ATTAINMENT

Explanations for the low educational attainment of Chicanos—male and female—typically target the individual, the educational institution, or Mexican/Chicano culture. Educational failure or success as an individual concern is a predominant theme among educators and scholars. In this view, educational achievement rests largely on the efforts of individuals, since overt legal barriers to education have been abolished by civil rights legislation (Sowell, 1981, 1982, 1984). Critics of this interpretation point to the large numbers of Mexican American students who leave school without a diploma (45 percent) and argue that, in spite of civil rights legislation, many unsolved problems in education remain (National Commission on Secondary Education for Hispanics, 1984). In fact, a majority of Mexican-origin students attend urban schools where the student population is predominantly minority (Orfield, 1983). In these schools, Chicanos achieve less and drop out at higher levels than students in predominantly white schools (Espinosa and Ochoa, 1986). Persistent low Chicano educational attainment limits employment options and rates of socioeconomic mobility—all of which point to the important role schools play in maintaining racial boundaries.

Bowles and Gintis (1976), in a major critique of schooling in the United States, contend that the school's basic function is to reproduce a hierarchically organized class society. A meritocratic ideal, which attributes success only to individual hard work, can mask institutional practices—such as IQ testing and curriculum placement (tracking)—that limit the level and quality of education received by working-class and minority children (compared to middle- and upper-class children). In addition, other research indicates that many teachers have low academic expectations of working-class and minority children (Percell, 1977; James Irvine Foundation, 1982). Thus, within schools, both organizational practices (such as curriculum tracking) and social dynamics—in particular, relations between teachers and students—can negatively affect educational achievement.

The fact of being female can impede the educational attainment of all girls, including Chicanas. Teachers give boys more positive feedback and direct more criticism against girls (Cherry, 1975). Within families, parents typically expect their sons to be more ambitious, highly educated, and career-oriented than their daughters (Hoffman, 1977; Block, 1979). In contrast, daughters are expected to be kind and nurturing and to prepare for good marriages. Research on Mexican-origin families reports similar expectations for Chicanas (Mirandé and Enríquez, 1979; Chacon et al., 1982; Solorzano, 1986).

Other research on Chicano education argues that Mexican-Chicano culture does not place a high premium on education (Ringawa, 1980). In particular, a low esteem for education is supposedly the reason for limited involvement by Mexican parents in school activities and irregular communication with teachers and counselors. Recent scholarship counters this logic by pointing out that inadequate English-language skills often bar parental involvement in school activities (Carter and Segura, 1979). Further, parents from working-class backgrounds with limited education feel at a disadvantage when interacting with school personnel, whom they regard as the "professionals" (Lareau, 1984). Finally, cultural variations between Mexican and Anglo families may not be as critical to the process of educational attainment and future occupational success as perceptions of the local opportunity structure (types of jobs available to their reference groups of family and friends) (Ogbu, 1978; Romo, 1984; Moore, 1976).

As the research cited here shows, we need to analyze individual, institutional, familial, and cultural features to understand the dilemma of Chicana education. In this essay, I will analyze factors that influence the schooling experience of a selected sample of Chicanas, so as to understand their barriers to education. When we understand the conditions that have impeded the educational attainment of Chicanas who slipped through the educational cracks, we can perhaps devise strategies that overcome problems in the schooling process.

METHODOLOGY AND SAMPLE PROFILE

To identify and analyze barriers to educational attainment of low-achieving Chicanas, I conducted in-depth interviews of twenty adult Chicanas without high school diplomas or sufficient academic preparation to enter the job of their choice.[2] The interviewed women were selected from the 1978–79 or 1980–81 cohorts of an adult education/employment training program, Servicios Educativos para Adelantar, or SEPA (a pseudonym for a real agency in a city in the Greater San Francisco Bay Area). This program assisted Latinos without high school diplomas or "good" academic skills in obtaining a GED (General Education Diploma) and sufficient academic or employment skills to enter a variety of semiskilled clerical, service, and factory jobs in the Greater San Francisco Bay Area.

Typically, the Chicanas in this study came from lower- and working-class urban backgrounds.[3] All but one attended racially mixed schools in the San Francisco Bay Area. Two Chicanas went to schools with a large number (approximately 20 percent of the student body) of Chicano/Latino students. One Chicana attended a predominantly white school in a middle-class suburban area. When they were interviewed (1985), the average age of the respondents was 27.5 years. Half of the Chicanas were second-generation U.S. citizens (at least one parent was born in Mexico). The rest of the Chicanas were third-generation U.S. citizens with both parents born in the United States.

This essay is based on data gathered from the respondents on family and education. The women interviewed for this study do not represent all Chicana low achievers. However, since they are high school dropouts, low achievers, and eventual entrants into semiskilled jobs—characteristics shared by many Mexican-origin women—their educational experiences will strike resonant chords among other women who have not succeeded in school.

FAMILY OF ORIGIN

The family of origin is a critical arena where the acquisition of education can be either supported or thwarted. These Chicanas' early socialization in the family and extended kin networks emphasized values traditional to their local communities and to society at large. A majority of the Chicanas reported being taught "traditional" female roles. Susana said: "In our family it [socialization] was different. My mom loved us both [my brother and me], but we were treated differently. I mean, she treated me like a girl. She couldn't treat me like a guy anyway."

In Susana's family and in a majority of the families of the interviewed Chicanas, girls were expected to learn housework from their mothers, care for their brothers and younger siblings, obey their parents unquestioningly, and respect their elders. Most of the Chicanas attended church services regularly as children. They expected to marry, have children, and work—if the work did not lower the quality of family life. The gender-specific role expectations noted here also are found in other research on Chicano families (Mirandé and Enríquez, 1979), Hispanic families (Farris and Glenn, 1976), and families in general (Chodorow, 1979; Epstein, 1979; Sokoloff, 1980).

This emphasis on maintaining traditional gender roles can conflict with high educational attainment by Chicanas (Mirandé and Enríquez, 1979; Vásquez, 1982). Family characteristics often associated with low educational attainment include family instability, low value for education, and lack of parental encouragement to pursue schooling (Ringawa, 1980; Mahan and Johnson, 1983; Evans and Anderson, 1973). The families of the low-achieving Chicanas did not meet these conditions; instead, nearly all the respondents reported that their parents valued education and had urged them to do well in school. Parental encouragement ranged from a general exhortation to attend school and do well to a more active monitoring of achievement, exemplified by Laura's mother: "My family was always pushing 'school and get a good education.' When you're raised that way, then you go out and work for it. We used to always have to bring our report cards home. And when I had a C or lower—whew! I had to get A's or B's—that's what my mom wanted."

A more typical view of the parental role in education was offered by Julia: "Well, they [parents] mostly tried to raise us as best as they could. Both of my parents didn't graduate. They cared, but they were just naive about what was going on. They let us choose what we wanted. But we never really talked about it. We never thought about what we would do after high school." Julia, like most of the other Chicana respondents, felt that her parents "cared" about her education even though they were not actively involved in it.

In general, few Mexican parents are actively involved in schools (e.g., participate in Parent-Teacher Associations or attend "open houses"); but the reasons for this lack of involvement are not as obvious as was once thought. That is, it does not necessarily reflect a low esteem for education or a lack of interest in their children's educations. Rather, Chicano/Mexicano parents from working-class and/or limited English-speaking backgrounds are rarely well informed about school activities and the importance of their participation in the schools their children attend (United States Commission on Civil Rights, 1972; Carter and Segura, 1979).

Other evidence (Lareau, 1984) suggests that different levels of parental involvement in schools reflect social-class differences more clearly than racial or ethnic differences. Lareau found that middle-class parents viewed schooling as a shared responsibility, whereas working-class parents regarded their children's educations as the responsibility of professional educators. They did not deem it appropriate for them (as nonprofessionals) to intervene in the schooling process. This study offers insight into the parent-school relationship of the respondents' families, given their predominantly working-class backgrounds.

The Chicanas indicated that their parents valued education but encouraged them to do well in school for different reasons. About one-third of the sample were urged by their parents to finish high school and pursue higher education in order to marry a man with good employment prospects. As Lydia said: "With my mom . . . Well, my dad was never really into education. My mom was more like, well, you should go to school and meet a doctor and get married." In families such as Lydia's, educational attainment was viewed not as an end in itself or as the precursor to a professional career. Instead, encouragement to do well in school was shaped to fit traditional gender-role expectations and the primacy of the family in a Chicana's life.

In contrast to Lydia's situation, two-thirds of the respondents indicated that parental educational encouragement was not related to improving their marriage prospects. In this group, women reported being urged by their mothers to do well in school to prepare for professional careers. As Jenny said: "My mom wanted all of us to be like lawyers and professionals—well educated. You know how parents want their kids to be something big. Well, my aunt wanted that for us [too]. . . . What they didn't have, they wanted us to have. That's how it goes, you see? They want us to be better than them. And I want that for my daughter." Jenny's comments illustrate the commonly felt pressure to achieve a degree of school (and career) success that had eluded their parents.

Parental support of education took many forms. In general, parents worked hard in physically demanding jobs to buy or rent houses in areas that had "better" schools; and, when necessary, they bought educational materials such as encyclopedias or books. The pressure compounded the pain Chicanas felt when they did poorly in school. Ester recalled: "When I heard my family call me a failure—well, it hurt—and worse—I began to believe it. . . . Of course, my mother never knew any better and my father didn't know what to do either. He had never gone to school."

When she was called a failure by her family, Ester felt resentful and hurt, particularly since their disparagement reinforced the negative sense of self she had formed in school. Currently a single parent, Ester is immersed in her son's education. She participates in different school activities and volunteers in the classroom. She says: "I'm doing everything I can to give him the chance I never had." If and when her son graduates with a high school diploma, Ester will feel successful at last.

The Chicanas in the present sample felt pressure to meet parental expectations in both the educational and the familial arenas. They received mixed messages from their parents. On the one hand, they were expected to conform to traditional female roles that centered on family life; on the other hand, Chicanas were pressured by their families to do well in school and even to aspire to professional careers. The gulf between both sets of expectations is a conflict relevant to women outside the present sample. In spite of the potential conflict between these expectations, the Chicanas remembered having a variety of career aspirations as young children. Alma, currently a clerical worker, spoke of her early love of astronomy. Lydia, a sales clerk on maternity leave, had dreamed of being a dentist. Susana, currently unemployed, had wanted to be an interior decorator. Their dreams faded before they entered junior high school—replaced by fears of failing.

Although the families of the respondents had encouraged educational attainment, they could not provide the necessary tools to enhance achievement. The school system was the critical component in these young women's educational attainment and inadequate career preparation.

EDUCATION

The school system has not been successful in educating Chicano children in the United States. Forty-five percent of all Mexican-American students leave school without a high school diploma (National Commission on Secondary Education for Hispanics, 1984). Among Chicanos in the California public schools, only 23 percent are performing "satisfactorily" at each grade level (California Assembly Office of Research, 1984a, 1984b).

The Chicanas in this study discussed both negative and positive features of their school experiences. Their accounts, while painful in many instances, point to areas in the social organization of schooling that need to be addressed. Specifically, they recounted instances of teacher insensitivity, counselor neglect, unchallenging and monocultural curriculum, and disparagement by non-Chicano peers.

Teacher Instruction

Teacher instruction is central to the schooling process. Within the boundaries set by the school (e.g., class size and class composition), teachers instruct students. The type and quality of that instruction vary across and within schools (Coleman et al., 1966; California Assembly Office of Research, 1984b; California State

Department of Education, 1984). Minority students, including Chicanos, are usually relegated to general education classes that are held in less esteem than college preparatory classes (Carter and Segura, 1979; National Center for Education Statistics, 1980). In these classes, instruction is often remedial rather than academically challenging (Oakes, 1985; Persell, 1977).

In the present study, all but one of the respondents were placed in general education programs; one Chicana was in a remedial education program. To the respondents, teachers rarely appeared interested in their subject matter or in whether or not the individual Chicana actually learned. As Alma said, "Not too many teachers take the time to make sure you learned. It was just—'All right, class—did you understand it? Fine.' And that was it. And you're over here asking yourself—'Uh, what did she say?' Then you look around and ask your friend, or whatever." All too often, Alma and the other Chicanas were faced with teachers who appeared inattentive toward their educational needs or did not believe that they had the ability to succeed in school.

Detachment from student learning, coupled with low student expectations and unimaginative teaching (e.g., doing dittoed worksheets for most of the class period), constitutes "indifferent instruction." Under conditions of indifferent instruction, "passing" students often performed below grade level, never getting help that would raise their educational performance. Chicanas who were passed in classes irrespective of their academic performance now realize that both indifferent instruction and "passing" impeded the quality and quantity of their education. As Cynthia said:

> The teachers there [her high school] they would just pass you so they wouldn't have to deal with you anymore. Now, not all of them did that, but . . . like my history teacher did that. I was getting D's. I mean, you could see that I needed help or tutoring. But he just passed me with D's. Of course then I didn't realize what was happening. I didn't trip off it then—I just thought "all right!" But *now* I'm paying for it. Maybe if he would just have taken a little time—but maybe I should have asked for help too. But I didn't because it would have made me feel stupid. I was just, I guess, intimidated.

Chicanas like Cynthia were not held accountable by teachers and were passed even though they had not mastered the course content. As a consequence, half of the respondents gradually fell further and further behind classmates until they dropped out of school. The others managed to complete high school, but without good academic skills.

The teacher insensitivity endured by many of the Chicana dropouts both shamed and intimidated them. As Ester described:

> You don't have teachers being positive with some kids. I know what happened to me. This teacher in elementary school pulled out a folder—a math folder—and in front of the whole class said, "Look, class—look at Ester's folder. Isn't it impressive?" Then she opened up my folder and revealed that it was completely empty!

> I was so shamed. The other kids in the class didn't do anything. No one laughed or said a word. Some of them lowered their heads. I wanted to . . . [shrugged her shoulders]. But my school years were full of this type of incident.

Insensitive teaching methods perpetuated Ester's low-achievement patterns; she and other low-achieving Chicanas could not be "shamed" into achieving. Instead, Ester withdrew emotionally from this class, thereby insulating herself from feeling the same pain the next time she was publicly humiliated. By the time she was in the ninth grade, her emotional disaffection from the classroom was so intense that she left high school without a diploma. Other research demonstrates that Ester's experiences are common among the Chicano population (United States Commission on Civil Rights, 1972, 1974; Carter and Segura, 1979).

The Chicanas felt that teacher attitudes underlying instructional activities were major barriers to educational attainment. Particularly troublesome to the respondents was their perception that neither teachers nor counselors "cared" about their presence or achievement in school. As Antonia said: "I don't remember any teachers telling me to go on with my education. I was always 'passed on,' even when I didn't learn anything. No one ever discussed college with me. No, there weren't any counselors who talked with me about this. No one cared."

The sentiment that "no one cared," cited here by Antonia, reverberated throughout the Chicana sample. The Chicanas based this assessment on the fact that not one of them remembered having a teacher in elementary school who encouraged them to do well or helped them to master difficult course content. Further, not one Chicana remembered being told that "she was smart" or that she should consider college as part of her future. Lydia explained why teacher "caring" was so important to the respondents:

> The teachers I had—forget it! Mr. Delgado was the only one who really cared. He'd just scold me in a nice way—but really *cared* about us. He told me, "Look, Lydia—you're someone *important!* And you should let that person come out. I know you can do it!" He'd always say that to me. He'd say, "Don't do it for me or for anybody else—but do it for yourself." He used to tell me that a lot. And I always felt that he cared.

Teacher "caring" was valued by Lydia because of the underlying message that she was important—but only rarely was this message conveyed to, or received by, the Chicanas during their school years. Instead, they felt unimportant or unworthy.

Counseling

In addition to indifferent teachers and instruction, the respondents indicted the counseling provided by their schools. In these schools, counselors were responsible for curriculum advising, class scheduling, and educational placement. Ultimately, the counselor decided whether a respondent was placed in a college preparatory program, in a general education program, in remedial classes, or in work-experience programs.

Counselors often use standardized testing as a guide for placing students in educational programs, yet research clearly demonstrates that standardized testing has cultural biases unfavorable to minority students. In particular, Chicanos and blacks rarely do well on these tests and therefore are rarely placed in academic programs; as a result, racial segregation is reinforced in schools (Roos, 1984; Kent and Ruiz, 1979; Carter and Segura, 1979; United States Commission on Civil Rights, 1972).

In the present study, not a single Chicana reported that her counselor had suggested that she take a college preparatory program. Three Chicanas took several college preparatory classes on the advice of Chicano acquaintances in local colleges. The information these Chicanas received, however, was not adequate to prepare them to compete successfully in college.

In general, the Chicanas knew very little about college requirements and did not enroll in classes that would qualify them for either college or good jobs. As Julia said:

> I was never talked to [by counselors] about college. Not in high school, not in junior high. Never. College was something I did after I left high school and got my GED. But when I was in high school I didn't even know about college. I didn't know such a thing existed—or *could* exist for *me*. And I went to two different high schools.

For Julia and the other Chicanas, schooling was not a pathway to college and professional careers; instead, it was an interlude before work and marriage. These women had not been encouraged or counseled to think otherwise by educational professionals.

Another way that counselor actions (or inactions) hampered the educational achievement of the respondents was through class scheduling. Julia elaborated on this process:

> You know, I went from a straight A student to a straight D student. . . . By the end of the year I dropped out. It had started slowly, though. You see, another problem was the scheduling they started at —— High. This meant that you had two classes in the morning, then a TWO-hour break! When they did that, it was just awful. I would go to my first two classes, then in two and a half hours I was supposed to be ready to go back to the rest of my classes. Well, after two and one-half hours I just wasn't going back to classes. They still have that, too.

Julia's experience demonstrates that class schedules, which are arranged for administrative convenience, can interfere with student achievement—in this case by making class attendance difficult. About one-third of the Chicana respondents reported this type of scheduling problem.

Curriculum

If teaching and counseling methods left much to be desired, yet another major source of discontent among the Chicana respondents was the lack of a culturally relevant curriculum. School curricula tend to be monocultural, reflecting mainly the achievements of Anglo-Americans. Sitting daily in classrooms that ignored their culture and history, Chicanas felt alienated from their school settings. These feelings were particularly keen since a majority of the respondents attended schools that had courses in black history and culture. Cynthia said: "That's another reason I didn't like —— High. They had black history, but they didn't have anything for Chicanos. There should have been more equal time. I wanted it. Hey—I bet I would've gotten an A if they would've had Chicano history there."

Nearly all the respondents agreed with Cynthia that schools should include a more diverse curriculum, and most asserted that if such a curriculum had been integrated into their educational programs, they would have been more motivated to attend classes and achieve.

Peer Interaction

Peer interaction was another area of concern for the Chicanas. They often experienced racial or cultural hostility from their peers—both white and black. Cynthia said:

> I used to have some problems in high school. Like this one white boy used to tell me: "Why don't you go back to Tijuana?" And I didn't know *what* to tell him. Because he was white and . . . I was in the ninth grade. I remember I had this milkshake in my hand. So I just threw it at him and walked away from him. I used to have a lot of problems like that with the whites. I didn't like them. I mean, I wanted to like them, but they didn't like me. So I didn't like them. They used to think I was just stuck-up. But I wasn't. I just preferred being with the other Hispanics. But *they* didn't understand that.

The racial harassment experienced by Cynthia can negatively affect Chicano educational attainment by making school an unpleasant place to attend, and this harassment usually leads to a segregatory social life. Cynthia interacted almost exclusively with her own racial/ethnic group—a preference daily reinforced by "problems" with some white students. Segregatory social behavior—the penchant of Chicanos to congregate with each other—has been depicted negatively and is even offered as a cause of their low educational attainment. In fact, Chicanos often try to provide positive reinforcement to attend classes, as respondents indicated. For example, as Lydia expressed it: "My friends—they thought I was the one who would make it. They pushed me a lot. If some of the guys saw me cutting class, they would drag me to class and tell the teacher that my locker had been stuck. They were very supportive of me a lot."

In this case, as in others, peer interaction was a positive force to attend classes. In other cases, however, peers provided little incentive to attend school, as Elisa indicated when discussing her school years: "I did poorly in high school. I was young and just messing around with my friends. But the teachers didn't really care about you either."

Although peer interaction can contribute to low attendance in classes, it is not the major factor in low educational attainment and eventual dropping out, as Elisa's words indicate. Elisa, Cynthia, Lydia, and the other respondents repeatedly emphasized that their educational attainment and achievement were hindered more by teacher and counselor neglect; had Elisa's teachers shown more interest, she might have been less susceptible to whatever negative peer effects were present.

Youth Employment

Another problematic area for the respondents was their participation in youth employment programs. Eighty percent of the respondents were scheduled by counselors into work programs designed to assist low-income youth monetarily and to help them acquire work experience. The economic goals of these programs were often actually at odds with the educational progress of the Chicana respondents. Laura explained:

> There were problems, I know, with some people who couldn't keep up their grades and work too. When I was a senior they finally began to get strict about that. They started to enforce the rule that you had to have a certain grade point average to be in the [work] program. Before that they hadn't really checked. But after, Mr. Mendez started checking up—he started cracking down on us. Because the Chicano dropout was so bad that *we* started a tutorial program and got college students to help out.

Laura voiced several issues important to a majority of the Chicana respondents. First, she pointed to the negative effect that the youth employment program had on the achievement levels of many Chicanos who were marginal students. Second, she emphasized that the school did not correct this situation until a Chicano teacher involved himself with the employment program as part of his efforts to help address the "dropout" problem of his Chicano students. Finally, she explained that the school district's recalcitrance to provide programs that might reverse low Chicano educational attainment had compelled Chicano students to search for educational assistance beyond their local school.

Unlike Laura, a majority of the Chicanas did not have an advocate who tried to balance their economic needs with their academic needs. Instead, counselors placed them in work-experience programs without regularly reviewing their academic progress. This experience, coupled with a general education as opposed to college preparatory program, virtually precluded them from entering college.

Without a strong support base in schools to promote their educational achievement, 55 percent of the Chicana respondents "slipped through the cracks" and dropped out before high school graduation: only 45 percent acquired a high school diploma. After graduation, even these women did not have sufficient skills or knowledge to obtain stable employment that offered security and opportunities for advancement. Twenty percent entered state colleges but left during their first year. Although they had sufficient education to qualify for a variety of semiskilled jobs (mostly clerical), this group of Chicanas lacked a mode of entry into the job of their choice. The desire to improve their employability and educational skills drew the Chicana respondents to SEPA.

THE SEPA PROGRAM

The Chicanas chose to enter the SEPA adult education program to obtain the educational skills and credentials necessary for stable jobs. They chose SEPA for several reasons. First, many other Chicanos who had been "unsuccessful" in high school were able to obtain a GED and secure employment after completing the SEPA program. Second, SEPA specialized in educating Chicanos/Latinos and offered culturally diverse instruction, small classes, and bilingual teachers. Third, during the years before 1982, SEPA offered small educational stipends to low-income Chicanos through the (now-defunct) CETA program.

The most important reason the Chicanas chose SEPA was that it had proved successful in preparing students for the GED. The Chicanas in this study needed to choose a program that increased their chances to obtain a GED. Susana said:

> I went there because I knew that I had dropped out of school and I figured I'd go back to school at SEPA and get my GED. You know—try to make a go out of it. I told myself—"I can make a go out of it. I can go to *this* school and get my GED!" Studying for the same thing over and over—being so far behind—making up for all those years—I mean, it was really hard!

"Making up for all those years" was extremely difficult for the Chicana dropouts. But obtaining a GED was a critical step toward building a positive self-image; in addition, it enhanced the employment options of the Chicanas. Julia described both the practical and the symbolic value of the GED:

> The GED is important. It's a step up that's behind you—so that now you can go forward. Now I know that I *can* do something. Now the doors are open. It's up to *me* now. Before, when you don't have your GED, you can blame your failure on not having your diploma. But now it's all up to me. And I feel a lot better about that.

The GED allowed them greater access to jobs, but earning a GED was a moral victory as well; it enabled them finally to succeed in a school setting. Earning a GED helped to reverse the negative self-esteem acquired by indifferent instruction, insensitive teachers, and low educational attainment. Further, acquiring a GED gave them a sense of control over their lives that they had lost after nine to twelve years in the public schools.

SEPA's success with low-achieving students is related both to the structure of the program and to the quality of the students' relationships with their teachers, counselors, and peers. Julia praised this strongly interactive approach.

> What I thought was good was that they taught you at different levels. You had the chance to move up. That was different than in high school where you were always at the same level. In high school if you were behind you stayed behind. But at SEPA they taught you so that you moved up! There was nothing holding you back.

Ester reminisced:

> I had a Latino teacher. He took me through math, step by step. He showed me that math was just a puzzle and that I could figure out how to put it all together. Then the positive aspects of learning began to set in. Self-confidence stepped in slowly but surely. Then I started going to classes and got to know Hispanics—my own people [said softly, almost lovingly]. And I began to feel better about them and about myself!

Both Julia and Ester point to several features of SEPA that enhanced their desire to learn and their educational attainment. First, SEPA demystified the schooling process. Students knew the purpose of each class and recognized that the program would help them acquire suitable employment or access to additional education. Second, the SEPA educational program was individualized. Each student was tested to ascertain his or her written and verbal competency in the GED subject areas (math, science, social science, and English). A learning program was constructed by a teacher and a counselor, who discussed the goals and objectives with the student—a far different approach from that of the usual impersonal bureaucracy. Third, SEPA's teachers actively involved themselves in the education of their students. All the teachers worked in a small classroom setting (between ten and twenty students) supplemented by tutors recruited from local colleges, and they used innovative teaching methods to motivate the Chicanas to learn and complete homework assignments. The Chicanas wrote plays collaboratively, kept journals, and held debates about events in Chicano history. Fourth, the teachers used a diverse or multicultural curriculum, much of which they created. Fifth, all the teachers were perceived by the students as sensitive and caring.

Regarding the teachers, Cynthia said: "Well, the teachers were different. And they had teachers from different backgrounds—not just Hispanics—so that's not it. But the teachers seemed to care about you. They made you feel comfortable and not embarrassed to ask questions." The teachers of SEPA conveyed a positive message to the Chicanas—that they were important and could learn. SEPA's learning environment helped the Chicanas feel better about themselves and reversed the negative self-images they had developed in school. Feeling better about themselves, and studying in a program that offered them consistent feedback about their educational progress, the Chicanas obtained either their GEDs or the educational skills to improve their employment options. Thus, SEPA caught and even rescued the Chicana respondents who had fallen through the cracks of the public school system.

CONCLUSION

The educational and familial experiences examined here reveal the multidimensional nature of the impediments faced by the respondents as they struggled to become educated and force us to reevaluate the stereotypical explanations for low Chicano educational achievement. Though conventional wisdom perceives Chicano/Mexicano families as having low regard for education, the parents of the Chicana respondents repeatedly encouraged them to do well in school. Few parents, however, actually intervened in the schooling process. Far from being simply a racial or ethnic matter, this reluctance conforms to a more general working-class pattern of leaving educational concerns to educational professionals, as observed in another study (Lareau, 1984).

Within schools, teacher and counselor actions channeled Chicanas into nonacademic programs offering a lower quality of instruction. Their placement into general education curriculum tracks effectively restricted their early life chances, and neither teachers nor counselors encouraged the Chicanas to attend college or prepare for professional careers. Diffident instruction, lack of teacher caring, and inadequate counseling constrained the educational chances of the respondents. Teachers and counselors may not have explicitly vocalized racial ideology, yet inadequate instruction and subtly negative attitudes helped reinforce the existing system of social stratification. Consequently, the historically low levels of Chicana educational attainment, and their subsequent overrepresentation in the lower echelons of the labor market, have not changed materially.

When contrasted to their experiences in the schools, the experiences of the respondents in SEPA point to ways to improve the quality and amount of secondary education Chicanas receive. At SEPA, teacher innovation in the classroom, multicultural curriculum, and teacher "caring" and involvement motivated students to do well in the classroom. Furthermore, consistent monitoring of student progress prevented the Chicanas from staying at the same level throughout their time at SEPA; they were *expected* to achieve. Students were taught the skills to pass through the doors to different curriculum paths. Finally, students were given positive reinforcement and encouragement whenever possible by teachers and other school staff, allowing "the positive aspects of learning to set in."

The success this group of Chicanas enjoyed at SEPA demonstrates that effective educational programs can be designed and implemented. Our challenge as educators is to study both the negative and the positive features of schooling, so that we can design educational programs that will stop Chicanas from slipping through the cracks in the educational system of the future.

NOTES

1. In this study, *Chicano/a* refers to persons (male and female) of Mexican descent born in the United States or raised here since early childhood. It is used interchangeably with the term *Mexican American*. *Mexicano/a* refers to immigrants from Mexico, who are in this study distinct from Chicanos. The term *persons of Mexican origin* includes both. *Latino/a*, *Spanish origin*, and *Hispanic* are broader terms that refer to persons of Spanish and Latin American heritage. For additional information on the origins and use of the term *Chicano* (especially its political implication), see Tienda (1981), Peñalosa (1970), and Barrera (1979).

2. The information reported here complements my other research on barriers to employment and occupational mobility of Mexican-origin women in secondary types of jobs (Segura, 1986).

3. I determined the class position of the respondents by considering (a) the economic resources available to them; (b) the social and cultural milieu in which they lived; (c) parental occupations and educational attainment; (d) educational attainment of siblings; (e) memories of economic difficulties; and (f) their own assessments of the class positions of their families (e.g., "We were workers" or "My family was poor"). In general, if the respondents had parents working in unskilled or semiskilled jobs (such as plasterer or hotel maid), I categorized them as "working class." Parents in professional jobs (such as teacher) were classified as "middle class."

REFERENCES

Barrera, Mario.

1979. *Race and Class in the Southwest: A Theory of Racial Inequality*. Notre Dame, Ind.: University of Notre Dame Press.

Block, Jeanne H.

1979. "Another Look at Sex Differentiation in the Socialization Behavior of Mothers and Fathers." In *Psychology of Women: Future Directions of Research*, ed. J. Sherman and F. L. Denmark. New York: Psychological Dimensions.

Bowles, Samuel, and Herbert Gintis.

1976. *Schooling in Capitalist America*. New York: Basic Books.

California Assembly Office of Research.

1984a. *Making High Schools Work for Linguistic Minorities: A Research Partnership*. Sacramento: California Assembly Office of Research, April 9.

1984b. *Overcoming the Odds: Making High Schools Work*. Sacramento: California Assembly Office of Research, March 22.

California State Department of Education.

1984. *California High School Curriculum Study: Paths through High School*. Sacramento: California State Department of Education, January 5.

Carter, Thomas P., and Roberto D. Segura.

1979. *Mexican Americans in School: A Decade of Change*. New York: College Entrance Examination Board.

Chacon, Maria, et al.

1982. *Chicanas in Postsecondary Education*. Stanford, Calif.: Center for Research on Women, Stanford University.

Cherry, L.
1975. "The Preschool Teacher-Child Dyad: Sex Differences in Verbal Interaction." *Child Development* 46:532–535.
Chodorow, Nancy.
1979. *The Reproduction of Mothering*. Berkeley: University of California Press.
Coleman, James S., et al.
1966. *Equality of Educational Opportunity*. Washington, D.C.: U.S. Government Printing Office.
Epstein, Cynthia Fuchs.
1979. *Woman's Place*. Berkeley: University of California Press.
Espinosa, Ruben, and Alberto Ochoa.
1986. "Concentration of California Hispanic Students in Schools with Low Achievement: A Research Note." *American Journal of Education* 95, no. 1: 77–95.
Evans, Francis B., and James G. Anderson.
1973. "The Psychocultural Origins of Achievement and Achievement Motivation: The Mexican American Family." *Sociology of Education* 46:396–419.
Farris, Buford, and Norval Glenn.
1976. "Fatalism and Familism among Anglos and Mexican Americans in San Antonio." *Sociology and Social Research* 60:393–402.
Gandara, Patricia.
1982. "Passing through the Eye of the Needle: High Achieving Chicanas." *Hispanic Journal of Behavioral Sciences* 4, no. 2:167–179.
Hoffman, L. W.
1977. "Changes in Family Roles, Socialization, and Sex Differences." *American Psychologist* 32:644–657.
James Irvine Foundation.
1982. *Hispanic Participation in Higher Education: A Focus on Chicanos and Other Hispanics in California*. Princeton, N.J.: James Irvine Foundation.
Kent, Jaylene, and Rene A. Ruiz.
1979. "IQ and Reading Scores among Anglo, Black and Chicano Third- and Sixth-Grade School Children." *Hispanic Journal of Behavioral Sciences* 1, no. 3: 271–277.
Lareau, Annette Patricia.
1984. "Social Behavior and the Family-School Relationship in Two Communities." Ph.D. diss., University of California, Berkeley.
Mahan, Guy, and Charles Johnson.
1983. "Portrait of a Dropout: Dealing with Academic, Social, and Emotional Problems." *NASSP Bulletin* 67, no. 462:80–83.
Mirandé, Alfredo, and Evangelina Enríquez.
1979. *La Chicana: The Mexican American Woman*. Chicago: University of Chicago Press.
Moore, Joan W., with Harry Pachon.
1976. *Mexican Americans*, 2nd ed. Englewood Cliffs, N.J.: Prentice-Hall.
National Center for Education Statistics.
1980. *Achievement of Hispanic Students in High Schools: Background Characteristics and Achievement*. Washington, D.C.: U.S. Government Printing Office.
National Commission on Secondary Education for Hispanics.

1984. *Make Something Happen*. Washington, D.C.: Hispanic Policy Development Project, National Commission on Secondary Education for Hispanics.

Oakes, Jeannie.
1985. *Keeping Track: How Schools Structure Inequality*. New Haven, Conn.: Yale University Press.

Ogbu, John U.
1978. *Minority Education and Caste: The American System in Cross-Cultural Perspective*. New York: Academic Press.

Orfield, Gary.
1983. *Public School Desegregation in the United States, 1968–1980*. Washington, D.C.: Joint Center for Political Studies.

Penalosa, Fernando.
1970. "Toward an Operational Definition of the Mexican American." *Aztlan* 1 (Spring): 1–12.

Persell, Caroline Hodges.
1977. *Education and Inequality: A Theoretical and Empirical Synthesis*. New York: Free Press.

Ringawa, Marcel.
1980. "Cultural Pedagogy: The Effects of Teacher Attitudes and Needs in Selected Bilingual Bicultural Education Environments." In *Ethno-Perspectives in Bilingual Education Research: Theory in Bilingual Education*, ed. Raymond V. Padilla. Ypsilanti: Bilingual Bicultural Education Programs, Eastern Michigan University.

Romo, Harriet.
1984. "The Mexican Origin Population's Differing Perceptions of Their Children's Schooling." *Social Science Quarterly* 65, no. 2:635–650.

Roos, Peter D.
1984. "Equity and Excellence." In *Make Something Happen: Hispanics and Urban High School Reform*, vol. 2. Washington, D.C.: Hispanic Policy Development Project, National Commission on Secondary Education for Hispanics.

Segura, Denise A.
1984. "Labor Market Stratification: The Chicana Experience." *Berkeley Journal of Sociology* 29 (Spring): 57–91.
1986. "Chicana and Mexicana Immigrant Women in the Labor Market: A Study of Occupational Mobility and Stratification." Ph.D. diss., University of California, Berkeley.

Snipp, C. Matthew, and Marta Tienda.
1984. "Mexican American Occupational Mobility." *Social Science Quarterly* 65, no. 4: 364–380.

Sokoloff, Natalie J.
1980. *Between Money and Love: The Dialectics of Women's Home and Market Work*. New York: Praeger.

Solorozano, Daniel Gilbert.
1986. "A Study of Social Mobility Values: The Determinants of Chicano Parents' Occupational Expectations for Their Children." Ph.D. diss., Claremont Graduate School.

Sowell, Thomas.
1981. *Ethnic America: A History*. New York: Basic Books.

1982. "*Weber* and *Bakke* and the Presuppositions of 'Affirmative Action.'" In *Discrimination, Affirmative Action, and Equal Opportunity: An Economic and Social Perspective,* ed. Walter E. Block and Michael A. Walker. Vancouver, B.C.: Fraser Institute.

1984. *Civil Rights: Rhetoric or Reality?* New York: Morrow.

Tienda, Marta.

1981. "The Mexican American Population." In *Non-metropolitan America in Transition,* ed. Amos H. Hawley and Sara M. Mazie. Chapel Hill: University of North Carolina Press.

United States Commission on Civil Rights.

1972. *The Excluded Student.* Report III: Mexican American Education Study. Washington, D.C.: U.S. Government Printing Office.

1974. *Toward Quality Education for Mexican Americans.* Report IV: Mexican American Education Study. Washington, D.C.: U.S. Government Printing Office.

Vásquez, Melba J. T.

1982. "Confronting Barriers to the Participation of Mexican American Women in Higher Education." *Hispanic Journal of Behavioral Sciences* 4, no. 2:167–179.

THIRTEEN

Gender and the Life Course

A Case Study of Chicana Elderly

Elisa Facio

The time of life known as late adulthood is generally dominated by women, whose lives, as they age, are more precarious than those of men. On the whole, elderly women are poorer than elderly men, live longer, and tend to live alone. A statistical comparison of aged Chicanos illustrates this point. Data from the United States Bureau of the Census (1982) indicate that 60 percent of all Chicano elderly are women and that 40 percent of these women have incomes at or below the poverty line. Contradicting the assumption that elderly Chicanas reside with families and/or spouses, more than two-thirds of these women live alone.[1]

Growth in the number of adults over the age of sixty-five has been reported among many groups, including the Chicano elderly population. With roughly 6 percent of the Chicano population over the age of fifty-five, scholars and policy-makers predict that escalating numbers of elderly will live in poor, isolated conditions. This prediction applies in particular to Chicana elderly; inasmuch as many older Chicanas face a precipitous decline in economic and social status, questions concerning the lives of these aged women demand critical examination. Focusing on the lives of Chicana elderly, this essay broadens our understanding of the social conditions that confront these women.

Two aspects of this study make it important and unique. First, it examines a growing population whose adjustment to aging has not been extensively studied. Chicanas have been described as passive and uncritically accepting toward growing old (see Coles, 1980; Sanchez-Ayendez, 1986; Sotomayer, 1973). The elderly Chicana's attempt to define or shape her old age is overlooked, although attention to gender in Chicano aging studies surfaced during the late 1970s and early 1980s (see Coles, 1974, 1980; Elsasser, MacKenzie, and Tixier y Vigil, 1980; Martinez, 1979; Melville, 1980; Ashley, 1985; Zepeda, 1979). Second, unlike other studies, this investigation examines the Chicana elderly outside of a traditional family context. Since a number of Chicana elderly live as single heads of households, it seems important to move away from a stereotyped paradigm that views women strictly within the family structure. This analytical separation allows for a better understanding of Chicana elderly lives, since many no longer identify themselves with a traditional family structure.

Researchers who have viewed Chicana elderly in a traditional family context have assumed that they are active primarily within their immediate families. For example, empirical research indicates that Chicana elderly are usually at the top of an age-related status hierarchy in an extended family network. Further, it is posited that Chicanas gain in status as they age. This research implies that family structures serve as the primary source of self-worth (see Markides, Martin, and Gomez, 1983; Martinez, 1979). In particular, Chicana aged are held in high esteem for their role as *la abuela* (grandmother). Families have also been noted for providing economic and social support (see Keefe, Padilla, and Carlos, 1979; Markides, Boldt, and Ray, 1986).

These assumptions, although based on historical research, may be of limited relevance in contemporary times. The growing number of Chicana elderly whose lives are no longer centered in the family leads us to question how these women acquire self-worth. What adjustments and adaptations do they make to accommodate this process? Additionally, what particular skills have they had to develop or modify in dealing with the unpredictable nature of their social and economic condition? I sought answers to these questions in a two-year qualitative study conducted in a northern California senior citizen center. Employing methods described by Barbara Myerhoff (1978), I conducted extensive fieldwork through the use of participant observation. In addition, I collected twenty oral histories from elderly Mexican women at the senior citizen center. Of the sixty to sixty-five women who were registered as regular participants at the center, I selected twenty who seemed to attend most frequently. I also attempted to target women who represented the diversity of the center. For example, I interviewed both the most verbal and the least outgoing members.

Because the sample in this study is small and fairly homogeneous, no claims are made that the findings are generalizable to all Chicana aged. I hope, however, that my work will contribute to an understanding of Chicana elderly in other situations and that it will stimulate more detailed observations of this population in the future.

The average age of the women interviewed was seventy-one. Of the twenty respondents, only one woman was married; the remaining nineteen were widows or had been separated or divorced from their husbands.[2] Household composition varied. One woman had an adult daughter living with her; the remaining elderly Chicano women lived alone, either in senior housing complexes, low-income apartment housing, or homes acquired thirty or forty years before. The average monthly income for the respondents (1987) was $420. The average amount of schooling was three years.

LATE ADULTHOOD: "THE DAY-BY-DAY ERA"

The term *late adulthood* suggests continuity, a period that is part of the entire life course and not a separate entity. The concept of the life course as a continuum involving growth and change is advocated by such authors as Daniel Levinson (1978), Gail Sheehy (1978), Alice Rossi (1985), and Roger Gould (1978). These writers postulate that growth and change take place primarily during early and middle adulthood (see Levinson, 1978:2–3). But the character of living is altered in fundamental ways during late adulthood—as a result of numerous biological, psychological, and social changes. This phase—like every other phase of the life course—has its own virtues and limitations and requires some amount of growth, change, adaptation, and adjustment. Consequently, this study assumes that the elderly are capable of realizing the potential value of late adulthood and making the adjustments that this period requires.

Researchers speculatively locate the late-adulthood period between the ages of sixty and sixty-five. The beginning of this period is marked by events such as illness, retirement, or both. People of this age may experience bodily or mental decline; with increasing frequency, friends and family members die or become seriously ill. Even the healthy and physically active are faced with many reminders of decreasing vigor and capacity. In addition, they must hear themselves described as "the elderly," "in their golden years," or "senior citizens"—expressions with negative connotations reflecting cultural anxiety about aging. Thus, the elderly face the difficult task of sustaining themselves as healthy adults rather than "an empty dry structure devoid of energy, interests or inner resources" (Levinson, 1978:35).

During late adulthood, concerns over time and health become central. The elderly need to make time worthwhile and meaningful; acquiring a sense of self-worth becomes a dominant theme vital to a sense of identity and significance. Increasingly, the elderly rely on each other for feedback to bolster their self-worth, primarily because they no longer live among those who witnessed the successes or failures of their lives. This dependency also stems from the fact that long-term goals are no longer realistically possible, since time is both limited and unpredictable.

Attendance at senior citizen centers has been interpreted as one means of establishing a life structure that enables the elderly to come to terms with their aging (Myerhoff, 1978). With respect to Chicano elderly, Cuellar (1978) views senior citizen centers as a means of creatively responding to the contradictions and discontinuities of old age.

CHICANA ELDERLY: DIFFERENTIATED LIFE PROCESSES

In general, the late-adulthood period for women is characterized by poverty and isolation. As Sheehy (1978:498) has stated, "They're not so much imperiled by heart attacks as by widowhood, and they must rehearse for enduring alone." Thus, it is imperative for these women to find a sense of self-worth and a means of independent survival.

The manner in which Chicana elderly women structure their lives during this period is not determined solely by gender, as outlined by Sheehy, but is also subject to the effects of race and class. Their status as women of Mexican descent and members of the lower socioeconomic class renders them especially vulnerable economically, socially, and politically. For example, class, race, and gender interact in the migration experience of the respondents. Many had come to the United States because their husbands were recruited into the low-wage labor sector in the Southwest. They, too, had frequently worked at low-paying jobs available to Chicanas. One respondent, Regina, typifies this experience: "We came to the United States in 1916 from Zacatecas, Mexico. We went to New Mexico [and] then to Arizona, where my father and brothers worked for the railroads. We [women] lived in camps, working in the fields while the men worked for the railroad companies."

Nearly half of the respondents married and immigrated to the United States either during or after the Mexican Revolution. At the age of fifteen, Angelina married and immigrated to Texas; like Regina, she has a work history of low-paying jobs. "I rented rooms out and worked as a waitress. I went to California to find better work. I cleaned houses. . . . I made $1.25 an hour. . . . Sometimes I would have to clean houses with five or six bedrooms in one day!"

Women such as Rosario, Mercedes, and Maria remained married to their spouses for more than twenty years. Their husbands demanded that they quit any jobs they held before their marriage in order to assume full responsibility for household and child-care duties. Rosario, for example, explains why she no longer "worked" after she married: "My husband worked for the railroads all his life, but I never worked anymore after I got married. . . . He wanted me to stay home and take care of the children. . . . I worked in the house . . . cleaning, cooking, taking care of the children."

Throughout their lives, the respondents' economic situation has ranged from varying degrees of poverty to working-class status. These women have been relegated to low-paying jobs as cannery workers, farm laborers, and domestics, as well as to the unpaid sector of homemaker. Both factors result in a common predicament: poverty during late adulthood. Thus, Chicana elderly face the challenge not only of developing a sense of self-worth but also of meeting subsistence needs. The task involving self-worth is generated within the aging process; however, the simultaneous operation of class, race, and gender factors makes economic survival a pressing late-adulthood concern for the Chicana elderly. Ironically, the caretaking duties traditionally associated with women benefit women in the later years, when caretaking and other gender-associated skills are useful socially and economically.

CENTER LIFE AND THE CHICANA ELDERLY

The senior center, which is located in a Chicano barrio, is primarily funded to provide nutritional and transportation services for the elderly. It is surrounded by railroad tracks and broken-down Victorian homes. The building, painted with murals, symbolically reflects Mexican/Chicano culture and the historical experiences of the community.

The inside of the center resembles a small school auditorium with a kitchen, stage, and partitioned office spaces. The faded yellow walls are covered with posters in Spanish and English containing information about health issues such as high blood pressure, heart disease, and the importance of a nutritional diet. In addition, small multicolored Mexican rugs decorate the walls. In the back of the center is a mural depicting Mexican/Chicano culture. The mural is more than decoration, however, as it symbolically projects images of the elderly themselves as survivors and sources of Mexican culture.

Within the center, the women have formed groups based on gender-specific tasks. One group, Las Abuelas (the grandmothers), consists of widowed women who are also grandmothers. They plan Catholic church activities associated with religious and traditional holidays and also devise arts-and-crafts projects, with the end products sold for their own profit. Of the roughly twelve members of this group, Maria, Josefina, and Sara are the most active and outspoken.

Maria, a widow who lives alone, is seventy-three and the mother of seven children. Maria projects a very strong and stern character; she walks very erectly, with her head held high, and expresses pride in her knowledge of Catholicism. The most active member of this group is probably Josefina. At seventy-seven years of age, she is full of life, friendly, and very confident. Like many of the seniors, she values education and the goodness of her children. Sara, also a widow, is eighty-four and appears frail and somewhat vulnerable. Sara always greets the other women of the group with prolonged embraces and seems to be seeking acceptance and attention. Unlike Maria and Josefina, she has only her membership in the group to call attention to her presence and bolster her sense of self-worth.

Las Abuelas play an important part in involving other seniors in church-affiliated events. For example, a cultural celebration that remains significant for this group is Día de los Muertos (Day of the Dead, or All Souls Day, celebrated on November 2), when deceased relatives are remembered and honored. Las Abuelas generally believe in spiritualism; thus, this celebration enables these women to maintain a "spiritual bond" with deceased relatives. Josefina explains: "What we did in Mexico during this celebration is that we went to the cemetery taking flowers, candles, and we prayed. . . . There is a bread called 'bread of the deceased.' . . . We used to buy it and eat it on that day to make sure that we were all there as one. And we do this because we believe it is a way to being spiritually close to the deceased." Maria adds: "We have this responsibility to all our past relatives. I am devoted to pray each day during the month of November for my husband who died fifteen years ago. This is a custom that we learned from our grandmothers and mothers."

More important, though, Las Abuelas must confront the fear associated with death and deal with their own mortality. For these women, such activities provide a means of coping with the inevitable passage of death.

A second group, the Crochet Club, was organized by Virginia to teach women how to crochet. This group meets almost every day to receive instruction and comments on their current pieces of work and to discuss strategies for selling their products. Virginia customarily seats herself at the center of a table, giving instructions and overseeing the women working on their projects. When asked about the reasons for organizing this group, Virginia replied:

> I used to work in the canneries. In the off-season, I would work at the sanitarium for tuberculosis patients. Used to clean and help the people walk around, things like that. They assigned me to work with women. That's when I learned to crochet. I would crochet scarves, hats, and sell them to the patients. When they would ask me to make something, I would tell them that they would have to pay me first. Then I started bringing in jalapeño peppers and sold them, too, because they liked them. When the hospital closed down, I kept crocheting things and sold them and worked in the canneries. That's how I've made a living. I'm not saying I'm good, but I started classes here with the other ladies. This way they have something to do and can make a little bit of money.

Two members of this group, Neves and Amelia, always sat together at the end of the table, observing and listening to Virginia. From their behavior, I assumed that they were new to the group. They would sit and work and seemed constantly to be smiling. I found that the warm, friendly faces of these women masked a fear of appearing ignorant to other group members as well as to other seniors in the center. If they projected a self-assured image, they seemed to believe, no one would bother them, and they would be protected from the inquiries of the curious. At times, I had difficulty conversing with them—not because they were unfriendly but because their dispositions did not allow me to cross any boundaries. This behavior is not uncommon, since the activities at the center create an atmosphere where individuals are judged and categorized (see Myerhoff, 1978).

For Neves and Amelia, participation in such a group generated an opportunity for being seen and honored, a way of securing visibility and receiving attention. A knowledgeable and confident image meant a positive self-worth, an image and a self-evaluation that they would not be able to obtain in the outside world.

Trini and Rosa responded differently to my presence. At times, I sensed that they were "performing" for me. They appeared to know exactly what they were doing. When I came around to sit with them and observe their work, they became much more efficient. When they asked me if I knew how to crochet, I told them that it looked too difficult, and this gave them the opportunity, in a sense, to compete with me on equal ground. Through their knowledge of crocheting, they were able to establish a sense of power. This power struggle between young and old would surface again and again. I, the younger person, symbolically reflected "youth," an oppressive constituent of society to the old. Thus, they attempted to refute stereotypical notions of inadequate, nonproductive individuals, and their efficient crocheting techniques let them display their existence and their worth to someone from the outside world.

A third group is called the Center Volunteers. The women in this group are responsible for center maintenance. They also set tables for and serve the noon meals. Their tasks include placing tablecloths, condiments, and beverages on the tables and serving lunches in an assembly-line fashion. These volunteers, all women, arrive as early as 8:30 A.M. to begin their tasks, which require anywhere from two to three hours. In return, the volunteers receive free meals.

Rosario, Hipolita, Antonia, and Marequita are distinguished from the others by their aprons with "Volunteer" written across the front. Marequita is mainly in charge of serving coffee. She stands off to one side of the serving line, with the coffee machine placed on a small table. I spent a considerable amount of time with her, because she has been a member since the center opened. Marequita's physical movements were slow and cautious, making her appear somewhat passive. With each cup of coffee that she filled, I was informed about the center and its members.

> I volunteer because I need something to do with my time and I get free meals . . . saves me a little bit of money. I don't want to be like some of these people, they take whatever they can. A lot of them steal the salsa on the tables. They bring jars or use their milk cartons and slip them into their bags. . . . But that's life, and I still like to come here. We dance, sing, and I like the birthday celebrations.

I then asked her if there was a difference in aging among women and men. She replied:

> You know, the men and women are different here at the center. . . . The men look like they're lost; they're real quiet. Life is hard for all of us. We're poor, a lot of us get sick . . . we get arthritis. We're just waiting, but here at the center, we can wait together. We just thank God that he brings us here every day.

Membership in such groups generates opportunities for these women to be seen, respected, and honored and thereby to establish a sense of self-worth. Because their lives away from the center are largely determined by forces beyond their control, these elderly women often are preoccupied with honor and self-worth (Myerhoff, 1978:39). Hence, activities and group organizations are markets of existence and a display of worth. Chicana elderly women have constructed life at the senior center as a surrogate world, within which people can interact, take part in meaningful activities, and retain a measure of control over their lives.

Interestingly, I found that the women as a group are more complex, active, and assertive than the men. Men in the senior center are quieter and more vague and are becoming more obsolete than the women—at least they seem to feel that they are. In his study of migrant families, Velez (1978) has shown how networks of women are transformed into instruments for political and economic action. For example, familial networks have been instrumental in pro-union activities such as the United Farm Workers struggles of the mid-1960s and the Watsonville cannery strike of the mid-1980s. Men do not characteristically become engaged in such networks; and as they become older, they participate less actively in social life. Cuellar (1978) reports similar findings among Chicano elderly of East Los Angeles.

As in all social arenas, a number of distinctions are made between the appropriate roles for men and women. With aging, the stereotypical expectations of female behavior are better defined than those of the male. The roles that women assume at the center largely reflect the division of labor by gender that characterized their families. Las Abuelas, for example, continue their role as facilitators of religion and of handcrafts. Likewise, activities such as crocheting, preparation of meals, and maintenance of the living space are patterns of domesticity that have been extended from the domestic sphere and are now performed at the senior center.

The data suggest that the condition of women in late adulthood stems from the system of patriarchy. In this system, as Hartmann (1981) has pointed out, women are relegated to the "private" sphere—the domestic domain of household maintenance, child care, nurturance, and interpersonal relationships. On the other hand, men assume responsibility for the "public" sphere—the world of work, providing for the family's economic subsistence. This distinction between public and private domains remains prevalent throughout the aging process.

In addition, the principle of patriarchy is not exclusive to the domestic domain. As mentioned earlier, Chicana women have historically been concentrated in low-paying jobs, determined by the interplay of class, race, and gender. Thus, during late adulthood, Chicana elderly women find themselves poorer than men and more seriously challenged to develop alternative means of economic subsistence. The selling of crafts and crocheting products supplements monthly incomes. Volunteer work at the center in exchange for free meals constitutes a means of labor; with each meal costing fifty cents a day, or ten dollars monthly, they save a substantial amount of money. The household work that these women formerly did in their homes has shifted to sites such as the center, where domestic tasks also have become extensions of wage-earning capacities.

What enables Chicana elderly women to maintain a distinct sense of continuity in the aging process? One plausible explanation is that the roles allocated to the elderly are predominantly associated with the "private" sphere. As Myerhoff (1978:62) points out, "Retired people in society, both women and men, are expected to spend their time socializing, taking care of themselves, passing the days pleasantly, attending to the quality of life and interpersonal concerns." With the loss of work, men in general lose their link to the public sphere. As a result, the retired man loses not only his ability to earn money but also his sense of self-worth and autonomy. Although men are expected to involve themselves in the private sphere after they retire, they usually have had little experience in this sphere and often have been taught to regard it as demeaning. Accordingly, women have an advantage over men, since their primary responsibilities—associated with the private domain—continue to be viable in the later years.[3] As illustrated by the center's activities, Chicana elderly women utilize skills of the private sphere that have been historically prescribed by gender. This structure allows Chicana elderly women to exert a strong sense of vitality, dominance, and power. Through the senior center's groups and activities, Chicana elderly are able to display their ability to establish interpersonal relationships and to care for themselves as well as others.

The foregoing discussion illustrates the complexity of the late-adulthood period, especially for Chicana elderly women. Patriarchy constrains women to the private sphere, but their skills associated with this domain become relatively more viable during the later years, so that their lives have a distinct continuity. However, this same set of constraints historically has relegated women to low-paying jobs; as a result, they usually must live in poverty throughout late adulthood.

CONCLUSION

For Chicana elderly women, life at the senior center is established as a distinct world within the larger society. Two conditions characterize the center's members: continuities between past and present circumstances and social isolation. Several marked similarities exist between circumstances of Chicana adulthood and old age: immigrant experience, development of sound survival strategies, poverty, and the challenge of developing a sense of self-worth during old age.

Since the traditional Chicano family structure no longer serves as the primary source of self-worth for Chicana elderly, they must try to develop a sense of self-worth outside the family unit. The senior center allows Chicana elderly to pursue this task successfully. This task, however, is influenced by the contradictory nature of gender and the dynamics of the aging process. On the one hand, gender overwhelmingly contributes to the economic deprivation of Chicana elderly. On the other hand, the division of labor associated with gender and the caretaking duties traditionally linked with women become beneficial for Chicana elderly in establishing self-worth.

This task also is facilitated by the "expressive" nature of old age. The elderly are expected to establish life structures on the periphery of society—apart from the world of work and society in general. Thus, for these women, the challenge in acquiring a positive self-worth calls on their lifelong experiences associated with the private sphere.

For Chicana elderly women, the constraint of gender prescribes the form that the late-adulthood structure takes. Inasmuch as gender historically has relegated

Chicana elderly women to low-paying, menial occupations, many live on or near the poverty levels. Consequently, vital economic concerns have challenged these women to develop alternative means of supplementing monthly incomes. At the same time, the nature of late adulthood, as it is defined today, allows Chicana elderly women to display their capacities and abilities in maintaining continuity in the life course.

NOTES

1. The United States Bureau of the Census (1980a) indicates that more than 47.7 percent of Spanish-origin women over fifty-five years old residing in California were widowed. The Census Bureau, however, does not specifically report the marital status of Chicano women over fifty-five or household compositions. The statistical information reported is a rough estimate at best.

2. The status of widowhood requires clarification. Of the nineteen respondents who were categorized as widows, only eight women actually were widows. The others had been previously separated or divorced and simply called themselves widows. Widowhood for these eleven women was merely symbolic. It gave them a status that provided a sense of identity and position among this aged community.

3. The argument that women are better able to cope with poverty and isolation is based on participation observation and on informal discussions with the men in the center. Also, detailed conversations with both the director and the assistant director provided further information about all the elderly who attended the center.

REFERENCES

Aguirre, Ben E., and Abbie Bigelow.
1983. "The Aged in Hispanic Groups: A Review." *International Journal of Aging and Human Development* 17:177–201.

Alford, Robert R., and Roger Friedland.
1985. *Powers of Theory*. New York: Cambridge University Press.

Almaguer, Thomas.
1975. "Class, Race, and Chicano Oppression." *Socialist Revolution* 5:71–99.

Alvirez, David, Frank D. Bean, and Dorie Williams.
1981. "The Mexican American Family." In *Ethnic Families in America,* ed. C. H. Mindel and R. W. Habenstein. New York: Elsevier.

Ashley, L. M.
1985. "Self, Family, and Community: The Social Process of Aging among Urban Mexican-American Women." Ph.D. diss., University of California, Los Angeles.

Baca-Zinn, Maxine.
1975. "Political Familism: Toward Sex Role Equality in Chicano Families." *Aztlan* 6:13–26.
1979. "Chicano Family Research: Conceptual Distortions and Alternative Directions." *Journal of Ethnic Studies* 7:59–71.
1980. "Employment and Education of Mexican American Women: The Interplay

of Modernity and Ethnicity in Eight Families." *Harvard Educational Review* 50: 47–62.

1982. "Chicano Men and Masculinity." *Journal of Ethnic Studies* 10:9–44.

Bacerra, Rosina M.

1983. "The Mexican-American: Aging in a Changing Culture." In *Aging in Minority Groups,* ed. R. L. McNeely and J. N. Cohen. Beverly Hills, Calif.: Sage.

Barrera, Mario.

1979. *Race and Class in the Southwest: A Theory of Racial Equality.* Notre Dame, Ind.: University of Notre Dame Press.

Bastida, Elena.

1984. "Reconstructing the Social World at 60: Older Cubans in the United States." *Gerontologist* 24:265–270.

Becker, Gaylene.

1980. *Growing Old in Silence.* Berkeley: University of California Press.

Boone, Margaret S.

1980. "The Uses of Traditional Concepts in the Development of New Urban Roles: Cuban Women in the United States." In *A World of Women,* ed. E. Bourguignon. New York: Praeger.

Boswell, Thomas D., and James R. Curtis.

1984. *The Cuban-American Experience.* Totowa, N.J.: Rowman and Allanheld.

Cantor, Marjorie H.

1979. "The Information Support System of New York's Inner City Elderly: Is Ethnicity a Factor?" In *Ethnicity and Aging,* ed. D. E. Gelfand and A. J. Kutizk. New York: Springer.

Carrasquillo-Morales, Hector Anibal.

1982. "Perceived Social Reciprocity and Self-Esteem among Elderly Barrio Antillean Hispanics and Their Familial Informal Networks." Ph.D. diss., Syracuse University.

Clark, Margaret.

1969. "Mexican American Aged in San Francisco: A Case Description." *Gerontologist* 9:90–95.

Coles, Robert.

1974. *The Old Ones of New Mexico.* Albuquerque: University of New Mexico Press.

1980. "Una Anciana." In *Growing Old in America,* 2nd ed., ed. B. Hess. New Brunswick, N.J.: Transaction Books.

Cowgill, Donald O., and L. D. Holmes.

1972. *Aging and Modernization.* New York: Appleton-Century-Crofts.

Cuellar, José.

1978. "El Senior Citizens Club: The Older Mexican-American in the Voluntary Association." In *Life's Career, Aging: Cultural Variations on Growing Old,* ed. Barbara Myerhoff and Andrei Simic. Beverly Hills, Calif: Sage.

Dowd, James J.

1980. *Stratification among the Aged.* Monterey, Calif.: Brooks/Cole.

Dowd, James J., and Vern L. Bengtson.

1978. "Aging in Minority Populations: An Examination of the Double Jeopardy Hypothesis." *Journal of Gerontology* 33:427–436.

Doyle, Ruth T., and Olga Scarpetta.

1982. "Roles and Relationships within the Puerto Rican Family." In *Hispanics in*

New York: Religious, Cultural and Social Experiences. New York: Office of Pastoral Research, Archdiocese of New York.

Elsasser, Nan, Kyle MacKenzie, and Yvonne Tixier y Vigil.
1980. *Las Mujeres: Conversations from a Hispanic Community.* Old Westbury, N.Y.: Feminist Press.

Estes, Carroll L., et al.
1984. *Political Economy, Health and Aging.* Boston: Little, Brown.

Fitzpatrick, Joseph P.
1971. *Puerto Rican Americans.* Englewood Cliffs, N.J.: Prentice-Hall.

Flores-Ortíz, Yvette.
1978. "The Impact of Acculturation on the Chicano Family: An Analysis of Selected Variables." Ph.D. diss., University of California, Berkeley.

García, Alejandro.
1984. "Life Satisfaction of Elderly Mexican Americans." *Journal of Minority Aging* 9:30–38.

Gould, Roger.
1978. *Transformations.* New York: Simon and Schuster.

Graebner, William.
1980. *A History of Retirement.* New Haven, Conn.: Yale University Press.

Guillemard, A. M.
1983. "The Making of Old Age Policy in France." In *Old Age and the Welfare State,* ed. A. M. Guillemard. Beverly Hills, Calif.: Sage.

Hartmann, Heidi.
1981. "The Unhappy Marriage of Marxism and Feminism: Towards a More Progressive Union." In *Women and Revolution,* ed. Lydia Sargent. Boston: South End Press.

Hochschild, Arlie.
1973. *The Unexpected Community: Portrait of an Old Age Subculture.* Englewood Cliffs, N.J.: Prentice-Hall.

Jackson, Jacquelyne Johnson.
1985. "Race, National Origin, Ethnicity, and Aging." In *Handbook of Aging and the Social Sciences,* ed. R. Binstock and E. Shanas. New York: Van Nostrand Reinhold.

Keefe, Susan E.
1984. "Real and Ideal Extended Familism among Mexican Americans and Anglo Americans: On the Meaning of 'Close' Family Ties." *Human Organization* 43:65–70.

Keefe, Susan E., Amado M. Padilla, and Manuel L. Carlos.
1979. "The Mexican-American Extended Family as an Emotional Support System." *Human Organization* 38:144–152.

King, Lourdes Miranda.
1979. "Puertoriqueñas in the United States: The Impact of Double Discrimination." In *The Puerto Rican Woman,* ed. E. Acosta-Belen and E. H. Christensen. New York: Praeger.

Korte, Manuel.
1980. "Theoretical Perspectives in Mental Health and the Mexicano Elders." In

Chicano Aging and Mental Health, ed. M. Miranda and R. Ruiz. Rockville, Md.: National Institute of Mental Health.

Levinson, Daniel.
1978. *Seasons of a Man's Life.* New York: Ballantine.

Madsen, William.
1964. *The Mexican-Americans of South Texas.* New York: Holt, Rinehart and Winston.

Maldonado, David, Jr.
1975. "The Chicano Aged." *Social Work* 20:213–216.
1979. "Aging in the Chicano Context." In *Ethnicity and Aging,* ed. D. E. Gelfand and A. J. Kutizk. New York: Springer.

Markides, Kyriakos S., Joanne S. Boldt, and Laura A. Ray.
1986. "Sources of Helping and Intergenerational Solidarity: A Three-Generation Study of Mexican Americans." *Journal of Gerontology* 41:506–511.

Markides, Kyriakos S., Harry W. Martin, and Ernesto Gomez.
1983. *Older Mexican Americans: A Study in an Urban Barrio.* Austin: University of Texas Press.

Martinez, Maria Zuniga de.
1979. "Los Ancianos: A Study of the Attitudes of Mexican Americans Regarding Support of the Elderly." Ph.D. diss., Brandeis University.

Melville, Margarita, ed.
1980. *Twice a Minority: Mexican American Women.* St. Louis: Mosby.

Miller, Michael V.
1978. "Variations in Mexican American Family Life: A Review Synthesis of Empirical Research." *Aztlan* 9:209–231.

Mirandé, Alfredo.
1977. "The Chicano Family: A Reanalysis of Conflicting Views." *Journal of Marriage and the Family* 39:747–756.

Mirandé, Alfredo, and Evangelina Enríquez.
1979. *La Chicana: The Mexican American Woman.* Chicago: University of Chicago Press.

Moynihan, Daniel P.
1965. *The Negro Family: The Case for National Action.* Washington, D.C.: U.S. Department of Labor.

Myerhoff, Barbara.
1978. *Number Our Days.* New York: Simon and Schuster.

Neugarten, Bernice L.
1985. "Interpretative Social Science and Research on Aging." In *Gender and the Life Course,* ed. A. Rossi. New York: Aldine.

Newton, Frank Cota-Robles, and Rene A. Ruiz.
1980. "Chicano Culture and Mental Health." In *Chicano Aging and Mental Health,* ed. M. Miranda and R. Ruiz. Rockville, Md.: National Institute of Mental Health.

Nuñez, Francisco.
1975. "Variations in Fulfillment of Expectations of Social Interaction and Morale among Mexican Americans and Anglos." Master's thesis, University of Southern California.

Pedraza-Bailey, Silvia.
1985. *Political and Economic Migrants in America: Cubans and Mexicans.* Austin: University of Texas Press.
Perez, Lisandro.
1986. "Immigrant Economic Adjustment and Family Organization: The Cuban Success Story Reexamined." *International Migration Review* 20:4–20.
Phillison, Chris.
1982. *Capitalism and the Construction of Old Age.* London: Macmillan.
Portes, Alejandro, and Robert L. Bach.
1985. *Latin Journey: Cuban and Mexican Immigrants in the United States.* Berkeley: University of California Press.
Queralt, Magaly.
1983. "The Elderly of Cuban Origin." In *Aging in Minority Groups,* ed. R. L. McNeely and J. N. Cohen. Beverly Hills, Calif.: Sage.
Richmond, Marie La Liberte.
1980. *Immigrant Adaptation and Family Structure among Cubans in Miami, Florida.* New York: Arno Press.
Riley, Matilda White.
1985. "Age Strata in Social Systems." In *Handbook of Aging and the Social Sciences,* ed. R. Binstock and E. Shanas. New York: Van Nostrand Reinhold.
Ross, Jennie-Keith.
1977. *Old People, New Lives.* Chicago: University of Chicago Press.
Rossi, Alice S., ed.
1985. *Gender and the Life Course.* New York: Aldine.
Rubel, Arthur J.
1966. *Across the Tracks.* Austin: University of Texas Press.
Salgado, R.
1985. "The Puerto Rican Family: Present Realities and Future Developments." In *Recent Trends in Puerto Rican Migration.* Washington, D.C.: National Puerto Rican Coalition.
Sanchez-Ayendez, Melba.
1986. "Puerto Rican Elderly Women: Shared Meanings and Informal Supportive Networks." In *All American Women: Lines That Divide, Ties That Bind,* ed. J. B. Cole. New York: Free Press.
Schmidt, Adeny, and Amado M. Padilla.
1983. "Grandparent-Grandchild Interaction in a Mexican American Group." *Hispanic Journal of Behavioral Sciences* 5:181–198.
Sena-Rivera, Jaime.
1979. "Extended Kinship in the United States: Competing Models and the Case of La Familia Chicana." *Journal of Marriage and the Family* 41:121–129.
Sheehy, Gail.
1978. *Passages.* New York: Bantam Books.
Sokoloff, Natalie J.
1980. *Between Love and Money.* New York: Praeger.
Sotomayor, Marta.
1973. "A Study of Chicano Grandparents in an Urban Barrio." Ph.D. diss., University of Denver.
Torres-Gil, Fernando Manuel.

1978. "Age, Health, and Culture: An Examination of Health among Spanish Speaking Elderly." In *Hispanic Families,* ed. Miguel Montiel. Washington, D.C.: National Coalition of Hispanic Mental Health and Human Service Organizations.

United States Bureau of the Census.

1980a. *Detailed Population Characteristics: California.* PC80-1-D6. Washington, D.C.: U.S. Department of Commerce.

1980b. *General Population Characteristics.* PC80-1-B1. Washington, D.C.: U.S. Department of Commerce.

1982. *Politics of Aging among Elder Hispanics.* Washington, D.C.: U.S. Government Printing Office.

1983. *1980 Census of Population: General, Social and Economic Characteristics. Part 1: United States Summary.* Washington, D.C.: U.S. Government Printing Office.

1985. *The Hispanic Population in the United States: March.* Current Population Reports: Population Characteristics. Series P-20, No. 422. Washington, D.C.: U.S. Department of Commerce.

1986. *Statistical Abstract of the United States.* Washington, D.C.: U.S. Government Printing Office.

1987. *Marital Status and Living Arrangements: March.* Current Population Reports: Population Characteristics. Series P-20, No. 423. Washington, D.C.: U.S. Department of Commerce.

Velez, Carlos.

1978. "Youth and Aging in Central Mexico: One Day in the Life of Four Families of Migrants." In *Life's Career; Aging: Cultural Variations on Growing Old,* ed. Barbara Myerhoff and Andrei Simic. Beverly Hills, Calif.: Sage.

Zepeda, M.

1979. "Las Abuelitas." *Agenda* 9:10–13.

FOURTEEN

Conclusion

Adela de la Torre
Beatríz M. Pesquera

Returning to our *pláticas,* we will conclude our anthology. For it is the voices and insights of our *colegas* that will help determine future directions of Chicana scholarship. Our hope is to highlight not only the achievements of our scholarship but also the barriers confronting our work. Within these contradictions of barriers and success, acceptance and disdain, recognition and indifference, our scholarship will be produced—and in time, we hope, will flourish.

Since the 1980s, a small number—but a critical mass—of Chicana scholars have been placed in selected universities and colleges. Many face challenges for survival within the academy. As the educational pipeline narrows, these women speak out to us of the contradictions they face in their daily lives that threaten and mold the future direction of their scholarship. By identifying the obstacles before them, they are able to discover what is needed to build for the future.

Adaljisa Sosa Riddell: Well, first of all, there is a low critical mass; we are overstressed and overworked. Another obstacle is getting academia to accept our work. We are told to produce, but we are not given the right to produce what we want to say. There are other obstacles, like access to publications. But I think people are beginning to recognize that there is really something potentially there.

Deena González: We're the ones who spend more contact hours with students. We're the ones who spend more contact hours with each other, in just trying to keep each other alive and going. We're the ones that spend the most time ensuring that our students' and our voices are represented on every committee. So I think we are right now the hardest-working people in the academy—the hardest-working group. As a result of that, we take time away from publishing. We take time away from family life. We take time away from community life to do that kind of work. It's just not easy. We don't have the institutionalized support systems that we need to flourish. We're not flourishing. I see us truly not flourishing, but maintaining.

Emma Pérez: The obstacles we face are that we're usually the pioneers, first going into a department, the first to get tenure, the first to publish on these kinds of issues. This forces us to be superwomen. One way to overcome this isolation is through strategizing, because if we do not strategize, then we're locked into individual components throughout the Southwest, making it very easy for the sexism, the racism, the elitism to get us and for people to try to inch us out of our places.

Angie Chabram Dernersesian: In the production of Chicana scholarship, the greatest obstacle within the academy is institutional racism. This takes on many forms, including the tendency to undervalue the cultural production of people of color in general and women of color in particular, and the tendency to isolate young, intelligent Chicana scholars in disciplinary ghettos, such as mainstream departments, which have no other Chicanos or Chicanas on the faculty, which assign the Chicana academic the unwritten service obligation of integrating the discipline, and which are unable to offer any type of intellectual support because of ignorance of Chicana scholarship trajectory and current debates. There is another domain in which institutional racism leaves its scar on the psychology of the Chicana intellectual. Here I am referring to the unprofessional behavior that is often directed toward Chicana intellectuals in the form of racial slurs implicating her people as a whole or her subject matter. It is a supreme irony that, in a place which consciously claims itself the bastion of intellectual thought, the minority critic is deprived of the public discourse.

So, in my opinion, one of the greatest obstacles to intellectual development is the academy itself—an academy that has refused to take its mission seriously. If we are to overcome these institutional obstacles, we must engage in widespread institutional reforms and education of traditional mainstream sectors. That is, we must assist the mainstream in leaving behind attitudes, practices, and beliefs that imprison it in the current dynamic of token representation and underrepresentation of ethnic minorities.

Antonia Castañeda: The same obstacles that have existed historically exist for us as Chicanas in society. No matter how we cut it, the structures of patriarchy, male domination, racial domination, and particularly class domination have not fundamentally changed. Maybe they have elasticized a little bit—they've always elasticized to let one or two of us in—but fundamentally those structures remain, and we brush up against those structures.

Denise Segura: First of all, in the post–affirmative action era that I think we're in, Chicanas are a suspect category in the sense that as "tokens" we are viewed as people who got to the university as part of a movement, rather than by "merit." I just gave a commencement speech at Santa Barbara where I tried to make the point that "merit" and "quality" are nebulous concepts that change with the times and the persons in charge. Research indicates that people like to think they represent "quality," and, further, they think people like them in similar jobs also represent "quality." The university is notoriously homogeneous. Chicanas represent a departure from the standard. They don't look like the other faculty. They are not male or white. Hence, their quality and merit are automatically suspect. The onus is on Chicanas to "prove" themselves in ways that white men and women are not obliged to do. Yes, they all want diversity. But what does that mean? They don't mean they want someone who radically departs from the sacred standards of the discipline. They mean a white, male sociologist in drag—or, in my case, masquerading behind a brown female mask. The fact that I have a husband and three children, things that make me diverse—my race, gender, and family status—are things that pose barriers to my "success" in the university. They pose barriers to many if not most Chicanas striving to survive in a university setting—an environment designed by white males.

Elisa Facio: It starts with the fundamental way the university is organized. Then there is the whole publishing arena, controlled by people who just cannot see, or just refuse to acknowledge, the importance of the kind of work we are doing. I think we need to look at the situation very critically, and as a group we will figure out collectively how to survive in the institution. One way we have done that is by networking, the MALCS institute, NACS, for what it is—at least it provides a vehicle to get together and voice our opinions. Through things like that and informal groups, we have collectively gotten together and brainstormed and figured out how we survive, how we integrate our issues, how we make our voices heard.

Norma Alarcón: The need for an alternative space in the first place was created by the exclusion from institutionalized programs. If you are excluded from the institutionalized programs and you still think that your questions and the position from which you want to raise them have validity in academia as well as the political arena, then you are not going to abandon the questions. What you do is create the space where you can pursue them. I think that women have been doing that for a long time. Of course, it also works against us because what happens is that we create the alternative space because we are not included as fully as we want institutionally, and we're always living from hand to mouth. At some point energy runs out, and the project is abandoned for a while and then we go into it all over again. That is why our history seems so interrupted, and it is difficult to theorize it because of those interruptions. So these alternative spaces that we have managed to create, like MALCS, become one of the major outlets for self-expression that later can be rethought and rewritten somewhere else.

The barriers and issues discussed by many of *las colegas* provide the backdrop for our future research agenda. The inherent contradictions that we as Chicanas experience in our daily lives in the academy serve also to push us forward to develop our scholarship for the 1990s. Thus, our last question more directly asks *las colegas* to identify their collective hopes for the evolution of Chicana studies in the 1990s.

Adaljisa Sosa Riddell. As far as Chicana scholarship, it's like a little foot that goes out there, just kind of tentatively, somebody steps on it, it pulls back a little, and then it tries again and again. But eventually, I think we aren't going to be so cautious and we are not going to pull back. So I think probably—I would say maybe three years from now—a lot of women are going to take the deep plunge and come out with theories that are in their heads, in their hearts. Women are going to put on paper what they are saying, behind closed doors, in all the sessions we hold.

Emma Pérez: There are so many issues that our Chicana feminist academic community has not dealt with. We haven't successfully dealt with homophobia, with people who are physically different, with issues of age. We are going to have to challenge ourselves about that. The more we grow, the more Chicana academic scholars we have, then the more diverse the group will be. We are also going to have more middle-class women. Certainly, most of the women that I know that came out of the seventies were working class and had a real intimate connection with working-class communities through our mothers and fathers and our families. This isn't to say that middle-class people can't be radical. I think class background leads to a different kind of focus.

Norma Alarcón: We have learned a lot in the past ten to fifteen years, and I think that we have yet to realize what we have actually learned. I don't know about you, but I feel overwhelmed at what I have learned, because we are working two or three sides of a street—sometimes not out of desire but out of coercion. But when you are working two or three sides of a street, you're learning so much that you can't assimilate it all, because some of it is contradictory, conflicting, and you have to sort it out. So I personally think that a lot of our major work is still to come, out of what we actually already do know but have not articulated—because you can't articulate all of it at the same time; at least this is the way I personally feel about it in terms of my intellectual trajectory in the academy. I think the field is going to explode, it's going to multiply, it's going to become very rich and very fertile and very exciting.

Deena González: We're moving in the direction of creating a field called Chicana studies, and that to me is still primary. In that field, we include all the intersections and cross sections and tensions that arise around the issues of class, race, ethnicity, social location, sexuality and sexual preference, sexual politics, and community involvement. I also think that in the next ten years, we are going to have some real major battles around particular political stances—around where are work is going.

Rosa Linda Fregoso: I am hoping that we move beyond strict disciplinary boundaries and begin to question, from a Chicana feminist perspective, some of the theoretical assumptions of our respective disciplines. Twenty years ago, Chicano studies was conceived as an alternative and interdisciplinary field. Yet, for various historical reasons, the interdisciplinary nature has never been fully realized. Instead, *interdisciplinary* came to be understood to mean that different scholars from various disciplines come together under the umbrella of Chicano/a studies in departments, conferences, or anthologies. It seems that Chicana scholarship is more open to the dismantling of narrow and artificial disciplinary boundaries. I see us evolving in this direction.

Angelina Veyna: I foresee a florescence in a lot of the different disciplines and a coalescence of disciplines. These will bring about new paradigms, new frameworks to explain our experiences, and a new scholarship of our own. We can't depend on U.S. scholarship or Latin American scholarship or Mexican scholarship: Chicana scholarship is the fruition of our own ideas. Another issue that we will have to face is developing our own resources for the dissemination of the research that we do. Right now it just doesn't work out, because editors end up using the criteria of general disciplines, general literary guidelines, to assess what we have, and we don't necessarily have to or want to fit within those paradigms. I think one of the key issues that we are going to have to deal with is developing our own mechanisms for disseminating information. It may mean developing our own Chicana journals.

Antonia Castañeda: I would have us come together in collectives, address the issues, grapple with them, and train each other. To take everybody's material and question it and challenge it and analyze it and reformulate it from a Chicana perspective, taking into account all these central issues that I have already mentioned of gender, race, class, and sexuality.

Angie Chabram Dernersesian: An important item in Chicana scholarship should be the search for interdisciplinary paradigms, collaborative efforts, and the exploration of new forms of scholarship, which can begin to effectively address the pernicious division between disciplines, between Chicana academics, and between Chicano and Chicana academics. I think the most important objective in Chicano scholarship in the nineties and thereafter is the need for collaboration through working seminars and research institutes that support Chicanas and Chicanos in their efforts to consolidate fragmentation and often unnecessary duplication of efforts.

Vicki Ruiz: Five years ago, many of us would not have recommended graduate school to our worst enemy. But certainly we recognize that the future of Chicana studies depends on the recruitment of our students into graduate education. Perhaps—I will use this qualifier because I don't want to be accused of being overly optimistic—perhaps we can make the experience more humane for those who come after us. My hopes for the future center around not only the augmentation of our numbers but the persistence of the sisterhood we share and our commitment to Chicana agency and voice.

Elisa Facio: The focus on gender is very important. But we are really seriously questioning what the issues are in the community. We are beginning, or attempting, to speak on behalf of what is going on in the community. We don't want to create scholarship just for the sake of creating scholarship; there is real concern about what is happening to women's lives.

We end this anthology, these *pláticas,* with some reflections on the process of "Building with Our Hands."

Beatríz Pesquera: As you listen to the voices of our *compañeras,* you can hear that tension, from mounting frustration and deep-seated anger, which somehow has to be controlled, maintained, and channeled.

Adela de la Torre: What is positive here is a realization that finally there is a critical mass—that, despite the institutional hurdles, we challenged the existing academic canons and fashioned new directions in scholarship. We are beginning to develop a new generation of Chicana scholars who bring Chicanas from the margin to the center of social inquiry.

Beatríz: We are not *las sufridas,* the suffering victims. It is a question of an analysis of our particular social relationships within an institution in which we have never had a presence. The flip side of the hardships is going to be the exhilaration of being involved in this kind of enterprise. As many of the women have said, the work of the eighties has been building a community of scholars, talking about our questions collectively, beginning to research some of those questions. There is a very strong sense of a collective engagement with questions.

Adela: There certainly is a spirit of collectivity, something that underlies all struggles when you're looking at the Chicana experience.

Beatríz: Many of us came together on the basis of a shared political experience, which has been an important contribution of our intellectual development. There has always been this important link to the political environment. The kind of knowledge that we are generating is politically invested to empower our communities.

Adela: If you look at the research agendas, most of the women focus on issues that affect our community. Many of us feel that it is critical to be involved in the academic enterprise; at the same time, we are trying to maintain our own moral legitimacy in our respective communities. And that effort creates problems in terms of the types of research we do, the types of publications we obtain, and the types of reviews we get.

Beatríz: What initially bound us together was our interest in researching the Chicana experience. So we were not drawn together because of a particular allegiance to a discipline, theory, or methodology but, rather, because we shared a concern about Chicanas' lives. So we created a safe space in which to discuss this concern.

Adela: What drew us together was a hunger for knowledge, information, a space to share experience. This hunger forced us together and was instrumental to our development in our intellectual pursuits.

Beatríz: Efforts in the eighties involved building community and generating new approaches to research. The nineties are going to be the "decade of the plunge"; that is, Chicana scholars will more forcefully confront issues of patriarchy and sexual politics in all areas of research. We can take certain risks now, because we now have a community of *compañeras*.

Adela: We also will see further critical discourse about the direction of Chicana studies—debates on selected methods, theoretical frameworks, and topics. Ethical questions linked to the application of our work to public policy and political empowerment of our communities are questions that will merit center stage in the nineties.

Beatríz: Issues of disciplinary boundaries versus a more holistic approach to our work have certainly been alluded to by a number of the *compañeras*. Many more of us will certainly go beyond the constraints of traditional disciplines. This move raises issues, as before, regarding outlets for our publications. It is quite conceivable that a journal will emerge to accommodate our needs. To be bold, I predict that by the end of the decade it will be possible to enter a Ph.D. program in Chicana studies.

Adela: Beatríz, this really has been an incredible learning process for us and for all the *compañeras* involved. I really don't know how we can end this.

Beatríz: Well, I find that often what best expresses my sense of being is Chicana poetry. I think we should end with a stanza from the poem "Beneath the Shadow of the Freeway," by Lorna Dee Cervantes, which inspired the title of our anthology:

> and in time, I plant geraniums.
> I tie up my hair into loose braids,
> and trust only what I have built
> with my own hands.

INDEX

Compositor:	ComCom
Text:	10/12 Baskerville
Display:	Baskerville
Printer and Binder:	Haddon Craftsmen